Financing Politics

Politics and Public Policy Series

Advisory Editor
Robert L. Peabody
Johns Hopkins University

Mass Media and American Politics
Doris A. Graber

Congressional Procedures and the Policy Process
Walter J. Oleszek

Interest Groups, Lobbying and Policymaking
Norman J. Ornstein
Shirley Elder

Invitation to Struggle: Congress, the President and Foreign Policy
Cecil V. Crabb, Jr.
Pat M. Holt

Financing Politics

Money, Elections and Political Reform

SECOND EDITION

Herbert E. Alexander
University of Southern California

Congressional Quarterly Press
a division of
CONGRESSIONAL QUARTERLY INC.
1414 22nd Street N.W., Washington, D.C. 20037

Cover Design: Richard Pottern

Printed in the United States of America

Library of Congress Cataloging in Publication Data

Alexander, Herbert E.
Financing politics.

Bibliography: p.
Includes index.
1. Elections — United States — Campaign funds.
I. Title.

JK1991.A6797 1980 324.7'8'0973 80-10884
ISBN 0-87187-182-3

To
Nancy, Michael,
Andrew and Kenneth

Contents

Tables and Figures

Table

Figure

Foreword

Money, and what it can buy, has always been important in American politics. George Thayer, a campaign historian, describes one of George Washington's first attempts at public office:

> When he ran for the Virginia House of Burgesses from Fairfax County in 1757, he provided his friends with the "customary means of winning votes": namely 28 gallons of rum, 50 gallons of rum punch, 34 gallons of wine, 46 gallons of beer, and 2 gallons of cider royal. Even in those days this was considered a large campaign expenditure, because there were only 391 voters in his district, for an average outlay of more than a quart and a half per person.
>
> — George Thayer, *Who Shakes the Money Tree?* (New York: Simon & Schuster, 1973), p. 25

The basic methods for raising money and gaining votes have changed over the centuries. Providing liquor and music at campaign rallies has given way to emphasis on television spots and the use of direct-mail solicitations. Still, money as a resource remains central to attracting candidates and winning elections.

Dr. Herbert E. Alexander of the University of Southern California tells how and why money is important in this, the second edition of his book, *Financing Politics: Money, Elections and Political Reform.* The earlier work, published in 1976, has been substantially revised and updated to incorporate intensive examinations of campaign financing practices, especially in the 1976 and 1978 national elections. Dr. Alexander also speculates about the import of money on politics and what lies ahead in the 1980s.

For almost two decades the author has been widely recognized as the nation's leading authority on how political money is raised and spent. In 1961-62 he served as executive director of President Kennedy's Commission on Campaign Costs. As the director of the Citizens' Research Foundation, the principal private organization collecting and publishing campaign financing statistics, Dr. Alexander brings to this book a mastery of his subject, and he grounds it with a historical perspective.

Financing Politics focuses upon issues that reflect the basic structure and processes of our democratic system — who runs for office and how their campaigns are financed; how money is raised and to whose advantage; where it comes from and how it is allocated in campaigns; and the myriad attempts to regulate the use of money in national and state elections.

In addition to its comprehensiveness, *Financing Politics* is the most up-to-date treatment of the problem. It covers the major legislation passed from 1971 to 1979 — the Revenue Act of 1971 (containing the presidential election tax checkoff provisions), the Federal Election Campaign Act (FECA) of 1971 and the important modifications to FECA contained in the Amendments of 1974, 1976 and 1979. (Summaries of each of these laws are contained in the appendix.)

Never before, in such a relatively brief time frame (1971-1980), have so many fundamental changes in electoral reform taken place. In the process, the rules of the game have been extensively altered. Not until the beginning of the 1980s has the United States had in place a working election regulation system of some stability. As the author notes, it was a system that had "taken most of the previous decade to enact and 'debug.' "

The book begins with a fundamental question: Given that a democracy is based on "one person, one vote," how can this be equated with an unequal distribution of wealth, and hence a distorted capacity to influence election outcomes? The balance of Chapter 1 is given over to a historical survey of campaign practices and an assessment of the problems created by the rising costs of running for office in the mid-twentieth century.

Chapter 2 examines the response to rising costs, namely reform efforts leading to passage of the FECA and the subsequent Amendments. The main focus is upon their legislative history, major provisions and the problems that have been encountered in their implementation.

Who puts up the money for political campaigns? Chapter 3 examines the role played by individuals, especially large contributors such as W. Clement Stone, Richard Mellon Scaife and Stewart R. Mott. The role of the centimillionaires was drastically eclipsed in the presidential election of 1976. (For example, Stewart Mott, heir to a General Motors fortune, contributed $822,592 in 1972, about half of which went to Democratic presidential candidate George McGovern. In 1976 Mott's total federal political gifts were limited by law to $25,000.) In 1976, for the first time, candidates for the presidential nomination and the presidency received governmental funds to subsidize the campaigns. Federal contributions amounted to almost $24 million in the primary campaigns (spread among 15 candidates), and more than $43 million for the general election (Carter vs. Ford).

One consequence of public financing of presidential elections has been to funnel more individual funds and, especially, group funds into congressional elections. Chapter 4 describes the enhanced role of corporate, labor and other political action committees (PACs), in campaign politics.

Chapters 5 and 6 provide detailed analyses of the impact of the new campaign reform legislation on the 1976 presidential and congressional elections and the 1978 House and Senate races. In 1976 public funding helped Carter offset Ford's incumbency advantage. The congressional elections of 1978 were marked by a "taxpayers' revolt," which contributed to moderate gains by Republicans in both houses of the national legislature.

Political campaign reform also was instrumental at the state and local levels. These experiences are described and analyzed at length in Chapter 7.

In his closing chapter, Professor Alexander becomes future oriented. If public financing seems to be working at the presidential level, why isn't it likely to be extended to congressional races? What is the probable impact of the continuing growth of PACs? How reasonable are the existing levels of expenditure and contribution limits? How can the political system be modified so as to encourage broader participation on the part of individual citizens?

The second edition of *Financing Politics,* like the first, cannot supply easy answers to these or even broader questions of democratic governance. How can we attract stronger candidates to run for public office when the positions themselves are held in declining repute? How do we maintain and promote faith in the viability of our public institutions in an era increasingly characterized by crises, foreign and domestic?

This book continues to be essential reading for all those who would like to understand the fascinating and interwoven relationship between money, politics and electoral reform.

Robert L. Peabody

Preface

This second edition of *Financing Politics* was triggered by the knowledge that political finance data is quickly outdated. There are congressional elections every two years, presidential elections every four years and much political activity in the intervals. Moreover, new rules governing federal elections have gone into full effect, giving us in 1976 the first experience with the public funding of presidential campaigns. Accordingly it was decided to update the book with the latest information available in 1980.

Material that has been added analyzes the electoral reform movement of the 1970s and its impact on public policy. New trends, such as the rapid growth of corporate political action committees, are examined. The evolution of the Federal Election Commission, a young agency when this book first was written, is discussed in the context of its powers and operating methods. The first edition chapter on the 1974 election was replaced with one on the 1978 congressional election. Similarly, the 1972 chapter was replaced with a new chapter on the 1976 congressional and presidential elections. The chapter on nonfederal election reform laws was rewritten in light of the states' experiences with those laws.

The literature since the first edition has brought significant analyses of the consequences of the election laws; these studies are discussed and reference is made to them in the text, chapter notes and bibliography.

Taken together, the substantial changes amount to almost a complete rewriting of the earlier edition. Chapters were reorganized and condensed, resulting in a shorter book that I believe will be more interesting to students and more useful to political science teachers who have limited time to spend on this subject.

Special thanks are due to Mike McCarroll, vice president and general manager of Lexington books, D. C. Heath and Co., for permission to use materials, including tables and appendices, from my book, *Financing the 1972 Election,* published by D. C. Heath and Co.

Some historical data are derived from my article, "Financing Presidential Campaigns," in *History of American Presidential Elections, 1789-1968,* Arthur M. Schlesinger, Jr. (editor), Volume IV, New York, Chelsea House Publishers with McGraw-Hill, 1971. I appreciate the permission given by Chelsea House for use of materials from that article.

The thinking about reform and its implications is taken in part from an article the author wrote, entitled, "Rethinking Election Reform," in *The Annals, Political Finance: Reform and Reality,* May 1976. Permission to use parts of the article has been granted by *The Annals.*

I am happy to thank members of the staff of the Citizens' Research Foundation for their devotion and help in the first edition, on which much of the second edition continues to be based: John M. Fenton, for editorial assistance; Linda Y. Sheldon, for editorial and typing assistance and preparing the bibliography; Gloria N. Cornette for important contributions during the book's preparation; and Jean Soete for all her help.

In the second edition, again CRF staff devotion and help were essential: Brian A. Haggerty for editorial assistance, rewriting and redrafting throughout; Jennifer W. Frutig, my research assistant, Brigitte Huke-Clausing, a former editorial assistant, and Joseph Peek, a former research assistant, all of whom helped draft or rework chapters; Robert H. Pickett, for typing help; and Gloria Cornette, CRF's administrative coordinator, who always lightens my burdens and generously provides help and time in ways too numerous to list.

Jean L. Woy, political science editor in the Book Department of Congressional Quarterly, was especially helpful in her editorial suggestions and added immeasurably to the final product. John L. Moore did a masterful job of editing and proofing. I also want to thank Professor Robert L. Peabody, advisory editor of this series for the Congressional Quarterly Press.

Herbert E. Alexander

Financing Politics

1

Money and Elections

The American system of government is rooted in the egalitarian assumption of "one person, one vote," but, like all democracies, it is confronted with an unequal distribution of economic resources. The attempt to reconcile the inequalities lies at the base of the problem of money in politics.

The difficulties of financing political campaigns are widespread; few candidates or political committees have found satisfactory ways of meeting the expenses necessary to compete in a system of free elections. And the implications of the ways in which we finance our politics are many. Affected are: candidates at all levels, from the White House to the courthouse, in both the nominating and electing phases of the electoral process; the two-party system and the structure of each party; and the decision-making process and public policy.

Scores of millions of dollars are needed — and spent — to elect our public officials. Consider the following:

- In 1952 about $140 million was spent on elective and party politics. By 1976 the costs rose to $540 million, nearly four times as much.
- More than 500,000 public offices, from president to the proverbial dogcatcher, are filled by election in the United States, yet federal and state constitutions contain few provisions for the necessary — and costly — campaigns.
- In some states a campaign for the U.S. Senate may cost more than 10 times the salary paid to the winner during his term of office.
- The annual budgets of the major national party committees, such as the Republican National Committee and the Democratic National Committee, run several million dollars even in nonelection years — the size of the budget of a small corporation.
- The electorate is expanding and well dispersed in urban, suburban and rural areas. The development of communications media

makes it easier — but also more costly — to carry on political campaigns.

These items add up to an important fact: Money — lots of it — is essential to the smooth conduct of our system of free elections. If one considers how much is spent in this country each year on chewing gum or cosmetics, the $540 million does not seem overwhelming. It can be considered the cost of educating the American people on the issues confronting them. But there are several crucial questions for citizens in our democracy:

What effect has money on the ideal of equality of opportunity to serve in public office?

Is the person of little or no wealth disadvantaged in trying to enter public life?

Can the poorly financed candidate win nomination or election?

Do special interest groups exercise undue influence through their contributions?

What effects have the reforms of the 1970s had on the ways we elect our officials?

We shall return to these questions many times in this book, and will try to answer some of them.

MONEY AND POWER

In virtually all societies, money is a significant medium by which command over both energies and resources can be achieved.[1] The distinguishing characteristics of money are that it is transferable and convertible without necessarily revealing its original source. These are obvious advantages in politics.

Money is convertible into other resources. It buys goods, and it also buys human energy, skills and services. Other resources, in turn, can be converted into political money through the incumbent's advantages of public office, for example, in awarding contracts and jobs, in controlling the flow of information and in making decisions. Skillful use of ideology, issues and the perquisites or promises of office attract financial support to political actors — in legitimate forms as contributions or dues, or in unethical or illegitimate forms such as those involved in recent years in the cases of Senator Thomas Dodd, Bobby Baker, Spiro Agnew, and, of course, Watergate.

The convertibility of money, then, makes the financing of politics a significant component of the governing processes of all but the most primitive societies. But money is symbolic. The deeper competition is for power or prestige or for other values. In this sense, money is instrumental, and its importance is in how it is used by people to try to gain influence, or is converted into other resources, or used in combination with other resources, to achieve political power. Because of its universality, money is a tracer element in the study of political power. Light thrown upon transactions involving money illuminates political processes and behavior and improves our understanding of the flows of influence and power.

Power is distributed unequally in society; it does not vary directly with wealth, status, skill, or any other single characteristic. Rather, degree of power is determined by many such factors, no one of which stands alone and no one of which has meaning unless related to the purposes of the individual and the environment in which he or she acts. So money is but one element in the equation of political power. But it is the common denominator in the shaping of many of the factors comprising political power, because it buys what is not or cannot be volunteered. Giving money permits numbers of citizens to share in the energy that must go into politics. In relatively affluent America, many individuals find it easier to show their support for a candidate or their loyalty to a party by writing a check than by devoting time to campaign or political work. Of course, most citizens have no special talent for politics, or they will not give their time, so money is a happy substitute and at the same time a means of participation in a democracy. If money is considered as a substitute for service, however, it does not require so firm a commitment; for example, one might give money to both parties, but one is less likely to give time to both. Money has an advantage over service, however, in that it is not loaded down with the personality or idiosyncrasies of the giver.

The problem of reconciling the "one person, one vote" theory with the unequal distribution of economic resources is compounded if one considers the operation of the American constitutional and political systems. The framers of the Constitution foresaw many of the problems that were to confront the new Republic and met them straight-on. But for the most part they warned against the divisiveness and factionalism of political parties, as experienced in Europe, while at the same time requiring the election of officers of two of the three branches of government. Most state constitutions also failed to provide institutional means for bridging the gap between the citizen and the government, while they too were requiring the popular election of numerous public officials. The gap was closed by the advent of political parties. The party system, however, never has been accorded full constitutional or legal status, nor has it been helped much financially by governments at the state and federal levels until recent years.

Of course, the Founding Fathers could not have foreseen all the developments that were to occur once the Republic began functioning. They could not have foreseen the rise of a highly competitive two-party system, nor the huge growth in the number of popularly elected officials, nor the direct election of U.S. senators, nor nomination campaigns, nor the democratization of the presidency, nor the advent of universal suffrage, nor the development of costly communications media — nor indeed the necessity for contenders to spend heavily on direct-mail appeals designed to raise still more.

American history has witnessed an ever-expanding electorate, from the abolition of property qualifications through women's suffrage to civil rights legislation of the 1960s and the lowering of the voting age to 18 in the 1970s — all in addition to normal population growth. In 1919, for example, we doubled our voting potential by adopting the 19th Amendment, granting nationwide suffrage to women. In the 1960s, big strides were taken to register blacks, with consequent increases in campaign costs, while the 26th Amendment added millions of voters 18 to 20 years old to the electorate.

COSTS OF EARLY AMERICAN ELECTIONS

Before 1972, it was more difficult to measure all the costs of presidential campaigns, since money traditionally was spent at the national, state and local levels by a multitude of committees and individuals (with no central accounting system necessary). Yet, because of the prominence of presidential elections, more historical information is available about them than about most other categories of election campaigns.

John Quincy Adams, sixth man to hold the office, argued that the presidency should neither be sought nor declined. "To pay money for securing it directly or indirectly," he asserted, was "incorrect in principle." [2] These were noble sentiments, but, in fact, all presidential candidates since George Washington have had to worry about campaign costs. From torchlight parade to "telethon," someone has had to pay expenses.

Table 1-1 shows the amounts spent by national-level committees on presidential candidates in the general elections since 1860, though the figures for years before 1912 are less reliable. A general upward movement in spending is revealed, with some startling differences in particularly intense contests. Much of the increase in expenditures over time is related to the growth in the size of the electorate and to general price increases. If expenditures are calculated on a per-vote basis, the sharp increase in costs is a recent phenomenon, beginning with the 1952 elections, the year, significantly, when the freeze on licensing of new television stations was ended; within the next four years, the number of commercial stations had quadrupled.[3]

Printing

Since the Republic's founding, printing has been the most basic campaign expense. In 1791 Thomas Jefferson asked Philip Freneau to come to Philadelphia, gave him a part-time clerkship for foreign languages in the State Department and made him editor of the *National*

Table 1-1 Costs of Presidential General Elections, 1860-1976

Year	*Republican*		*Democratic*	
1860	$ 100,000	Lincoln*	$ 50,000	Douglas
1864	125,000	Lincoln*	50,000	McClellan
1868	150,000	Grant*	75,000	Seymour
1872	250,000	Grant*	50,000	Greeley
1876	950,000	Hayes*	900,000	Tilden
1880	1,100,000	Garfield*	335,000	Hancock
1884	1,300,000	Blaine	1,400,00	Cleveland*
1888	1,350,000	Harrison*	855,000	Cleveland
1892	1,700,000	Harrison	2,350,000	Cleveland*
1896	3,350,000	McKinley*	675,000	Bryan
1900	3,000,000	McKinley*	425,000	Bryan
1904	2,096,000	T. Roosevelt*	700,000	Parker
1908	1,655,518	Taft*	629,341	Bryan
1912	1,071,549	Taft	1,134,848	Wilson*
1916	2,441,565	Hughes	2,284,590	Wilson*
1920	5,417,501	Harding*	1,470,371	Cox
1924	4,020,478	Coolidge*	1,108,836	Davis
1928	6,256,111	Hoover*	5,342,350	Smith
1932	2,900,052	Hoover	2,245,975	F. Roosevelt*
1936	8,892,972	Landon	5,194,741	F. Roosevelt*
1940	3,451,310	Willkie	2,783,654	F. Roosevelt*
1944	2,828,652	Dewey	2,169,077	F. Roosevelt*
1948	2,127,296	Dewey	2,736,334	Truman*
1952	6,608,623	Eisenhower*	5,032,926	Stevenson
1956	7,778,702	Eisenhower*	5,106,651	Stevenson
1960	10,128,000	Nixon	9,797,000	Kennedy*
1964	16,026,000	Goldwater	8,757,000	Johnson*
1968	25,402,000	Nixon*	11,594,000	Humphrey
1972	61,400,000	Nixon*	30,000,000	McGovern
1976 [a]	21,786,641	Ford	21,800,000	Carter*

* indicates winner

[a] 1976 represents the first time public funding was used for presidential elections. The Republican National Committee spent an additional $1.4 million on Ford's campaign. The Democratic National Committee spent an additional $2.8 million on Carter's campaign.

SOURCES: 1860-88 Republican and 1860-1900 Democratic: The best available figures, although disputed, are from the *Congressional Record,* Vol. 45 (61st Congress, 2nd Session. April 18, 1910), p. 4931, as cited in Louise Overacker, *Money in Elections* (New York: The Macmillan Co., 1932), p. 71n; 1892-1924 Republican and 1904-24 Democratic: Overacker, *Money in Elections,* p. 73; 1928-44: Louise Overacker, *Presidential Campaign Funds* (Boston: Boston University Press, 1946), p. 32; 1948: Alexander Heard, *The Costs of Democracy* (Chapel Hill: The University of North Carolina Press, 1960), pp. 18, 20; 1952-60: *Financing Presidential Campaigns.* Report of the President's Commission on Campaign Costs (Washington, D.C.: April 1962), p. 10; 1964: Herbert E. Alexander, *Financing the 1964 Election* (Princeton, N.J.: Citizens' Research Foundation, 1966); 1968: Herbert E. Alexander, *Financing the 1968 Election* (Lexington, Mass.: D. C. Heath and Co., 1971); 1972: Herbert E. Alexander, *Financing the 1972 Election* (Lexington, Mass.: D. C. Heath and Co., 1976); 1976: Herbert E. Alexander, *Financing the 1976 Election* (Washington, D.C.: Congressional Quarterly Press, 1979).

Gazette, the subsidized organ of the Anti-Federalists. The Federalists had been financing their own paper, the *Gazette of the United States,* with money from Alexander Hamilton, Rufus King and from public printing subsidies.[4]

The system of a newspaper supporting, and being supported by, one or another political faction quickly developed. Editors' fortunes rose and fell with the political success of their patrons. Newspapers vilified candidates mercilessly, and various factions spun off their own papers.

Much early campaigning for the presidency took place in newspaper columns. As late as 1850, when a wealthy backer wanted to further the political ambitions of James Buchanan, he contributed $10,000 to help start a newspaper for Buchanan's support.[5] In 1860 Lincoln secretly bought a small German weekly in Illinois for $400 and turned it over to an editor who agreed to follow the policies of the Republican Party and to publish in both English and German.[6]

During the early 1800s, books, pamphlets and even newspapers often were handed from person to person until they were no longer readable. All that campaign publicity caused a reaction that seems quite modern. A letter writer to the *Charleston Gazette* complained that "We are so beset and run down by Federal republicans and their pamphlets that I begin to think for the first time that there is rottenness in the system they attempt to support, or why all this violent electioneering?"[7]

By 1840 more than just the printed word was used to spread the story. Pictures, buttons, banners and novelty items appeared. According to one observer, William Henry Harrison's campaign that year had "conventions and mass meetings, parades and processions with banners and floats, long speeches on the log-cabin theme, log-cabin songbooks and log-cabin newspapers, Harrison pictures, and Tippecanoe handkerchiefs and badges."[8]

Active Campaigning

Active campaigning by the presidential candidates themselves is a fairly recent phenomenon. Andrew Jackson retired to the Hermitage after he was nominated, though his supporters did hold torchlight parades and hickory pole raisings. Political rallies came into their own in the mid-1800s. Campaigns provided an opportunity for a widely scattered population to meet and socialize. Orators were judged by the length — not the content — of their speeches: a two- or three-hour speech was not uncommon.

Stephen A. Douglas decided to barnstorm the country in his 1860 campaign against Lincoln, a practice not really tried again until 1896 when William Jennings Bryan, the "Boy Orator," traveled 18,000 miles giving some 600 speeches to at least five million people.[9] His opponent, William McKinley, by contrast, sat on his front porch and let the people come to him; special trains were run to his hometown of Canton, Ohio, with the railroads cooperating by cutting fares. The costs of these early forays into personal campaigning by Douglas and Bryan are not known, but since both candidates lost, they probably were not considered worthwhile expenses.

COSTS OF MODERN ELECTIONS

With the growth of the electorate has come a sharp increase in the cost of reaching it either directly through jet travel or indirectly through the mails and mass media. Politics today has become a major industry.

In 1952, the first presidential election year for which total political costs were calculated, it was estimated that $140 million was spent on elective and party politics at all levels of government. Twenty years later it was three times that much — $425 million.

The 1972 total represented a huge jump of 42 percent over the 1968 amount and a significant actual increase in spending beyond the factor of inflation. But the 1976 expenditure of $540 million, though a 27 percent increase over 1972, fell short of the 33 percent rise in the cost of living during the four-year period.

In 1976, for the first time, public funds were used to pay some of the costs of presidential primary and general election campaigns, with the money coming from taxpayers' optional use of an income tax form checkoff setting aside $1 of their payment for the campaign fund. The federal funding and related prohibition of private contributions for the presidential general election made considerable private and special interest money available for other political uses, including congressional, state and local campaigns.

Spending in 1976 also tended to be lower than it might have been because Watergate had turned off some previous contributors and new federal laws requiring disclosure of political donations had an inhibiting or chilling effect. The diminished role of wealthy "fat cat" contributors will be discussed later in this chapter.

Even with public funding, presidential campaigns still account for the largest portion of the country's total political bill. The Citizens' Research Foundation has estimated that $160 million of the $540 million spent on 1976 campaigns, 30 percent of the total, went for presidential campaign costs.[10] Included in the $160 million are the costs of prenomination campaigns, some dating from 1973, third-party and independent expenditures, and national party and convention committee spending.

Congressional campaigns spent a larger share of political money in 1976 than they did previously, partly because private participation in the presidential campaign was limited and partly because more money was made available by a growing number of political action committees (PACs) formed by business, labor and other special interest groups.

Figure 1-1 The Campaign Spending Dollar in 1976.

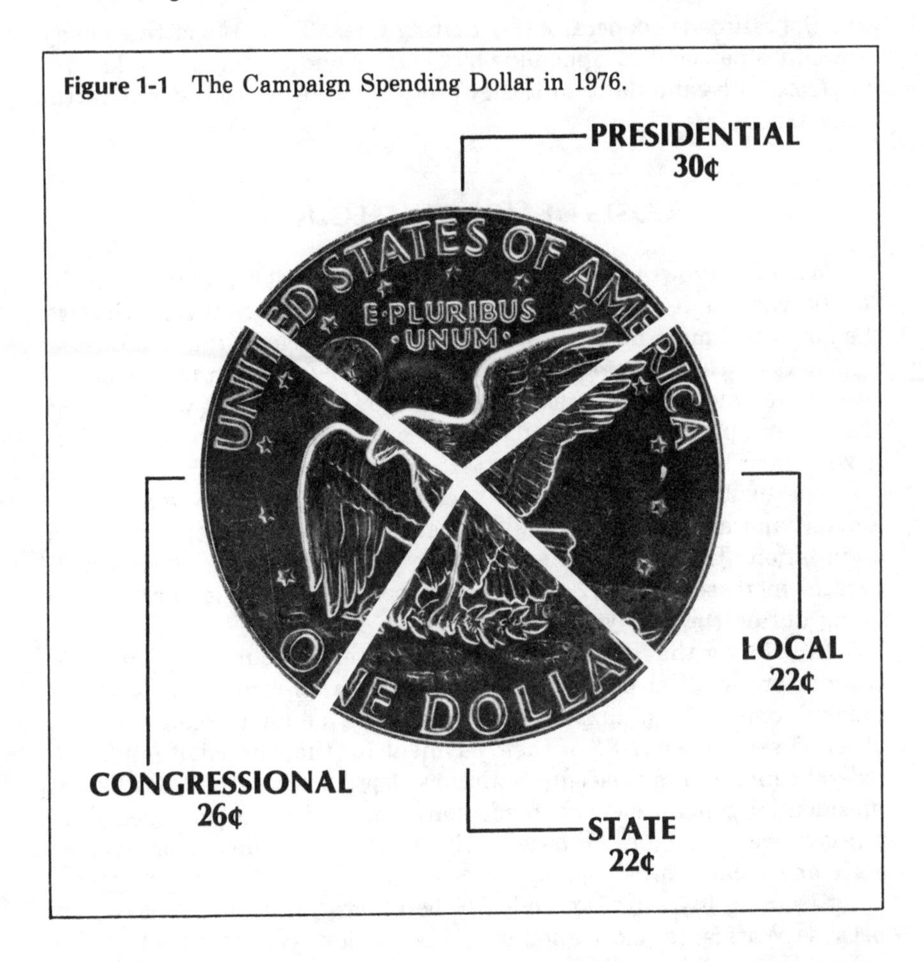

About $140 million, 26 percent of the $540 million total, was spent on campaigns involving 35 Senate seats and the 435 House of Representatives' seats.[11] The remaining $240 million was evenly divided between state and local elections and ballot issues, each accounting for about 22 percent of the total.

WHY COSTS RISE

The 1976 elections marked a major escalation in reported political spending. One reason is that political spending was more meticulously reported than in prior years. The Federal Election Campaign Act Amendments, which took effect January 1, 1975, require that most persons or committees expending significant funds to influence the outcome of a federal election shall file reports with the Federal Election Commission (FEC). The amendments grant the FEC broad oversight and enforcement authority to ensure disclosure of campaign receipts and expenditures at the federal level, including senatorial and congressional campaigns.

Another reason for the increase in reported spending is the inflation factor. From 1972 to 1976, the Consumer Price Index rose by 33 percent. Communications costs, in particular, skyrocketed. In such areas as media, advertising and public opinion polling, cost increases exceeded 30 percent; these items are now the basic components of political spending.

The hotly contested struggle for the presidential nomination in the Democratic Party also pushed up reported spending in 1976. An unprecedented $16 million had been spent by December 31, 1975; more than $46 million was consumed before the struggle was concluded. Moreover, an unusual, highly competitive contest took place for the Republican presidential nomination. Even so, including Ford's general

Figure 1-2 Total Political Spending in Presidential Election Years and Indexes of Total Spending, Total Votes Cast for President and Consumer Prices, 1952-1976

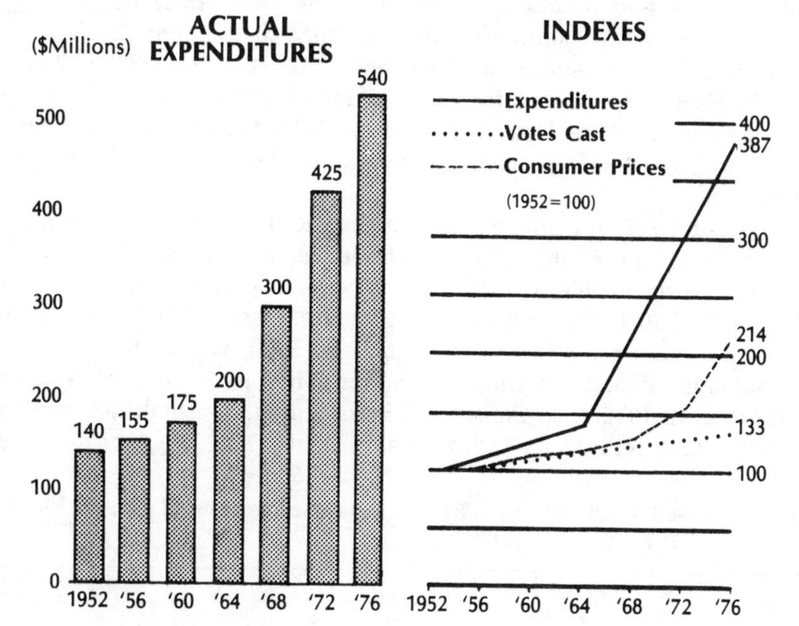

SOURCES: Expenditures 1952-76, Herbert E. Alexander, *Financing the 1976 Election* (Washington, D.C.: Congressional Quarterly Press, 1979), p. 166, derived in part from Alexander Heard, *The Costs of Democracy* (Chapel Hill, N.C.: The University of North Carolina Press, 1960), pp. 7-8; consumer price index and votes cast for president, U.S. Bureau of the Census, *Statistical Abstract of the United States: 1979*, 100th Edition (Washington, D.C.: Government Printing Office, 1979), pp. 483 and 513.

election spending of about $23.3 million, Ford and Reagan together spent less ($49.5 million) in 1976 than Nixon alone had spent ($61.4 million) in his 1972 reelection campaign.

Impact of Radio and TV Spending

The quantum jump in campaign spending that began in the 1950s can be attributed in considerable measure to the use of television. Between the 1948 and the 1952 elections enough Americans had bought television sets for the medium to figure seriously for the first time in the 1952 campaigns; by then, it was estimated that there were 19 million television sets and 58 million viewers.[12]

Candidates who choose to use broadcasting facilities pay dearly for the opportunity. Spending in the 1976 presidential campaigns for television and radio combined amounted to $16.9 million, 36 percent of the $46 million spent on the presidential general election that year.

Radio. Radio was first used in the 1924 election. In that campaign, the Republicans opened their own stations in their eastern campaign headquarters and broadcast every day from October 21 until election day, spending $120,000 for air time (one-third the amount they spent on either pamphlets or speakers). The Democrats spent only $40,000 on air time in 1924. Four years later, the new medium was more fully utilized by both parties: The Democrats spent $650,000 and the Republicans, $435,000. Such levels of spending for radio were fairly constant for 20 years.

After television came into wide use, candidates continued to buy radio air time. In the 1968 general election, radio costs were double what they had been in 1964, while TV costs were only 55 percent higher. Between 1968 and 1972, TV costs in the general election declined $2.5 million while radio costs increased slightly by $200,000. In the 1976 presidential campaign, approximately one million dollars more was spent on radio than in 1972. The Carter and Ford campaigns combined reported spending $2.8 million for radio time.

Table 1-2 Radio and Television Expenditures for Presidential General Election Campaigns, 1952-76, by Party

Year	*Republican*	*Democratic*
1952	$ 2,046,000	$1,530,000
1956	2,886,000	1,763,000
1960	1,865,000	1,142,000
1964	6,370,000	4,674,000
1968	12,598,000	6,143,000
1972	4,300,000	6,200,000
1976	7,875,000	9,081,321

Some candidates prefer radio to TV because it is much cheaper per message. They also like radio for its potential to reach "trapped" audiences, such as commuters traveling to and from work, and its ability to pinpoint special groups, such as in the ethnic radio appeals made in 1972 by the Nixon forces.

Television. With television came sharp increases in the cost of broadcast time. When Adlai Stevenson was told that one television speech would cost $60,000 he said: "Now every time I start to put a word on paper, I'll wonder whether it's an expensive $10 word, or a little, unimportant word like 'is' or 'and' that costs only $1.75." [13] Abraham Lincoln's successful 1860 campaign cost $100,000. A century later, that much was spent for a single half-hour of television air time.

The highest level of broadcast spending came in 1968. That year Richard Nixon had a carefully programmed campaign calling for noncontroversial television spots and live regional broadcasts which featured the candidate answering prescribed questions from a panel of well-rehearsed supporters. The total of $58.9 million that Federal Communications Commission (FCC) reports show was spent in 1968 by candidates at all levels was 70 percent above the total spent only four years earlier ($34.6 million). On the presidential level, about $12.6 million was spent on broadcasting for the Nixon campaign, and about $6.1 million worth of broadcasting was devoted to the Humphrey campaign; these were large amounts in relation to the value of the dollar at that time.

The 1972 broadcast spending totals were only slightly above the 1968 totals. Given the overall increase in all political spending from $300 million to $425 million, broadcast spending declined as a proportion of the total from about 20 percent in 1968 to 14 percent in 1972. Among the reasons for this decline was the emergence in importance of nonbroadcast media of communications, such as direct mailing, and the provisions of the 1971 election law, which will be explained in Chapter 2.

Much of the decline was accounted for by a drop in Republican presidential broadcast spending — down from $12.6 million in 1968 to $4.3 million four years later. Recognizing that what became known as the "selling of the presidency" [14] by TV in 1968 had in fact done little to bolster their candidate's showing in the polls, the Nixon campaign made a major shift in campaign strategy in 1972 to emphasize spending on direct mail aimed at particular groups in the electorate. Nixon's opponent, George McGovern, spent $6.1 million for air time.

In the 1976 presidential general election campaigns, more money was spent than in 1972 for TV broadcast time, but the total still was lower than the comparable 1968 total. Public financing and spending limits led Carter and Ford to channel large portions of their funds into advertising that would enable them to reach the largest number of voters. Inflated network costs also accounted for the increase. In 1972 the cost of a network minute was approximately $40,000; in 1976 it jumped to about $90,000 and even higher, to about $120,000, for selective prime time.

Ford and Carter allocated about half their general election budgets to media and related expenses. Carter spent $10.3 million on media, including $7.8 million to buy TV air time. Ford spent $11.5 million for media, $6.4 million of it used to purchase television broadcast time.

Compliance

The 1976 presidential nominees incurred additional costs trying to comply with reporting requirements of the 1971 Federal Election Campaign Act (FECA) and subsequent amendments. The 1976 amendments sought to mitigate this burden by exempting from the definitions of contribution and expenditure — and consequently from expenditure limitations — money paid for legal or accounting services to comply with the FECA or tax laws applying to political activity.

Compliance requirements caused particular problems during the 1976 prenomination campaigns. The traditional cash flow problems were compounded by the newly enacted contribution limits and by the need for timeliness and accuracy in making claims for certification of matching funds. Candidates had to maintain control over expenditures in each primary state to stay within the legislated spending limits and to conform to required accounting procedures. The 20 percent overage allowed in spending ceilings for fund-raising and the exemption of compliance costs required separate accounting. In addition, the 1976 amendments and FEC regulations belatedly allowed all compliance-related expenditures not only to be accounted for separately, but to be divorced from statutory limitations and, if necessary, to be paid from money raised separately to cover compliance costs.

Fulfilling the requirements led to increased accounting, bookkeeping, computer and legal costs, partly to ensure conformity with the disclosure and limitations sections of the law and partly to prepare submissions for matching funds. The magnitude of the compliance costs incurred during the prenomination period is indicated by data made available by the three most expensive campaigns, those of Ford, Reagan and Carter. Gerald Ford spent $581,000 on compliance, 4.3 percent of his primary expenditures and 12.5 percent of the matching funds received. Ronald Reagan's compliance expenses came to about $550,000 or 4.4 percent of the primary costs and 12.3 percent of the matching funds. Jimmy Carter spent $348,000 on compliance or 2.8 percent of the primary campaign budget and 9.8 percent of the matching funds received.

Fund Raising

Fund-raising expenses also have become a major cost component in campaigns for federal office. The FECA contribution limits make it necessary for candidates to undertake broadly based drives that often are more expensive than soliciting a smaller number of large contributors. The 1974 law sought to take these costs into account by allowing a 20 percent overage beyond expenditure limits for fund-raising operations.

The 1976 Carter and Ford campaigns illustrate some of the costs of raising money. The Carter prenomination campaign expended $1.2 million on fund raising, approximately 10 percent of its primary expenditures. Carter's early political success was built on a comparatively small base of contributions, which increased with each victory. Forty-four percent of the $1.2 million went for meetings, fund-raising events and benefit concerts; 15 percent went for postage and delivery; and 14 percent for printing costs. The remainder was spent on telethon, mailing list, mailing label and computer time costs and on buying and selling bumper stickers, buttons, pins and T-shirts.

The President Ford Committee reported prenomination fund-raising expenditures of $2.2 million, approximately 16 percent of primary expenditures. Ford officials at first concentrated on attracting larger contributions. But when they switched to a broader-based approach, receipts accelerated. The early financial difficulties embarrassed the incumbent's campaign, but did not significantly hamper it.

Supplementing Ford's personal solicitation and direct-mail appeals were a large number of fund-raisers, some of which charged admission as low as $10 a person. The more typical event, however, was high-priced and surrounded an appearance by Ford, a GOP member of Congress, or administration officials. The costs of such affairs, which also helped involve local community leadership, were relatively low.

Professionalization of Politics

Candidates incur additional costs by retaining political specialists. Some consultants run the candidate's entire campaign, advising on basic strategy decisions, such as what issues the candidate should stress or how best to utilize limited time and funds. Others specialize in polling, fund raising, organizing volunteers or media advertising. Some consultants handle only particular aspects of a campaign; for example, putting voters' names on computer tapes for direct-mail appeals, fund raising or election day get-out-the-vote reminders. Other firms provide automated telephone equipment and operators who can make thousands of calls to voters, play a message from the candidate or record responses.

The proliferation of consulting firms points to the increasing professionalization of electoral politics. This trend is irreversible but has been criticized on the grounds that profit-making companies have no base or interest in the candidate's constituency and often supplant established party organizations and traditional volunteer campaign staffs. Few party organizations, however, are geared to provide services with the competence and reliability that some professional consultants demonstrate. Further, campaign managers often have looked upon volunteers as of marginal help. With the complexities of new regulations regarding disclosure and limitations, some campaign directors feel that the amateur efforts are more often a burden than a boon.

REGULATION OF CAMPAIGN FINANCE

Until Watergate and other recent scandals brought intense scrutiny to the role that money plays in U.S. elections, reform of the political finance system since about the turn of the century invariably yielded piecemeal legislation which, ironically, may have helped further the very corruption that was the original target. The controls imposed by the legislation were mostly negative, restricting spending even as needs and costs were rising.

To prevent candidates from becoming obligated to special interests, limits were set on the amount of contributions. Funds from suspect sources or heavily regulated industries were prohibited. To dilute the "spoils system," career civil servants were protected from political demands for cash. If there was danger that partisans would dominate the airwaves, all sides were guaranteed equal opportunity for free time — although opportunities to buy time were equal only for those who could pay for it. One after another, traditional sources of political funds were cut off without provision for new sources of supply.

The application of new technology to political campaigns exacerbated the financial problems. The use of television, jets, polling and computers caused costs to mount and to outpace contributions. Consequently, political contributors, often large donors and special interests, were squeezed to give more. New contributors and new sources emerged as improved solicitation and collection systems developed with computerized mail drives and sophisticated fund-raising organizations. Labor and business pioneered in forming political action committees to raise funds and support candidates. Other organizations, especially trade associations, then peace groups, environmentalists and other issue-oriented groups, emulated them. Millionaire candidates raised the ante for other candidates, escalating costs but also focusing attention on wealth as a factor in electoral candidacy.

During the first half of the 1970s, federal laws regulating election campaigns were changed fundamentally — in the Federal Election Campaign Act of 1971, the Revenue Act of 1971, and in the FECA Amendments of 1974, which significantly altered both the 1971 enactments. From 1972 to 1976, 49 states also revised their laws regulating political money. The states undertook much experimentation, living up to their description by Justice Louis D. Brandeis as "laboratories of reform." [15]

Although there has been little uniformity in the recent laws governing political finance, certain patterns can be discerned. The regulations have taken three basic forms, each of which will be discussed at greater length later. Stated briefly, they are:

1. Public Disclosure — to provide the public, both during and after campaigns, with knowledge of monetary influences upon its elected officials and to help curb excesses and abuses by increasing the political risk for those who would undertake such practices.

2. Expenditure Limits — to meet the problems created by rising costs and by some candidates having more funds than others.

3. Contribution Restrictions — to meet the problems of candidates obligating themselves to certain interests. Both at the federal level and in some states, partial government funding now is provided for, making available alternative sources of funds to replace contributions that have been prohibited or limited.

This recent wave of reform, a tide unmatched since the Populists and Muckrakers triggered reform at the turn of the century, has been primarily an effort to improve a system perceived by many as fraught with favoritism and corruption. It had been widely felt in recent years that the American system of financing elections through sometimes secret, often unlimited private donations had given undue influence in politics and government to wealthy or well-organized donors at the expense of the unorganized public.

The Consequences of Reform

Reform is not neutral. When the rules of the game are changed, advantages shift and institutions change — sometimes in unforeseen ways. As Douglas Rae has pointed out,[16] election laws can be used — in fact are being used — as instruments to achieve certain political goals.

The problem of the election reformer in the final third of the 20th century is how to apply democratic principles to elections in an age of media politics, seemingly dominated by an atmosphere of dollar politics. The $61.4 million reported for Richard Nixon's successful campaign to retain the presidency in 1972 — the year of the last presidential campaigns conducted under the old election laws — represents six times the amount reported for John Kennedy's attaining that office in 1960 and more than 600 times the amount to elect Abraham Lincoln a century earlier. In the 1976 presidential campaigns — the year of the first such campaigns to be funded by public monies — Jimmy Carter spent $21.8 million of public funds in the general election in his successful effort to gain the presidency. As we have seen, $160 million was spent on all 1976 presidential campaigns. Concerning the effort to change the rules that govern this spending, several questions must be asked: Do expenditure limits mean there will be more or less communication between candidates and voters? Do contribution limits and expenditure limits encourage more competition, or do they favor incumbents or discriminate among candidates in differing jurisdictions and circumstances? How will government funding of political campaigns alter the political process? Will government intrusion be an opening wedge for control over various political activities? Are floors (minimal levels of public funding) better than ceilings or limits on spending?

The consensus among reformers and their supporters (who, at least since Watergate, appear to make up most of the citizenry), seems to be that democratic principles cannot be upheld in an atmosphere of unfettered and often unpublicized campaign fund raising and spending. The secrecy or incomplete disclosure surrounding political giving prior to the enactment of reforms permitted widespread abuses that at times constituted a fundamental corruption of the election process. Several events in recent years, some of which are described in the following chapters, have provided dramatic evidence of the corruption of political money that can occur at both the federal and state levels. Such events have given impetus to the reform movement.

DOES MONEY WIN ELECTIONS?

Popular lore has it that the candidate who spends the most wins and, on the surface, the record in recent elections would seem to bear this out. During the general election in 1976, since both Carter and Ford accepted public funding, each spent approximately the same amount. During the prenomination campaigns, however, both Carter and Ford outspent their opponents. Carter spent $12.4 million to gain the Democratic nomination. Four opponents who remained in the race with him through the late spring primaries — Governor Jerry Brown, Senator Frank Church, Senator Henry Jackson and Representative Morris Udall — together spent only slightly more than Carter alone spent. On the Republican side, Ford outspent his opponent, Ronald Reagan, $13.6 million to $12.6 million, on his way to a narrow convention victory.

Work and Organization

The outcome of an election, however, usually depends upon much more than money. Carter's capture of the Democratic nomination was in large part a result of the hard work and efficient organization of his campaign staff. Carter's early primary victories served to attract the funds he needed to continue his steady march. And the length of his campaign, lasting from 1974 through the Democratic convention, and participating in all the key primaries while other candidates dropped out along the line, had much to do with Carter's larger spending. Although Ford, the nation's first unelected president, did not enjoy all the advantages normally associated with incumbency, the fact that he occupied the White House no doubt brought him funds that otherwise might not have been available.

Voters sometimes refuse to respond favorably to frills, blitz campaigns or wealthy candidates. It is worth noting that despite the record spending on the presidential campaigns of 1972 the turnout of voters was the lowest since 1948. Survey data indicated that many persons did not vote simply because they were not interested or did not care for any of the candidates.[17]

A number of factors can compensate for a shortage of cash. Low-budget candidates may be campaigning in areas predominately favorable to their parties or they may be well-entrenched incumbents; they may be swept into office by a national trend or benefit from a presidential landslide. Any of these circumstances can bring victory if candidates have sufficient resources to enable them to present their qualifications and positions — sometimes merely their names and faces — to the voters.

Counterbalance

In broad terms, money can be considered as a countervailing force to a natural majority, or to large aggregates of voters, with the candidates of the minority party feeling compelled to spend more money than the candidates of the party that otherwise would command the most votes. For challengers to do so, however, is not always possible because the party out of power may have less money than the majority party if money, as is often the case, goes to those in power.

In 1976 the Carter campaign concentrated a major share of its budget on expensive broadcast time, in part because the candidate was new to the national scene and was running against an incumbent who enjoyed the advantages of free television broadcast of presidential events and actions.

During the 20th century, at the national level, Republicans consistently have had more money at their disposal than the Democrats, even when independent labor funds are added to Democratic spending. Yet, from the 1930s through the 1970s, the Democrats have been able to command a majority of voters more often than have Republicans. In his eight years in office, Dwight Eisenhower had a Republican-controlled Congress for only two years; Nixon and Ford from 1969 through 1976 faced large Democratic majorities in Congress.

In the 1936 presidential election, the Republican Party together with the wealthy Liberty League spent $9,411,095 (a total not topped until 1960) against the Democrats' $5,964,917. Yet, despite this 3-to-2 financial advantage, the Republicans carried only two states for their nominee, Alfred Landon. Some historians have expressed doubt that any of the presidential elections in the 20th century would have ended differently had the losing candidate been able to spend more money. The closer the election results, however, the greater the chance that any one factor could make a difference. For example, the Kennedy-Nixon contest in 1960, the Nixon-Humphrey race in 1968 and the Carter-Ford race in 1976 all were won by such small margins — less than 1 percent of the vote cast — that additional expenditures could well have changed the result.

The predisposition of voters, the issues of the moment, the advantages of incumbency and the support of various groups are always related to the final vote totals and are often more important than cash. Independent decisions by the news media — particularly TV — about what aspects of a campaign to cover can provide more exposure than advertising purchased by the candidates. Most campaigns now spend substantial amounts of travel money to put the candidate at events where free television coverage is certain. Campaign schedules are now drawn up with a view to obtaining media coverage, in time to make the morning or evening newspapers or to get on the evening newscasts. National nominating convention sessions are usually scheduled for prime viewing hours.

If not decisive, money at least is capable of reducing severe handicaps for most candidates. No candidate can make much of an impression without it, especially a maverick who contests the regulars or a candidate who challenges an incumbent.

How Much Is Enough?

One reason candidates seem to spend so lavishly is that little scientific evidence is available about the incremental value in votes of various levels of campaign spending and about the effectiveness of different campaign techniques. Traditionally, candidates spend as much as their supporters expect them to or as their opponents spend — and then some. New techniques win acceptance and to some extent displace older ones, but few candidates are willing to pioneer with unconventional methods alone. For example, although the electronic media are now widely used, the print media still comprise major expenditures in most campaigns. Indeed, new uses of old techniques develop. As an example, the print media have been enhanced by applications of computer technology, bringing increased use of direct mail that can be specially targeted to groups of potential voters or contributors. Contribution limits have produced pressures in the same direction, requiring candidates to attempt to reach a broader base of financial support by soliciting more small contributions. Matching fund plans have produced similar pressures. A provision in the 1974 Amendments, for example, requires that, to qualify for public funds, a candidate for the presidential nomination must receive a minimum number of contributions in 20 states.

Other new pressures are at work; for example, statutory expenditure limits as well as contribution limits lead to less money available for spending, forcing campaigns to undertake vigorous "cost-benefit" budgeting of available resources. This may lead to the reduction or elimination of certain marginal campaign activities. Of course, there is no agreement on what activities are considered marginal, and, in fact, marginality differs for the various levels of campaigning. Neither social science nor market research has been able to tell candidates what kinds of spending achieve the most per dollar; indeed, the impact will be different in a national or statewide campaign than in a local one. Perhaps half of all campaign spending is wasted — but no one knows which half. In any case, political campaigns are not comparable to advertising campaigns selling products such as soap. The candidate's personality and unanticipated events both impinge on campaigns in ways that cannot be controlled as easily as can the environment for selling commercial products.

Significant spending also occurs from largely psychological motives: The candidate spends to quiet his anxieties (in most campaigns, plentiful), to stimulate workers or to show that he attracts money and is serious about winning. For example, the high expenditures for President Nixon's 1972 reelection campaign grew in part from his need to build confidence in his ability as a vote-getter. Politicians often feel they must do something, anything, to keep the campaign going and morale high. The candidate's morale is bolstered when he sees his picture on posters or billboards along the route; some campaign managers spend a considerable amount of money just to keep the candidate happy and enthusiastic. Indeed, the costliest election is a lost election.

Relatively, the dollar price of U.S. elections is not high. The $540 million spent for campaigns in 1976 was less than the total of the advertising budgets for that year of the two largest corporate advertisers, Procter & Gamble and General Motors. It was a fraction of 1 percent of the amounts spent by federal, state, county and municipal governments — and that is what politics is all about, gaining control of governments to decide policies on among other things, how tax money will be spent. The $160 million spent to elect a president in 1976, including prenomination campaigns and minor-party candidates, was just under half of what Americans spend in one year on clock and table radios. And compared with what is spent in other nations on elections, the U.S. total is not excessive — our average costs fall somewhere near the middle, clustered with costs in India and Japan. The cost per voter in Israel is far higher than in the United States.

Nevertheless, U.S. political costs tend to be higher than in some countries because our political season is relatively short, and the intensity for each candidate is highest just before an election. Our system of elections creates a highly competitive political arena within a universe full of nonpolitical sights and sounds also seeking attention. Candidates and parties must compete not only with each other but also with commercial advertisers possessed of large budgets, advertising on a regular basis, often through popular entertainment programs on television and radio.

In this competitive situation, there are two conditions we can point to that, if all other things are fairly equal, enhance the power of money. First, we have found that money is most important in prenomination campaigns. Second, there is evidence that wealthy candidates do have a head start on those without wealth.

Importance of Prenomination Spending

Because of its ability to buy the kinds of services that produce name recognition and exposition of positions, money wields its greatest influence on campaigns — particularly presidential races — during the prenomination period. This is the period before the national nominating convention when the candidate's name and image must get publicity, when a number of organizations, national and local level, must be created to win delegates, when the serious national candidate probably will need to contest a string of primary elections in states across the country. Moreover, the number of presidential primaries increased from 15 in 1968 to 23 in 1972 and to 30 in 1976, with 37 scheduled in 1980.

John F. Kennedy's prenomination campaign of 1960 reported spending $912,500; additional outlays by state and local groups added unknown amounts to that total. In addition, Kennedy was able to threaten to spend enough money to discourage competition, as in California and Ohio.

The 1964 Republican prenomination fight was essentially a battle between Nelson A. Rockefeller's personal wealth and Barry Goldwater's broad financial base consisting of many small contributions from his conservative supporters. The $10 million spent for the 1964 Republican nomination campaigns doubled the record $5 million spent in the Eisenhower-Taft contest of 1952.

These totals, however, paled in comparison with the sums spent on the 1968 nomination when, for the first time since 1952, there was serious rivalry in both parties. In all, about $45 million was spent before Nixon and Humphrey finally got the major-party nominations. Nixon's campaign accounted for more than half the $20 million spent by the Republicans and Humphrey spent about $4 million of the $25 million expended by a large field of Democratic candidates that included Lyndon Johnson (before he decided not to seek reelection), Robert Kennedy (before his assassination), and Eugene McCarthy.

With Nixon's nomination assured in 1972, his Committee for the Reelection of the President directed most of its spending toward the general election. But the Democrats topped the record $25 million they had reported spending four years earlier. George McGovern, the eventual nominee, and 17 other candidates spent $33.1 million in the party's prenomination battle.

In 1976 candidates for the Democratic nomination spent more than $46 million, with Jimmy Carter accounting for $12.4 million of that sum.

On the Republican side, Gerald Ford and Ronald Reagan spent some $26 million on their prenomination campaigns. Prenomination spending in 1976 is treated in greater detail in Chapter 5.

Wealthy Candidates

Four of the last eight chief executives were considered wealthy men when they took office (Franklin D. Roosevelt, Dwight D. Eisenhower, John F. Kennedy and Lyndon B. Johnson). Personal wealth, however, was a factor only in the nomination of Kennedy. Adlai E. Stevenson and Barry Goldwater were well-to-do, but their fortunes bore no relation to their nomination or subsequent defeats; at most, their wealth may have helped them to enter politics. George McGovern, Hubert Humphrey, Harry Truman, Thomas Dewey, Richard Nixon (in 1960) and Gerald Ford were not even moderately wealthy when they became presidential candidates. Although Jimmy Carter may have been moderately rich when he entered presidential politics, his personal wealth does not appear to have been a factor in his attaining his party's nomination. The success of his family's peanut warehouse business, however, did permit Carter to guarantee loans to his campaign during a difficult period in 1976 when matching government funds were not available because of legal challenges to the then-new public financing system for presidential campaigns.

But, even though it was not a factor in the nomination of most recent presidential candidates, personal wealth has been an important factor in several modern political campaigns.

The most conspicuous examples of self-contributors on the record are the Rockefellers. When he appeared before the House Judiciary Committee in November 1974 as the vice president-designate, Nelson Rockefeller said that in his 18 years in public office he and members of his family had spent more than $17 million on his various political campaigns. He noted that this family spending had been necessary because "it's very difficult for a Rockefeller to raise money for a campaign. The reaction of most people is, 'Why should we give money to a Rockefeller?' "[18]

Rockefeller submitted to the Senate Rules Committee a summary of his own political contributions during the years 1957-74. He said his political spending since 1957 totaled $3,265,374, which included $1,000,228 in his own presidential campaigns, $80,599 in his New York gubernatorial campaigns, and $1,031,627 to the New York State Republican Party and local committees and clubs. In addition, Rockefeller's brothers and sister had supported his political activities with contributions totaling $2,850,000.

Another notable self-contributor, Milton J. Shapp, spent at least $6.5 million in his first two attempts to become governor of Pennsylvania. Shapp, who had made a fortune in the community television business, was successful on his second try, in 1970. He won reelection in 1974 without spending much money personally. But in 1976, despite personal wealth and public financing, Shapp was forced to drop out of the race for the Democratic presidential nomination because he lacked sufficient campaign funds. His wealth again became significant when the Federal Election Commission found that Shapp's campaign had fraudulently received $300,000 in matching funds; Shapp repaid the money from his personal account.

In 1971 passage of the Federal Election Campaign Act (FECA) diminished the role personal wealth could play in campaigns. But the Supreme Court, in a 1976 decision, *Buckley v. Valeo,* removed FECA's limits on a candidate's contributions to his own campaign. The law subsequently was revised to reinstate the personal and family limits in presidential and vice presidential elections, but only if the candidate accepts government funding. (The *Buckley* decision is discussed in Chapter 2.)

Spending limits for congressional campaigns in 1976 did not apply in any case because federal funding was not provided for those elections. Accordingly, there were several instances in 1976 of wealthy candidates spending considerable sums of their own money. In the Republican senatorial primary in Pennsylvania, for example, Representative H. John Heinz III financed almost 90 percent of his successful campaign against former Philadelphia District Attorney Arlen Specter with loans from his personal fortune — $585,765 out of a total of $673,869. Specter spent only $224,105 on the primary, according to his campaign reports; of this total, Specter lent his campaign $38,744. Counting the general election race, which he also won, Heinz made loans to his own campaign amounting to $2,465,500.

Two concerns usually are raised in discussions of wealthy candidates. One is that their personal resources give them too great an advantage over other candidates; the second is that their advantage gives the rich overrepresentation.

Advantages. Even with the limitations that now obtain on spending by a wealthy presidential or vice presidential candidate accepting government funds, wealth still would seem to bring a candidate incalculable advantages. His name makes news, and items about his family draw attention — all part of the process of building valuable name recognition. The budding politician from a wealthy family frequently is able to run for high office from the outset, whereas men and women of less wealth (with the possible exception of actors, athletes and astronauts) usually must begin at lower elective levels and earn their way upward.

Other advantages for wealthy candidates derive from their access to wealthy friends. Well-connected persons obtain credit with ease and can guarantee that loans or bills will be paid. Their ability to pick up the tab at lunches and dinners, to phone long-distance without worrying about the cost, is helpful too.

Superficially, at least, rich candidates seem less likely to seek personal gain from public office. They may, in fact, incur fewer obligations to contributors and thereby preserve more freedom of action — and wealthy candidates have at times used just such an argument in their campaigns. Milton Shapp in Pennsylvania freely acknowledged that he preferred to spend his own money and not be obligated to large contributors.[19] Republican Rep. Millicent Fenwick of New Jersey repeatedly has volunteered the information during her political campaigns that she has a net worth of more than $5 million.[20]

All this is not to say that wealthy candidates may not lose: they frequently do. But for many reasons, political realities continue to favor the wealthy candidate. Wealth propels, quickens and catalyzes. And it is only folklore that the average American admires the inpecunious candidate who wins elections on a shoestring. The voter has often cast his ballot willingly for the man who is well-to-do with an expensive organization and a substantial war chest. American voters have been strongly drawn to the Roosevelts, Tafts, Kennedys and Rockefellers.

Representation. As to the concern that the rich are overrepresented in politics, it is necessary to point out that wealthy candidates often are surrogates or in effect representatives of those who might not otherwise have strong voices in government. This tradition goes back to the Virginia squire who was the first president, and it carries up through such wealthy candidates as the late Robert Kennedy, with his appeal to the black and the poor voter. Kennedy's brother, Senator Edward M. Kennedy, continued in early 1980 to be the person many members of these two groups wanted to see in the White House.

Contrary to the common assumption, wealthy candidates are not all conservatives who represent vested interests. An Associated Press report in 1979 noted that at least 37 of the 100 U.S. senators had personal or family wealth or other assets that could qualify them as millionaires.[21] Those senators represented both ends of the political spectrum. Among the liberals, for example, were Democrats Kennedy of Massachusetts, Bill Bradley of New Jersey, Claiborne Pell of Rhode Island, and Republicans Jacob K. Javits of New York and Charles H. Percy of Illinois. Conservatives included Republicans Barry Goldwater of Arizona and S. I. Hayakawa of California.

To the extent that wealthy candidates help shore up the two-party system or give voice to minority interests, they make an important contribution to the political dialogue.

The main problem of wealth in elections may not be in the outcome of financially imbalanced contests but rather in depriving the voters of potential leaders who do not have the money to consider running for office.

NOTES

1. Derived from Alexander Heard, "Political Financing," *International Encyclopedia of Social Sciences,* (New York: The Macmillan Co. and the Free Press, 1968), XII, pp. 235-241.
2. *Memoirs of John Quincy Adams,* (1875, VII, pp. 468-470, as quoted in Jasper B. Shannon, *Money and Politics* (New York: Random House, 1959) p. 15.
3. For a brief history of the uses of radio and television broadcasting in political campaigns, see Herbert E. Alexander, "Financing Presidential Campaigns," in *History of American Presidential Elections 1789-1968,* ed. Arthur M. Schlesinger, Jr. (New York: Chelsea House Publishers in association with McGraw-Hill Book Co., 1971) pp. 3873-3875. Other historical information in this chapter is drawn from the same source.
4. Eugene H. Roseboom, *A History of Presidential Elections* (New York: The Macmillan Co., 1957), p. 25.
5. Shannon, *Money and Politics,* p. 21.
6. Shannon, *Money and Politics,* p. 23.
7. Jules Abels, *The Degeneration of Our Presidential Election: A History and Analysis of an American Institution in Trouble* (New York: The Macmillan Co., 1968) p. 83.
8. Roseboom, *A History of Presidential Elections,* p. 121.
9. M. R. Werner, *Bryan* (New York: Harcourt, Brace and Co., 1929), p. 95.
10. Herbert E. Alexander, *Financing the 1976 Election* (Washington: Congressional Quarterly Press, 1979). See Chapter 4.
11. Alexander, *Financing the 1976 Election.*
12. Newton N. Minow, John Bartlow Martin and Lee Mitchell, *Presidential Television* (New York: Basic Books Inc., 1973) p. 34.
13. Quoted in Robert Bendiner, *White House Fever* (New York: Harcourt, Brace and Co., 1960) p. 147n.
14. Joe McGinniss, *The Selling of the President 1968* (New York: Trident Press, 1969).
15. Louis D. Brandeis, "What Publicity Can Do," *Harpers Weekly,* December 20, 1923, p. 10.
16. Douglas W. Rae, *The Political Consequences of Electoral Laws* (New Haven: Yale University Press, 1967).
17. The Gallup Opinion Index, *Campaign '76* (Report No. 125) shows that nearly four of 10 nonvoters in 1972 did not vote because of lack of interest in politics or because they did not like the candidates.
18. Reported by UPI in *The Trentonian,* November 22, 1974.
19. Herbert E. Alexander, *Money in Politics* (Washington: Public Affairs Press, 1972) p. 44.
20. Richard E. Lyons, "Records Show 22 Millionaires in House, Despite Lack of Full Disclosure Law," *The New York Times,* January 4, 1976.
21. "19 Senators on Millionaire List," *Los Angeles Times,* May 19, 1979.

2

The Drive for Reform

For decades, official apathy toward serious reform of political finance was a Washington habit. The federal and state laws that were enacted tended to be predominantly negative — their chief purposes were to restrict ways of getting, giving and spending political money.

From the early twentieth century — when President Theodore Roosevelt proposed disclosure laws, a prohibition on corporate political giving and government subsidies — until 1961 several presidents went on record in favor of reform, but none took vigorous action.[1] President Kennedy was the first president in modern times to consider campaign financing a critical problem, and he showed this concern in 1961 by appointing a bipartisan Commission on Campaign Costs. This started the reform era but it was not until 1971 when, in the short space of two months, efforts to revise our antiquated system of political finance came to a sudden climax: Congress passed two measures — the Federal Election Campaign Act of 1971 (FECA),[2] which replaced the 1925 Federal Corrupt Practices Act, and the Revenue Act of 1971.

Until the time the Kennedy Commission was appointed, most of the laws affecting political finance were devised to remedy or prevent flagrant abuses. It evidently was assumed that honest politicians could afford to pay their campaign expenses with their own money or with "untainted" gifts. Efforts to free candidates from dependence upon any one person or interest group usually took the form of restricting or prohibiting contributions from presumably dubious sources. Moreover, arbitrary ceilings were set to prevent excessive spending.

As restrictive laws were passed, however, new methods of raising and spending money soon were devised. When the assessment of government employees was prohibited, attention swung to corporate contributions. When they in turn were barred, gifts from wealthy individuals — including many stockholders or officers in corporations — were sought. When direct contributions from the wealthy were limited by law, ways to circumvent the limitations were shortly found.

In this chapter we will briefly sketch the history of campaign finance regulation and describe the major laws that currently govern our system of electing candidates for federal office, including the public financing of presidential elections.

EARLY EFFORTS AT REGULATION

After the 1904 election — during which it was charged that corporations were pouring millions of dollars into the Republican campaign to elect Theodore Roosevelt — a move for federal legislation that would force disclosure of campaign spending led to formation of the National Publicity Law Association (NPLA). Under the banner of the NPLA were gathered such prominent figures as Charles Evans Hughes (later Chief Justice), William Jennings Bryan, Harvard President Charles William Eliot and American Federation of Labor President Samuel Gompers.

The first federal prohibition of corporate contributions was enacted in 1907. The first federal campaign fund disclosure law was passed in 1910. The following year an amendment required primary, convention and preelection financial statements and limited the amounts that could be spent by candidates for the House and Senate. The law was contested in a famous case in 1921 in which the U.S. Supreme Court overturned the conviction of Truman Newberry — a candidate for the Senate in 1918 who defeated Henry Ford in the Republican primary in Michigan — for excessive campaign spending.[3] The court held that congressional authority to regulate elections did not extend to primaries and nomination activities (most of the questionable expenses in Newberry's campaign had preceded the Republican primary). This narrow interpretation of congressional authority was rejected in 1941 in another Supreme Court case relating to federal-state powers,[4] but Congress did not reassert its power to require disclosure of campaign funds for prenomination campaigns until 1971.

Corrupt Practices Act

Relevant federal legislation was codified and revised, though without substantial change, in the Federal Corrupt Practices Act of 1925. That act remained the basic law until 1972, when the 1971 FECA became effective. Essentially, the law required disclosure of receipts and expenditures by candidates for the Senate and House (not for president or vice president) and by political committees that sought to influence federal elections in two or more states. The Hatch Act of 1940 limited to $5,000 the amount an individual could contribute to a federal candidate and the federal gift tax imposed progressive tax rates on contributions of more than $3,000 to a single committee in any year. But under both laws individuals could give up to that amount to multiple committees working for the same candidate. Thus, $25,000 or $100,000 or even larger gifts from one individual to one candidate were legally acceptable. The bar on corporate giving that had been on the books since 1907 was temporarily extended to labor unions in the Smith-Connally Act of 1943 and then reimposed in the Taft-Hartley Act of 1947.

The post-World War II years witnessed a series of congressional gestures, usually no more than congressional committee reports, toward reform. Presidents Truman and Eisenhower expressed concern about the methods used to raise money for political campaigns and, as ex-presidents, both endorsed the recommendations of Kennedy's Commission on Campaign Costs.

Commission on Campaign Costs

Kennedy had expressed much concern about campaign finance before he became president. He was sensitive to the advantages wealth gave a candidate. Having himself been accused of buying public office, he was aware of the public's cynicism. Before his inauguration, he set in motion the activities that led to creation of the Commission on Campaign Costs.

Taken as a whole, the commission's report[5] presented a comprehensive program for reforming the financing of the political system, covering not only federal legislative remedies but also bipartisan activities, certain party practices and state actions. One alternative presented for the first time called for matching funds (or matching incentives) for presidential candidates. Some of the proposals were not to be adopted for more than 12 years, but the report's purpose was more immediate: to get things moving in the field by detailing a comprehensive program for reform.

The recommendations were less than enthusiastically received on Capitol Hill, where certain members of Congress were distrustful of a presidential initiative in a field traditionally considered a legislative prerogative. Nor was there applause from such groups as the U.S. Chamber of Commerce, which was concerned that the tax incentive features would erode the tax base, or the labor movement, which objected to proposals on public reporting and tax incentives. Press comments were favorable, but election reform remained dormant for several years after Kennedy was assassinated.

The program was one of the few Kennedy creations to suffer seriously in the transition that followed his death. The White House gave the subject no public attention until 1966 when reports of criticism about the President's Club (a group composed of contributors of $1,000 or more, including some government contractors) and other political fund-raising activities moved President Johnson to act. In his 1966 State of the Union address he stated his intention to submit an election reform program. His proposals, however, were not transmitted until too late for passage by the 89th Congress.

Forerunners of the FECA

Although neither bill became effective, legislation considered by Congress during the Johnson administration — the Ashmore-Goodell Bill and the Long Act — helped pave the way for election reform measures that later became law.

Ashmore-Goodell Bill. In 1966 the censure of Senator Thomas Dodd of Connecticut for using political funds for personal purposes helped spark new interest in reform, and the House subcommittee on elections produced the bipartisan Ashmore-Goodell bill, the most comprehensive bill considered in Congress until that time. The bill was a mixture of the stronger portions of the Johnson and Kennedy proposals and of other bills and proposals. Most important, it called for a bipartisan Federal Election Commission to receive, analyze, audit and publicize spending reports by all candidates and committees in federal elections. A weakened version of the bill, eliminating the FEC as the single repository, passed the Senate the following year by a surprising 87-0 vote. The House failed to act, and the legislation died.

Long Act. The never-implemented Long Act was enacted by Congress in 1966 largely as the result of the persuasion and parliamentary skill of its sponsor, Russell Long of Louisiana, chairman of the Senate Finance Committee. The bill provided a federal subsidy for presidential elections, a scheme contrasting sharply with the Johnson administration's plan to provide tax incentives for political contributors. Caught off guard, the White House at the last hour chose to support Long's plan, shelving its own recommendation for tax incentives.

In the spring of 1967, Senators Albert Gore of Tennessee and John Williams of Delaware cosponsored an amendment to repeal the Long Act. Passage of the law had met with a negative reaction. One of the leaders of the floor fight for repeal was Robert Kennedy, who argued that the subsidy put a dangerous amount of power into the hands of the national party chairmen. Through promises of distribution of money in the general election, Kennedy argued, the chairmen would be able to influence the delegations of the large states to support the presidential candidate of the chairmen's choice. The Long Act was not formally repealed, but Congress voted to make it inoperative after May 1967.

LANDMARK LEGISLATION OF 1971

The Long Act and the Ashmore-Goodell bill might be termed the parents of the two laws that constituted a major turning point in the history of campaign finance reform: the Federal Election Campaign Act of 1971 (FECA), which replaced the Federal Corrupt Practices Act of 1925, and the Revenue Act of 1971.

Federal Election Campaign Act

The FECA of 1971,[6] which passed in January 1972, a month after the Revenue Act, required fuller disclosure of political funding than ever before — a factor that was to play a key role in the Watergate affair. Among its provisions, the FECA:

- Set limits on communications media expenditures for candidates for federal office during primary, runoff, special or general election campaigns. This provision was replaced in the 1974 Amendments[7] with candidate expenditure limitations on total spending (which were then in part declared unconstitutional by the Supreme Court in 1976).
- Placed a ceiling on contributions by any candidate or his immediate family to his own campaign of $50,000 for president or vice president, $35,000 for senator and $25,000 for representative, delegate or resident commissioner. This provision later was ruled unconstitutional by the Supreme Court, but the $50,000 limit was reinstated in the 1976 Amendments[8] for presidential election campaigns where the candidate accepts public funding.
- Stipulated that the appropriate federal supervisory officer to oversee election campaign practices, reporting, and disclosure was the Clerk of the House for House candidates, the Secretary of the Senate for Senate candidates, and the Comptroller General for presidential candidates and miscellaneous other committees. This provision was partially changed by the 1974 Amendments, which established the Federal Election Commission.
- Required candidates and their committees for the Senate and House to file duplicate copies of reports with the secretary of state, or a comparable officer in each state, for local inspection. This provision was designed to help provide information to local voters about the funding of campaigns.
- Required each political committee and candidate to report total expenditures, as well as to itemize the full name, mailing address, and occupation and principal place of business of each contributor, plus the date, amount and purpose of each expenditure in excess of $100; to itemize similarly each expenditure for personal services, salaries and reimbursed expenses in excess of $100. The $100 amount in both cases was raised to $200 by the 1979 Amendments.
- Required candidates and committees to file reports of contributions and expenditures on the 10th day of March, June and September every year, on the 15th and fifth days preceding the date on which an election is held, and on the 31st day of January. Any contribution of $5,000 or more was to be reported within 48 hours if received after the last preelection report. The dates of these filings were changed in the 1974 Amendments to include quarterly disclosures as well as one 10 days before an election and 30 days after an election.

- Required a full and complete financial statement of the costs of a presidential nominating convention within 60 days of the convention.

Revenue Act

The Revenue Act of 1971 provided tax credits or, alternatively, tax deductions for political contributions at all levels and also a tax checkoff to subsidize presidential campaigns during general elections. The act provided that political contributors could claim a tax credit against federal income tax for 50 percent of their contributions (to candidates for federal, state or local office and to some political committees), up to a maximum of $12.50 on a single return and $25 on a joint return (increased to $25 and $50 in the 1974 Amendments and to $50 and $100 in the Revenue Act of 1978, PL 95-600). Alternatively, the taxpayer could claim a deduction for the full amount of contributions up to a maximum of $50 on a single return and $100 on a joint return. (The deduction, which had been increased to $100 and $200 in the 1974 Amendments, was repealed in the 1978 law that increased the tax credit.)

The tax credits and deductions had an easy passage, but the accompanying tax checkoff provisions have had a long and stormy history. The checkoff represented a revival of a provision of the Long Act of 1966 but was revised to provide money directly to presidential candidates, not to the political party committees on their behalf. The checkoff provided that every individual whose tax liability for any calendar year was $1 or more could designate on his federal income tax form that $1 of this tax money be paid to the Presidential Election Campaign Fund; married individuals filing jointly could designate $2. This provision has remained in force ever since.

The Watergate events brought new pressures for reform. In May 1973 President Nixon proposed creation of a nonpartisan commission to study campaign reform. Nixon was by no means "out in front" on the issue. A week earlier, a House Republican leader, John B. Anderson of Illinois, had introduced a bill that he cosponsored with Democrat Morris K. Udall of Arizona calling for an independent Federal Election Commission. Nonetheless, it was almost two years before a new election law became fully operative.

1974 AMENDMENTS

Along with creation of the Federal Election Commission, the other major "firsts" in the 1974 Amendments to the FECA were the establishment of overall limitations on how much could be spent on political campaigning, and the extension of public funding to campaigns for the presidential nomination and to the national conventions.

Despite impetus given reform by the Watergate scandals, consideration of the measure was drawn out. Action on a Senate-passed reform bill was stalled throughout 1973 in the House, where the greater frequency with which its members run for reelection traditionally has made it a more conservative body when dealing with campaign reform. There the bill faced Wayne L. Hays of Ohio, chairman of the Committee on House Administration, a vocal opponent of public funding of elections.

In 1974 campaign reform was a major item on Congress' agenda. President Nixon sent his own proposals to Capitol Hill, but they pleased almost no one in Congress. The Nixon proposals were viewed by many as combining "safe" reforms with others that could not be passed. Nixon called public financing "taxation without representation." [9]

On August 8, 1974, a few hours before Nixon announced his resignation as president, the House passed, 355-48, a campaign reform bill that differed sharply from a second reform bill the Senate had passed while Hays was delaying consideration of the 1973 bill. The second Senate bill combined the original bill with a call for public funding of presidential and congressional primary and general election campaigns. The more limited House version provided for public funding of presidential nominating conventions and elections.

As finally passed by large margins in both chambers, the bill provided public financing only for presidential elections, including matching funds for the prenomination period, flat grants to the political parties for their national nominating conventions, and larger grants to the major-party nominees for their general election campaigns.

President Ford signed the bill October 15, 1974, in a White House ceremony to which all members of Congress were invited. A long-time opponent of public funding, the president expressed doubts about some sections of the law but said that "the times demand this legislation." [10]

Ford's reservations about portions of the bill were borne out when the Supreme Court in 1976 found parts of the legislation unconstitutional (discussed later in this chapter). Among the provisions of the 1974 Amendments invalidated by the *Buckley* decision were expenditure limitations on Senate and House campaigns, found unconstitutional because public funding was not provided for congressional elections. The 1974 Amendments also affected the development of political action committees, to be discussed in detail in Chapter 4.

Federal Election Commission

Established by the 1974 Amendments, the Federal Election Commission was formally organized in April 1975. It was designed to draw together the administrative and enforcement functions that previously were divided among the three supervisory officers — the Comptroller General, the Secretary of the Senate and the Clerk of the House of Representatives — as mandated by the FECA of 1971.[11]

The FEC had a stormy first year. It was in existence only nine months when the Supreme Court, in *Buckley v. Valeo*, declared unconstitutional the method by which the commission members were appointed (some by Congress, some by the president). That meant that for a time the commission could not enforce the FECA or certify matching fund payments to presidential candidates. Congress subsequently changed the procedure for appointing the members and the FEC was reconstituted.

From the outset, the potential conflict was apparent between the new commissioners' experience and friendships on Capitol Hill and their need for impartial handling of congressional elections. To achieve credibility as an independent agency, there was a clear need to establish the FEC's freedom from the Congress it was in part established to regulate. Some members of Congress, it turned out, did not want the FEC to be very independent where congressional elections were concerned.

This conflict was at the heart of a 1977 controversy over President Carter's nomination of John W. McGarry for FEC commissioner. Opponents of the appointment questioned whether the independence of the commission could be maintained if the nomination was approved. McGarry was a close friend of House Speaker Thomas P. O'Neill, Jr., D-Mass., and a counsel to the House Administration Committee. Republicans and the corporate community, fearing undue labor influence on the work of the FEC, resisted Senate approval of the nomination. After twice failing to receive such approval, Carter made a recess appointment of McGarry to the FEC in October 1978; he was reappointed in 1979 and this time was confirmed by the Senate.

Early FEC Regulations Rejected

Another problem for the FEC was — and continues to be — that the regulations it wrote had to be submitted to Congress along with an explanation and justification. If neither the Senate nor the House disapproved by a formal vote within 30 "legislative" days (days each house is in session), the commission could prescribe such regulation, and it would have the force of law.

Congressional review of regulations is unusual and tends to threaten the independence of the affected agency, in this case the FEC. Of course, FEC funds are appropriated by Congress, another potential pressure point. Commissioners claim the FEC seeks a balanced relationship with Congress, but discord developed very early in its existence. In fact, Congress rejected the first two FEC regulations, one dealing with congressional expense accounts and the other with "point of entry" — the question of which office would first receive reports from candidates for federal office.

Congressional Expense Accounts. In its initial proposed regulation, on congressional expense funds, the FEC, whether intentionally or not, served to alert Congress to the power the new agency could claim and to how that power might be perceived by some members to be directed at times against them or against traditional practices they did not want discontinued. This regulation, submitted to Congress in July 1975, dealt with the so-called "office slush funds," formally known as "constituent service funds," that usually come from contributions made outside the campaign framework. The money is used by some members to supplement funds provided by the government for day-to-day operations of congressional offices. These "office funds" are used for items such as newsletters, travel back home and office expenses beyond those authorized by Congress.

In its proposed regulation, the FEC held that money raised independently of appropriated funds "should be viewed as political and not legislative funds," [12] requiring disclosure in quarterly campaign finance reports. Even more controversial was the requirement that contributions and spending from the accounts be treated as campaign funds under the limitations set by law for the next election of the member maintaining the fund.

Congressional reaction was immediate and included threats to veto the ruling. The Senate subsequently did veto it by a one-vote margin (48-47).

A compromise version of the proposed regulation subsequently was further changed under pressure from some members of Congress. The FEC then deleted a $100 maximum on cash contributions. Since the election law set that limit on cash campaign contributions, the change put congressional office funding on a different basis. Similarly, the FEC retreated on its position that office account reports should be filed as attachments to campaign fund reports. Legislators objected that to do so would give the appearance that these funds represented campaign money, and they insisted on maintaining a distinction. The expense account reports were required once each year — on January 31 — but in election years quarterly reports were required.

It proved to be an unfortunate tactic for the FEC to seek to regulate a congressional custom before writing basic regulations dealing with the substance of the law, that is, disclosure, limitations and government funding. The FEC was responding to many requests for advisory opinions on many subjects, some of them marginal, but some from members of Congress who were persistent in seeking quick answers. Basic regulations were given lesser priority.

Point of Entry. The proposed point of entry regulation required that original copies of all candidate and political committee fund reports be filed first with the FEC; then the FEC would provide microfilm copies of the reports to the Secretary of the Senate and the Clerk of the House within two working days. Such a system would have provided more effective disclosure under efficient procedures, but it was rejected by the House.

Representative Hays, through whose committee the proposal had to move, argued that the law as it then stood sufficed and that the Clerk of the House "ought not to have a whole bunch of people handling these papers before they get to him."[13] The presumed prerogative of the House to receive the reports first was argued for two reasons: 1) The U.S. Constitution states that each house is the judge of its own membership, and hence custody of the original reports was essential in case any questions arose of contested elections or of unethical behavior in fund raising or spending; and 2) some members checked their disclosure filings with personnel in the Office of the Clerk of the House before filing verified reports, and they were concerned that the FEC would not provide the same service to help them to avoid possible violations of law.

Reluctantly, the FEC bowed before the opposition and revised its proposal — reversing the procedure so that candidates filed first with the clerk and the secretary, who then passed on copies to the FEC.

Both regulations that had been rejected by Congress were rewritten and, along with one on disclosure, had been cleared by Congress but not issued when the Supreme Court released its landmark decision, *Buckley v. Valeo.* While Congress rewrote the law to reconstitute the commission, three other proposed regulations that had been prepared were not submitted, and hearings on one other were canceled. Thus, the FEC was in operation for more than a year without a single regulation in force. A few days after the commission was reconstituted in May 1976, 10 sets of draft regulations were published for public comment. These incorporated provisions based on the 1976 Amendments.

Constitutional Challenge

In addition to its early liaison and communications problems with Congress, the new FEC's future was clouded almost immediately by a legal suit challenging not only the constitutionality of most of the major provisions of the 1974 Amendments but also the commission's very existence.

In *Buckley v. Valeo,* the courts confronted a difficult judicial task. There were dilemmas to be resolved that made the issue one of appropriate debate for the decade in which the United States marked its bicentennial. The problem, in its simplest form, was for the courts to balance the First Amendment rights of free speech and free association against the clear power of the legislature to enact laws designed to protect the integrity of the election system. Involved were questions of public discussion and political dialogue. Basically, the plaintiffs sought to ensure that the reforms, however well-meant, did not have a chilling effect on free speech or on citizen participation.

An unusual provision of the law had authorized any eligible voter to start federal court proceedings to contest the constitutionality of any provision of the law. The amendment, sponsored in the Senate by James

L. Buckley, New York Conservative-Republican, had been designed to speed along any case by permitting questions of constitutionality to be certified directly to the federal court of appeals, which was obliged to expedite the case. A case was brought a few days after the law became effective on January 1, 1975. Plaintiffs covered a broad spectrum of liberals and conservatives, individuals and organizations and included Senator Buckley, Eugene J. McCarthy, former Democratic senator from Minnesota, and Stewart R. Mott (a large contributor). Defendants included Secretary of the Senate Francis R. Valeo, the Attorney General, the FEC, the Clerk of the House, and three reform groups, Common Cause, the Center for Public Financing of Elections and the League of Women Voters.

On January 30, 1976, a little over a year after the case was initiated, the Supreme Court reversed many major points that had been considered and upheld by the court of appeals. The impact of the decision has been great not only on the regulation of federal elections but also on state and local law.

The central question was posed by Justice Potter Stewart during oral arguments: Is money speech and speech money? Or, stated differently, is an expenditure for speech substantially the same thing as speech itself, because the expenditure is necessary to reach large audiences by the purchase of air time or space in the print media? The decision resolved the conflict by asserting the broadest protection to First Amendment rights to assure the unrestrained interchange of ideas for bringing about popular political and social change. Accordingly, the court majority concluded that individual expenditure limitations imposed direct and substantial restraints on the quantity of political speech. This applied to limits on both individuals and on candidates in their personal expenditures on their own behalf as well as on spending by or on behalf of a candidate. However, an exception was made with reference to overall candidate expenditure limits, with the court holding that candidates who accepted public funding when provided by the government could also be obliged to accept campaign expenditure limits as a condition of the granting of the public money. The court made clear that independent spending by individuals and groups could be considered a protected form of free speech only if the spending were truly independent. Independent spending could not, then, be coordinated with the candidate or his campaign organization nor consented to by the candidate or his agent.

On the other hand, the court upheld the limits on individual and group contributions to campaigns, asserting that these constitute only a marginal restriction on the contributor's ability to engage in free communication. Saying that free expression rests on contributing as a symbolic act to help give a candidate the means to speak out, the court also asserted that the quantity of speech does not increase perceptibly with the size of the contribution. Hence limits on contributions were constitutional. The Supreme Court found that there was a real or imagined coercive influence of large contributors on candidates' positions and on their actions if elected, leading to corruption or the appearance of corruption, and it said that contribution limits were acceptable because they serve to mute the voices of affluent persons and groups while also restraining the skyrocketing costs of political campaigns.

The Supreme Court sustained all the disclosure requirements of the law, sanctioned the forms of public funding provided by the federal law, and upheld the concept of a bipartisan regulatory commission to administer and enforce the law so long as the agency was within the executive branch of the government and its members were appointed by the president. This last point required Congress to rewrite the law to reconstitute the FEC.

1976 AMENDMENTS

Although the Supreme Court required appointment of all members of the commission by the president within 30 days, the actual reconstitution of the FEC took 111 days. The proposed revision was complicated by the suggestion of controversial changes in the law. Among the proposals was one to extend public funding to senatorial and House campaigns. When Congress failed to act within the 30-day period, an additional delay of 20 days was granted by the Supreme Court. When Congress again failed to act promptly, the FEC on March 22, 1976, lost its executive functions, without which it could not certify payments of matching funds to candidates then seeking their party's presidential nomination. Until the law was revised, government funds could not be paid out, causing the candidates to economize while relying solely on private funds.

Much of the delay occurred because Congress was unable or unwilling to act promptly. President Ford requested a simple reconstitution to permit the FEC to continue to operate through the 1976 election. He argued against becoming bogged down in other controversial changes. Instead, Congress undertook significant revisions dealing with compliance and enforcement procedures, the issuing of advisory opinions, and the role of corporate and labor political action committees.

Within hours of being finally sworn in, in May 1976, the renewed FEC certified $3.2 million due for various candidates and $1 million to the major party national conventions. The FEC had continued to process submissions for matching funds while certifications were suspended.

The Ford campaign was relatively healthy financially throughout the hiatus. Ronald Reagan, Ford's main rival for the Republican nomination, charged that the president benefited from "interest-free credit" from the government, which billed the President Ford Committee while other candidates needed advance money before their chartered planes would fly. The effect on Ford's campaign was not clear, because Reagan went into debt in this period yet won primaries in Texas, Indiana, Georgia and Alabama, while Ford's cash advantage was slowly dissipated. The delays did not hurt Carter seriously, though he lost nine of the last 14 primaries in a winning campaign for the nomination. Given his momentum, prompt matching funds could have helped him in the later primaries.

1979 AMENDMENTS

Shortly before the 1980 presidential election year began, Congress after months of sporadic efforts enacted the 1979 Amendments to the FECA, without opposition in either house. President Carter signed the bill into law on January 8, 1980.[14] The amendments were designed to be "noncontroversial" to ensure passage, and many of the provisions were technical fine-tuning of the FECA after flaws and problems with it became obvious during the 1976 and 1978 elections. The new law's significance was that it represented some backtracking from the earlier stringent reform positions and some lightening of the burdens upon practitioners. Yet some changes were extensive. Essentially the bill simplified record keeping and public reporting requirements, increased the permissible role of state and local political parties, and refined the procedural requirements of the enforcement process.

Among its major provisions, the new law:

- Exempted candidates receiving or spending $5,000 or less from filing disclosure reports; the same applies to party committees under certain circumstances.
- Changed some political committee organizational requirements.
- Increased from $500 to $1,000 the amounts an individual can spend at his or her own home on behalf of a candidate or party without charge against the contribution limit.
- Permitted state and local party committees to pay the costs of certain voter registration and get-out-the-vote activities, and certain campaign materials used for volunteer activities.
- Raised the level of itemized reporting of contributions and expenditures from $100 to $200, and raised from $100 to $250 the threshold for reporting of independent expenditures.
- Reduced certain public reporting filings and changed filing dates.
- Required the Federal Election Commission to compile certain data.
- Permitted the FEC to initiate random audits but only when there is indication of significant violations.
- Clarified certain compliance and enforcement actions.
- Prohibited personal use of excess campaign funds except in limited circumstances.

- Raised from $2 million to $3 million the amount that major political parties may receive to operate their national nominating conventions.

Other limitations and provisions were left unchanged, and the laws regulating PACs were not revised. Two matters held up passage of the 1979 Amendments. The House and Senate differed on provisions relating to surplus funds and FEC audit authority. When these were resolved the bill passed.

AN EVOLVING FEDERAL ELECTION COMMISSION

The first chairman of the FEC, Thomas B. Curtis, resigned after one year. Curtis had threatened to resign several times during his term, and on April 30, 1976, he wrote a 23-page letter to President Ford requesting that he not be renominated when the commission was reconstituted.

Curtis raised two issues at the time of his resignation. First, he contended that a truly independent FEC, which he considered essential, would be possible only if the commissioners were part-time and able to continue drawing private income from their principal occupations. Congress headed in the opposite direction, however; the 1976 Amendments required the commissioners to relinquish their private business activities within a year of becoming members.

Second, Curtis raised questions about congressional controls on the FEC, stating that multiyear authorizations were desirable to avoid congressional pressure on the FEC's independence — a crucial point that Congress will need to deal with. The 1976 Amendments provided an authorization of $6 million but the appropriations have been increased in later years.

Upon its reconstitution, the FEC could not agree on a Democrat as chairman to succeed Curtis, a Republican. The members were divided over who best could deal with Congress. So in a compromise action Vernon W. Thomson, a Republican, was elected chairman and Thomas E. Harris, a Democrat, was elected vice chairman. The chairperson's term of office is limited by law to one year, presumably to avoid accretion of power by either party. The plan was to have bipartisan rotation of the chairmanship.

The current chairman of the commission is Robert O. Tiernan, one of the original members nominated by President Ford in 1975.

Four-Year Chairperson

In 1979 the Campaign Study Group of Harvard University's Institute of Politics recommended that the FEC chairperson be appointed to a four-year term and that he or she be responsible for administering the agency. The chairperson's responsibilities also would include appointing the staff director and general counsel and preparing the agency's budget. Under existing law, the commission decides administrative and fiscal business by majority vote; the chairperson represents the agency and presides over the commission meetings,[15] but has little authority. The Harvard Study stated:

> This intentionally "weak" commission structure creates . . . problems that need to be addressed: an absence of adequate accountability on the part of appointed officials; indirect delegation of responsibility to staff without adequate policy direction; and the likelihood that the staff, faced with such absence of direction, will either focus on non-controversial, minor paperwork matters, or, worse, assume policymaking functions properly reserved to publicly accountable officials.[16]

Appointments

The composition of the Federal Election Commission has been a continuing source of conflict. The opposing influences of labor and business frequently are brought to bear on appointments. The conservative and liberal wings of both parties screen each nominee, giving special attention to his or her views. Expertise and political cronyism often vie as criteria for appointments. Ideally, the commission should be comprised of elections experts or persons experienced in election administration, party or campaign management and running for office. In fact, according to some critics, appointments to the FEC have been unduly influenced by the appointees' political connections and leanings.

After taking office in January 1977, President Carter appointed four members, all to six-year terms. Three of these were new appointees; only Thomas Harris was an original member of the commission. Carter's nominations of Harris and Max Friedersdorf were confirmed by the Senate without controversy, but other Carter nominees aroused some opposition. Liberal Republican Samuel Zagoria eventually withdrew his name after his nomination met with strong opposition from the Republican leadership and from corporate interests. Another Republican, Frank P. Reiche, was opposed by conservative Republicans ostensibly because of his support of public financing, but was eventually confirmed. As noted, Democrat John McGarry's confirmation took almost two years.

Advisory Opinions

When Congress rewrote the law in 1976 to reconstitute the commission, it also set new standards for the FEC in writing advisory opinions (AOs) to guide candidates and other interested parties in complying with the law. The commission itself stopped issuing AOs following the 1976 Supreme Court decision and began evaluating them in light of the decision. Many of the 76 AOs that it had issued[17] through December 1975 were criticized by practitioners and scholars for being narrow and legalistic, for inflexibly following the rigidities in the law and for failing to consider traditional political practices.

The new standards set in the 1976 Amendments stipulated that the FEC cannot issue rules of general applicability but must apply AOs only to specific facts presented in a request. Any rules of general applicability must be incorporated into the regulations, which are subject to congressional approval. But the commission itself determines how broadly or narrowly to interpret the law.

The FEC responded in two ways to new requests for advisory opinions. It issued formal advisory opinions if they were applicable to specific factual situations. In other cases, the FEC issued responses to advisory opinions (AORs) which clearly stated that they were not formal advisory opinions but responses based on proposed regulations. While the AOs provided the full protections and immunities granted by the law, the responses to advisory opinions, which involved reliance on proposed regulations, did not afford the same protection to the requesters.

Political Action Committees Advisory. Perhaps the most controversial and widely publicized advisory opinion dealt with corporate political action committees (PACs).[18] It was entitled, "Establishment of Political Action Committee and Employee Political Giving Program by Corporation." However, it was widely called the SunPAC advisory opinion because it was written in response to a request submitted by the Sun Oil Co. The opinion was responsible for some of the delay in reconstituting the FEC, because the 1976 legislation incorporated provisions written in response to this AO.

In a 4-2 decision, the FEC voted to permit corporations to support the election campaigns of candidates for president, vice president, and the Senate and the House so long as the money came from voluntary employee contributions. However, it cautioned corporations that there is a potential for coercion in soliciting employees.

The commission's guidelines on solicitation were: first, that no superior should solicit a subordinate; second, that the solicitor should inform the solicited employee of the political purpose of the fund for which the contribution is solicited; and third, that the solicitor should inform the employee of the employee's right to refuse to contribute.

For the most part, the 1976 Amendments confined unions and corporations to soliciting their own members or stockholders and executives, except that twice a year corporate and union PACs can seek contributions, by mail only, from all employees not otherwise available to them for solicitation. The amendments as they apply to corporate, labor and trade association PACs are discussed in more detail in Chapter 4.

Voluntary Compliance

A major goal for the commission has been to induce voluntary compliance. After enactment of the 1971 FECA, expertise in fulfilling compliance requirements began to develop in the private sector, as candidates and political committees turned to lawyers, accountants and computer specialists for advice on how to comply. Numerous booklets, manuals and guides eased the early burden of compliance. Once it began functioning, the Federal Election Commission supplanted these as the major source of compliance information. It established a toll-free "hotline" to answer questions and held seminars throughout the country in preparation for the 1976 campaigns.

During the 1976 prenomination period, candidates and convention committees found increasing compliance costs particularly burdensome. In the general election campaign, public financing helped ease these financial problems for the two major presidential contenders. The 1976 Amendments and FEC regulations also belatedly allowed compliance-related expenditures to be counted separately and not be charged against statutory limitations. If necessary, money could be raised separately for this purpose.

Since the FEC's inception, compliance actions have dealt mainly with minor infractions. The 1976 Amendments reduced FEC powers and compliance action standards; they specifically forbade the commission to investigate or act on the basis of an anonymous complaint.

After investigation of a formal complaint, the commission must determine whether there is "reasonable cause to believe" that a violation has been committed and make public any determination. The commission must seek to correct the matter through "informal methods of conference, conciliation, and persuasion," conducted in a confidential manner. All attempts at conciliation, and all conciliation agreements, must be made public following resolution.

If a conciliation agreement is not reached, and if the commission determines there is "probable cause" to believe a violation has occurred, it may institute civil actions for relief, including temporary or permanent injunctions, restraining orders or other appropriate orders. The commission has the power to seek civil court enforcement of court orders and conciliation agreements. The commission also has the authority to refer certain serious offenses to the Department of Justice for criminal prosecution. These are "knowing and willful" violations involving the making, receiving or reporting of any contribution or expenditure having a value in the aggregate of $1,000 or more, or having a lesser value in certain cases.

Audits

The FEC's use of its audit authority drew considerable controversy during the commission's first four years, prompting Congress in 1979 to place some restrictions on that power.

Besides auditing presidential candidates to qualify them for matching funds, the FEC conducts audits of publicly financed campaigns after the candidate's withdrawal, the matching period or the campaign's end. By law, public funds not used for qualified campaign expenses must be returned. The auditors also monitor congressional campaigns, which are not publicly financed.

In 1975 the FEC conducted a 10-week audit tour to determine which presidential candidates were eligible for federal matching funds. The commission also randomly audited congressional campaigns that spent more than $35,000 in the case of Senate candidates and $25,000 in the case of House candidates. While the House was particularly critical, claiming the audits were a waste of money, the FEC did find significant discrepancies. For example, Pennsylvania Governor Milton Shapp was declared ineligible for federal funds after a post-election audit of his presidential campaign found misrepresentation. Shapp agreed to repay the matching funds, and some individuals involved in his campaign were fined.

In 1978 the FEC eliminated the random audit procedure and set up a schedule that gave top priority to candidates and committees needing assistance in reporting or record keeping.

The new policy showed that the FEC was willing to restrict the amount and scope of audits. Yet controversy continued over the commission's authority. The FEC audit of Carter's primary and general election campaigns aroused particular criticism. The Carter prenomination audit, released in March 1979, revealed minor discrepancies and technical violations that required an $8,000 repayment. Critics suggested the commission was not equipped to find anything but such minor infractions. The Carter general election audit, released in June 1979, required larger repayments, but it left unresolved certain matters relating to the 1976 campaign.

In 1979 the Campaign Study Group of Harvard's Kennedy Institute of Politics criticized the random audit program. It stated, however, that "the possibility of an audit serves to improve record-keeping and compliance." [19]

Partly because of widespread criticism of the Carter audits, and partly because of continued criticisms by some members of the House, the FEC contracted for two studies of its audit policies and procedures. Both reviewed the audit processes in depth, and both made significant recommendations for change.[20] The FEC then revised its audit policies.

In the 1979 Amendments, Congress eliminated the FEC's authority to conduct random audits and required a vote of four FEC members to conduct an audit after it determined that a committee had not substantially complied with the election campaign law.

Open Meetings

The FEC decided at the outset to be a "sunshine" agency, held regular open meetings except when dealing with personnel actions or enforcement, adopted a code of ethics for its members and employees and provided easy public access to its records and discussions, including the opening of a storefront public room for inspection of political fund reports. During 1975 the FEC processed 25,000 pages of filed reports and received from the three previous supervisory officers almost a million pages of filed reports for the years 1972-74. Emphasizing educating the public and seeking voluntary compliance, the commission mailed some 66,000 items during 1975 explaining the law. It continues to seek to provide ample information to induce voluntary compliance.

The FEC assumed responsibility for the Clearinghouse on Election Administration, which carries on activities and publishes studies relating to registration of voters, voting and election administration. Until 1979 the Clearinghouse served as a communication link among federal, state and local election agencies. It contracted with the Congressional Research Service of the Library of Congress to publish periodically a federal-state election law survey analyzing federal and state legislation and judicial decisions and also to issue an occasional survey of state election laws. But in the 1979 Amendments, the Clearinghouse role was pared back to deal with federal elections only.

PAST AND PROLOGUE

By the beginning of the 1980s, the United States had in place an election regulation system that had taken most of the previous decade to enact and "debug." Federal elections were subject to strict rules for disclosure of spending and contributions, with the role of the wealthy donor greatly diminished, and with public money available for the campaigns of presidential candidates. Unlike the negative reforms of the past, which attempted to prevent election abuses by telling candidates and vested interests what they cannot do, public funding was a positive step forward in that it provided a substitute for the source of funds that the law partially dried up.

The new election system was under the administration of an independent commission, and similar units throughout the country performed a similar function for state and local elections. The states' experience with campaign finance laws will be discussed in Chapter 7.

In the next chapter, we will look at the effect of the reform laws on a still-important source of campaign money: the individual contributor.

NOTES

1. This chapter is derived in part from: Herbert E. Alexander, *Money in Politics* (Washington, D.C.: Public Affairs Press, 1972), chaps. 11-13, pp. 183-251. Also see Louise Overacker, *Money in Elections* (New York: The Macmillan Co., 1932), p. 107; Alexander Heard, *The Costs of Democracy*

(Chapel Hill: The University of North Carolina Press, 1960), pp. 334-335; and David W. Adamany and George E. Agree, *Political Money: A Strategy for Campaign Financing in America* (Baltimore: The Johns Hopkins University Press, 1975).

2. For a case study of the enactment of FECA, see Robert L. Peabody, Jeffrey M. Berry, William G. Frasure and Jerry Goldman, *To Enact a Law: Congress and Campaign Financing* (New York: Praeger Publishers, 1972).
3. *Newberry v. United States,* 256 U.S. 232 (1921).
4. *United States v. Classic,* 313 U.S. 299 (1941).
5. *Financing Presidential Campaigns,* Report of the President's Commission on Campaign Costs (Washington, D.C.: Government Printing Office, 1962).
6. P.L. 92-225.
7. P.L. 93-443.
8. P.L. 94-283.
9. Christopher Lydon, "President Urges Campaign Reform with Gift Limits," *The New York Times,* March 9, 1974.
10. John Herbers, "Bill to Reform Campaign Funds Signed by Ford Despite Doubts," *The New York Times,* October 16, 1974.
11. Paul T. David, "The Federal Election Commission: Origins and Early Activities," *National Civic Review,* vol. 65, no. 6 (June 1976), pp. 278-283.
12. Richard D. Lyons, "Congress Leaders Fight Curbs on 'Slush Funds.'" *The New York Times,* September 15, 1975.
13. Warren Weaver, Jr., "Wayne Hays Today Will Again Tackle Election Board on Rule," *The New York Times,* October 20, 1975.
14. P.L. 96-187.
15. "Analysis of FEC Commissioned by House Recommends Giving Chairman More Power," *Campaign Practices Reports* (Washington, D.C.: Plus Publications Inc.), July 10, 1979, p. 8.
16. "Analysis of FEC," p. 9.
17. *Annual Report 1975,* Federal Election Commission, Washington, D.C., March 1976, pp. 30-32.
18. See Edwin M. Epstein, "Corporations and Labor Unions in Electoral Politics," in "Political Finance: Reform and Reality," *The Annals,* vol. 425 (May 1976), pp. 33-58; Michael J. Malbin, "Corporate PAC-backers Chart a Trail Through Congress," *National Journal,* April 10, 1976; Michael C. Jensen, "The New Corporate Presence in Politics," *The New York Times,* December 14, 1975; David Ignatius, "Firms Get a Slow Start in Inducing Employees to Give to Politicians," *The Wall Street Journal,* May 20, 1976.
19. "Analysis of FEC," p. 12.
20. *Federal Election Commission: Review of the Political Campaign Auditing Process,* conducted by Arthur Andersen & Co., September 1979, 65 pp.; and *Study of the Federal Election Commission's Audit Process,* conducted by Accountants for the Public Interest, September 25, 1979, 28 pp.

3

Sources of Funds: Individuals

The 1976 Supreme Court ruling on the new campaign finance laws left areas where "big money" still might influence campaigns — notably the unlimited spending permitted certain candidates in their own campaigns and the unlimited spending permitted the individual citizen so long as the effort is not coordinated with a candidate. On the other hand, the court upheld the $1,000 gift limit in the law, which greatly reduced the possibilities of a candidate's becoming beholden to large contributors. The effect of the reform laws becomes apparent when sources of campaign funds for the 1976 presidential election — the first to be conducted with public funding and under the contribution limits — are compared with sources of funds for earlier presidential election campaigns.

CAMPAIGN FINANCING — PRE-1968

Money collected from the candidates themselves and assessments on officeholders were sufficient to finance some of the earliest American presidential campaigns. Yet the system was expensive for those participating, and only a few could afford to run for office. Even after election, the salary was low, there was entertaining to do, and there were other demands on personal funds. Thomas Jefferson was almost insolvent when his last term of office as president was ended.[1]

By the 1830s, regular assessments were being levied on the government employees in the New York Custom House, and it was observed that those who refused to pay lost favor.[2] Soon, however, the money raised by collections and assessments was not enough.

Spoils System. Andrew Jackson is generally credited with bringing in the "spoils system," rewarding with favors and government jobs those who had contributed to campaigns. The payoff, of course, might include favorable government policies as well as jobs and contracts.

When August Belmont, the American representative of the House of Rothschild, set up the Democratic National Committee in 1852, he did so to raise funds for the party's presidential candidate, Franklin Pierce. His solicitations apparently were not successful, for it was reported that "at the opportune moment Belmont stepped in and contributed a large sum to the national committee. Thus the matter of funds was taken care of." [3] He would not be the last chairman to contribute to the party from his own pocket.

The Tycoon Era. With the end of the Civil War, the great corporations and individuals who had amassed fortunes from American industry began to pay a major share of presidential campaign costs. Grant is said to have entered office in 1869 more heavily mortgaged to wealth through campaign contributions than any candidate before him.[4] His $200,000 campaign (already double that spent for Lincoln's less than a decade earlier) was largely financed by men such as Commodore Vanderbilt, the Astors and Jay Cooke.[5] They represented the railroad and land grant interests which, along with major corporations, supplied most of the Republican money. Then, as later, only a small share of the wealthy were on the Democrats' side, but it included individuals such as Belmont, Cyrus H. McCormick and Samuel J. Tilden. Accordingly, the Democrats were only relatively disadvantaged.

Throughout the 1860s and 1870s, Jay Cooke held intimate fund-raising dinners in Washington, D.C., for the benefit of the Republican Party.[6] That businessmen should support the political party that most clearly favored their financial interests was accepted practice. "Frying the fat" was a phrase used to describe the means of acquiring campaign contributions from Pennsylvania manufacturers.

The Democrats attempted to raise money in the same way. In 1868 eight Democrats (including Belmont, still chairman of the Democratic National Committee) signed a business contract with the treasurer of the party in which each agreed to give $10,000 "to defray the just and lawful expenses of circulating documents and newspapers, perfecting organizations, etc., to promote the election of Seymour and Blair."

In 1876 the Democrats nominated Samuel J. Tilden, a millionaire said by some to be worth as much as $10 million.[7] Cartoonist Thomas Nast showed him supporting the Democratic campaign chest out of his own "barrel." [8] Actually, Tilden was notoriously tightfisted. He may have lost the election to Rutherford B. Hayes (though he led the Republican contender in both popular and, initially, electoral votes) because he was unwilling to spend enough money to win over more electoral votes.

James A. Garfield, in his presidential campaign in 1880, appealed to his managers to assess government employees for the money he would need. That was the last election, however, in which that source could be legally tapped.[9] Reformers had launched a concerted attack on that system, and the Civil Service Reform Act of 1883 began to protect federal workers from the demands of the parties for tribute money.

Mark Hanna. The financing of campaigns found its genius in Mark Hanna, who rose from wholesale grocer in Cleveland to maker of presidents because of his ability to raise funds for the Republican Party. In 1888 he raised more money than the Republican National Committee could spend; he returned the excess to the donors on a pro rata basis.[10]

In Hanna's view, there were few things that could not be bought with money; his battle to secure the Republican nomination for William McKinley in 1896 reportedly cost $100,000.[11] Hanna was named chairman of the Republican National Committee that year and proceeded to organize, on a scale never seen before, a campaign to elect McKinley. In a style that pioneered the fund-raising techniques of later generations, quotas were set and contributions were determined by ability to pay. Banks were assessed at one-quarter of 1 percent (.0025) of their capital. Life insurance companies, together with many other business organizations, contributed.

Hanna tried to make it clear that there were to be no favors in return for contributions; McKinley wanted to remain clean. In 1900 Hanna returned a $10,000 gift to a Wall Street brokerage firm which he believed was making a specific demand.[12]

The Republicans might not have had such easy access to large funds if the business community had not thought the stakes so large. The free silver issue threatened the existing economic policies of the United States and William Jennings Bryan and the people around him struck fear in many a Republican heart. These campaigns pitted the rich against the poor, the Eastern establishment against Western farmers.

William Jennings Bryan. Bryan never had access to funds in amounts the Republicans had. In 1896 he attempted to match the Republican campaign with resources of only $675,000, about 20 percent of the GOP total. Bryan lost some wealthy "Gold Democrats" to McKinley; most of the contributions Bryan did receive came from a group of wealthy silver mine owners.[13]

Of the $3.5 million that the 1896 Republican campaign is said to have cost, about $3 million was said to have come from New York City and vicinity and the rest from Chicago.[14] Harold L. Ickes, who worked in that election for McKinley, later wrote: "I never doubted that if the Democrats had been able to raise enough money, even for legitimate purposes, Bryan would have been elected." [15]

Theodore Roosevelt. Elected vice president in 1900, "TR" succeeded to the presidency on the death of McKinley in 1901. For his campaign in 1904, Roosevelt turned down the suggestion of Lincoln Steffens that he depend on small gifts of from $1 to $5.[16] He solicited funds from two of the country's richest men, railroad magnate E. H. Harriman and Henry C. Frick, a partner of Andrew Carnegie. According to one account, Frick later reported: "He got down on his knees to us. We bought the son of a bitch and then he did not stay bought." [17] Despite the immense corporate and private contributions to his campaign, Roosevelt showed little appreciation for the "hand that had fed him" as he began to attack the trusts and the men who had given to his campaign.

It took a long time to recognize the need to avoid obligations to special interests, though as early as 1873 in a speech at the University of Wisconsin, Chief Justice Edward G. Ryan of the Wisconsin Supreme Court had said: "The question will arise . . . which shall rule — wealth or man; which shall lead — money or intellect; who shall fill public station — educated and patriotic free men, or the feudal serfs of corporate capital."[18] Charles P. Taft, the brother of William Howard Taft, contributed $250,000 to his brother's campaigns in 1908 and 1912 because he did not want him to have to go begging to the large corporations or be under obligation to anyone as president.[19] In 1907 Roosevelt made several proposals to Congress to improve the political finance system, including government funding of political campaigns; one proposal, prohibiting direct corporate contributions to federal campaigns, was adopted that year and remains the law today.

Fund-Raising Dinners. The 1936 presidential campaign was one of the most expensive on record — the total was not exceeded until the 1960 race — and it gave birth to a new fund-raising technique that quickly became a staple, the $100-a-plate dinner. The technique is credited to Matthew McCloskey, a Philadelphia contractor and later treasurer and finance chairman of the Democratic National Committee, who arranged a dinner at the time of FDR's inauguration to raise money for the Democrats.[20] The idea spread quickly and widely; the $100-a-plate dinners, luncheons, breakfasts and brunches became common at all levels of the political system. With affluence and increased needs, the $500-a-plate and $1,000-a-plate affairs were held for more select groups. In 1968 Nixon held just one fund-raising dinner, but 22 cities were linked by closed-circuit television for that one event. The dinner grossed $6 million; the new profit, $4.6 million, was close to one-fifth the total cost of the campaign.

Big contributors continued to play a major part in the campaigns of the 1940s, 1950s and the 1960s. In 1948, for example, seven out of every 10 dollars (69 percent) contributed to the Democrats' national-level committees came from donations of $500 or more. In 1956 the comparable proportion for the Republicans was 74 percent. In 1964, 69 percent of the Democrats' money came from large donors; four years later, the Democrats' national-level committees received 61 percent of their funds from $500-plus donors.

1968 CAMPAIGN

In 1968 much more information about large contributors, both on and off the record, was available than ever before. That was especially the case in the prenomination period. Nixon, Eugene McCarthy and Robert F. Kennedy are believed to have had at least one $500,000 donor in their prenomination campaigns; McCarthy may have had two. One political contributor, Stewart R. Mott, divided $300,000 between Nelson Rockefeller and McCarthy. Initially, Mott spent $100,000 trying to persuade Rockefeller to run as an anti-Vietnam War candidate; then he turned to McCarthy.

One of the largest known contributions in 1968, just under $1.5 million, came to light unexpectedly. Until 1972 no federal law required disclosure of campaign funds in the prenomination period, and most campaign committees were legally set up in a state (such as Delaware) that had no disclosure laws. But for an unknown reason, one major Rockefeller committee was set up in New York, which did have a reporting law. The committee received $1,482,625 from Mrs. John D. Rockefeller Jr., Nelson Rockefeller's stepmother.

Mrs. Rockefeller's contribution was an unusual one in American politics in that she subsequently was required to pay gift taxes of $854,483. As gift taxes applied only to contributions in excess of $3,000, the larger donor normally would split up his gift into numerous smaller contributions made to multiple paper committees, all supporting the same candidate and established expressly for the purpose of tax avoidance.

The largest single contributor in the 1968 election was W. Clement Stone, chairman of the Combined Insurance Co. of America. Stone gave more than $2.8 million to the Republicans — all but $39,000 of that amount to Nixon to aid both his nomination and general election campaigns.

1972 CAMPAIGN

In terms of both numbers of individuals and amounts given, very large donors reached what seems almost certain to stand as their highest level of participation in campaign financing in the 1972 election. The information available about those largest of donors — contributors of $10,000 or more — indicates that they bankrolled the 1972 campaigns to an extraordinary degree. Just 1,254 individuals contributed a total of $51.3 million.[21]

Broader Data Base

Beginning with the 1972 election, much more than was ever known previously about sources of funds and categories of expenditures came to light, providing data for a more systematic analysis. The Corrupt Practices Act of 1925 did not apply to primary candidates, and it required reporting only by committees operating in two or more states. But adoption of the FECA in 1971 brought primaries and runoffs under coverage of the law. It also brought under coverage any committee raising or spending in excess of $1,000 and seeking to influence federal elections. These provisions led to geometric increases in information about both contributions and expenditures.

In the 1972 election, the General Accounting Office (GAO), the Clerk of the House, and the Secretary of the Senate each began to receive thousands of detailed reports. For the period covering April 7 (when the law took effect) to Dec. 31, 1972, the three offices together received well over a quarter-million pages of data, excluding instruction pages and audit notices.

Unfortunately, the reporting arrangement meant considerable overlap and duplication. A single committee supporting candidates for president, for the Senate and for the House, for example, was required to file reports containing the same information with the Comptroller General of the United States (head of the GAO), the Clerk of the House and the Secretary of the Senate. More than 1,000 committees — about a fifth of the 4,744 separate committees registered under the FECA — filed with two or three of those supervisory offices. Consequently, the problem confronting the student of campaign finance was to distinguish the discrete from the overlapping information.

Nevertheless, the massive amounts of data meant that journalists and scholars could study and report campaign practices in greater detail and with greater certainty than ever before.

Voluntary Disclosure

Spurred on by the new law and seeing a strategic campaign advantage, several of the presidential candidates voluntarily disclosed some of their contributions prior to April 7, 1972, adding considerably to the data base. Senator George McGovern, a Democratic contender, and Representative Paul N. McCloskey, Jr., a Republican challenger to incumbent President Nixon, made full disclosure of all contributions their central campaigns received. With varying scope and for varying times, partial disclosures were also made by four other Democrats — Senator Hubert Humphrey, New York Mayor John Lindsay, Senator Edmund S. Muskie and Alabama Governor George C. Wallace. In all, almost 1,500 contributions in sums of $500 or more were disclosed voluntarily by the six candidates. They totaled almost $4 million.[22] The other candidates flatly refused to make voluntary disclosures, though some data were subsequently collected and made public by the Citizens' Research Foundation from filings in states requiring disclosure where presidential primaries were held. Common Cause sued to force disclosure of the pre-April 7 receipts and expenditures of the Nixon reelection campaign. The legal action resulted in partial disclosure by court stipulation just before the November election; full disclosure was agreed upon and complied with in September 1973. Ironically, full disclosure meant that Nixon's campaign, otherwise noted for its secret funds and undercover operations, became the first presidential campaign in history fully on the record as far as its financing was concerned.

Big Contributors

The three largest contributors in 1972 gave a total of $4 million, the bulk of it to the presidential campaigns.

W. Clement Stone. The largest single contributor was again W. Clement Stone of Chicago, who donated $2,141,655.94. Stone, who began his insurance office with $100 and a rented desk and developed it into the Combined Insurance Co., contributed $2 million of the total to the Nixon reelection campaign in the pre-April period and $51,643.45 after disclosure became mandatory. He also made contributions ranging down from $11,500 to $500 to a number of congressional candidates and various committees. All but one were Republicans or Republican causes (the exception was an $8,411.54 donation to the reelection campaign of Democratic Senator Jennings Randolph of West Virginia). From 1968 to 1972, Stone and his wife, Jessie, contributed $7 million to political candidates and committees. With the exception of about $25,000, all of this money went to the Republicans, and most of it — more than $4.8 million — went to Nixon's 1968 and 1972 campaigns. These contributions may make Stone the largest contributor in American history.

Richard Mellon Scaife. The second largest contributor in 1972 was Richard Mellon Scaife, heir to the Mellon oil (Gulf), aluminum (Alcoa) and banking fortune, who gave the Republicans $1,068,000, most of it — $1 million — as a contribution to the Nixon campaign. As details of the Watergate scandal came to light, Scaife repudiated Nixon. In a May 1974 editorial in the *Greensburg* (Pa.) *Tribune-Review,* which he publishes, he called for Nixon's impeachment.[23]

Stewart R. Mott. The third largest 1972 contributor, Stewart R. Mott, heir to a General Motors fortune, was a McGovern supporter. Mott gave $822,592 in 1972 (not including some $25,200 in investment-loss deductions) to liberal and mainly anti-Vietnam-policy candidates and causes. Most of Mott's contributions went to the Democrats. Nearly half ($400,000) went to McGovern.

Others. Missing from the list of top givers in 1972, with the exception of Richard Mellon Scaife, are the names of the owners of the great American fortunes — the Fords, the Rockefellers, Whitneys and Astors, whose support had been crucial in earlier political campaigns, particularly those of Republicans. In 1972 those families were displaced by donors such as Stone, John A. Mulcahy, Anthony Rossi and Abe Plough. All of the latter could boast of Horatio Alger success stories. Mulcahy, a poor Irish immigrant in the 1920s, rose to the presidency of a steel industry equipment supplier and then became a major stockholder in a drug firm merger (Pfizer Inc.). Rossi, a former bricklayer and tomato farmer, born in Sicily, built Tropicana Products into a major company. Plough, chairman of Schering-Plough Corp., maker of St. Joseph's aspirin, began his career in 1908 as a door-to-door medicine oil salesman. Like Stone, all three were major backers of Nixon, with Mulcahy's $625,000 topping their gifts.

Along with Mott on the Democratic side the biggest contributors were Max Palevsky, at one time the largest stockholder in the Xerox Corp.; Martin Peretz of the Harvard faculty and his wife Anne, a Singer Co. heiress; and Dr. Alejandro Zaffaroni, the Uruguayan-born president of Alza Corp., a California drug research firm. All of these were among George McGovern's top contributors, replacing the traditional Democratic supporters such as the Lehmans, the Harrimans and others of earlier years.

Several of the largest 1972 contributors gave to both Republican and Democratic presidential campaigns. One so-called "split contributor," Meshulam Riklis, chairman of the board of Rapid-American Corp., was among a group of Democratic businessmen who met with McGovern in a New York hotel in January 1970. At the meeting he asked McGovern about his position on Israel (Riklis was an Israeli immigrant). McGovern answered that lasting peace in the Middle East could be achieved only by a negotiated settlement worked out by the United Nations. This position, not acceptable to Zionists, cost McGovern the support of some members of the Jewish community.[24]

Part of the gift of another of the largest split contributors, Minnesota soybean millionaire Dwayne O. Andreas, figured in the early unraveling of the Watergate affair. Andreas' check for $25,000, made out to the Nixon reelection campaign, was discovered in the Miami bank account of Watergate burglar Bernard Barker, a revelation that triggered a GAO audit of the Finance Committee for the Reelection of the President.

The Very Rich

The dominant allegiance to the Republican Party of wealthy persons — a fact of U.S. political history for decades — was never more apparent than in 1972. An analysis of the contribution patterns of the nation's centimillionaires (those with fortunes of $150 milion or more) shows that Republican money "outnumbered" Democratic money by better than 10 to 1 (Table 3-1). The Republican advantage was even more marked in 1972 than it had been in 1968 when centimillionaires also were studied.[25]

Centimillionaires. There were 66 centimillionaires on the 1968 *Fortune* list. Forty six of them (70 percent) were recorded as political contributors in 1968,[26] with total gifts of $3,705,000. Four years later, 63

Table 3-1 American Centimillionaires' Contributions in 1972 and 1968 Campaigns

	1972	*1968*
Number of Contributors	51	46
To Republicans	$5,550,896	$3,584,000
To Democrats	496,522	121,000
Miscellaneous	23,600	11,000
Totals	$6,071,018	$3,716,000

of those centimillionaires were still living and 51 of them (81 percent) made contributions to a political candidate or committee. Their contributions reported in 1972 amounted to $6.1 million, more than their gifts reported in 1968, when contribution disclosure laws were less stringent.

Twenty four of the 51 centimillionaire contributors in 1972 gave only to Republicans. Five gave only to Democrats.

Seventeen of the centimillionaires split their contributions, giving to both sides, though often only a nominal amount to one. But the largest Democratic contributor, Leon Hess, chairman of Amerada Hess Oil Co., gave $228,500 to Democrats (accounting for more than half of the total contributions of the centimillionaires to Democrats) and $252,500 to Republicans. Hess' donations to Republicans made him the second-largest contributor to Republicans in the centimillionaire group.

The Newly Rich. In 1973 *Fortune* compiled and published a list of 39 persons who had amassed the bulk of their wealth since the 1968 list was put together and who possessed fortunes of at least $50 million.[27] The new list did not include persons who had become wealthy entirely through inheritance.

Of those who were named, 28 (72 percent) contributed in 1972 to a political campaign or committee. Although the Republican contributions among this group in 1972 heavily outweighed the Democratic gifts, the advantage was not so overwhelming as it had been with the older, more established wealthy — about 3 to 1 Republicans compared with 10 to 1 on the earlier list. From the newly rich, the Republicans received $1,118,754 and the Democrats $321,865 ($4,000 fell in the miscellaneous category). Sixteen of the 28 gave only to the Republicans and two gave only to the Democrats.

Donors and Parties

Because of the expansion of information as well as particular interest in the election events of that year, Citizens' Research Foundation prepared a list of contributors whose aggregate contributions totaled $10,000 or more in 1972. The list was drawn from both governmental and nongovernmental sources.[28] This compilation shows that $51.3 million was raised from such contributors — more than four times the amount recorded in this gift category in 1968 when reporting requirements were less stringent.

The data show that 64 percent of the money given by these very large donors came from contributors who gave to only one party, so-called "straight party givers." Nearly half of the straight party money came from 82 individuals, each of whom gave an aggregate of $100,000 or more — some $14.3 million of the $33 million in straight party gifts.

Straight party contributions from the large donors to Republican candidates and party organizations amounted to more than twice the sum given to Democratic candidates and party organizations — $23.3 million to $9.4 million. The major beneficiary of large contributions was Nixon, who received $19.8 million in gifts from straight party contributions from these sources. In contrast, George McGovern's straight party contributors in the $10,000-and-over category gave him a total of $4.1 million.

Large contributors who split their gifts made political donations totaling $18.2 million in 1972. The split contributors tended to divide their gifts among different levels — giving, for example, to a presidential candidate of one party and a senatorial candidate of another. Or they supported the candidate of one party in the primary and then shifted their financial allegiance to the other party's candidate in the general election — in most cases, when their original primary candidate had lost the nomination.

1976 CAMPAIGN

The sources of funds for the 1976 presidential campaigns and the formulas for public funding in the prenomination and general election periods are considered in detail in Chapter 5. Some indications of those sources here, however, will allow a comparison to be made between the 1976 and earlier presidential elections.

Public Funding

In 1976 for the first time, candidates for the presidential nomination and for the presidency itself received government funds to subsidize their campaigns. The federal subsidies were intended in part to make up for the monies candidates no longer could seek from wealthy donors, since the 1974 FECA Amendments limited the amount of money individuals and groups could contribute.

During the prenomination campaigns, matching funds were provided for qualified presidential candidates. The U.S. Treasury contributed $23.7 million to the 1976 primary campaigns of 15 candidates (13 Democrats and two Republicans). During the general election campaign, the Treasury provided $43.6 million to the general election campaigns of Jimmy Carter and Gerald Ford.

Federal funding thus accounted for 35 percent of the money spent by the principal campaign committees of the primary candidates qualified to receive matching funds and 95 percent of the money spent by the principal campaign committees of Carter and Ford. Of the overall total of $160 million spent in relation to the 1976 presidential election, federal funds accounted for more than 42 percent.

Wealthy Donors

The 1974 FECA Amendments limited contributions by an individual to a candidate for federal office to $1,000 for each primary, runoff and general election and to an aggregate contribution of $25,000 for all federal candidates annually. Faced with this restriction, many wealthy donors continued to contribute in 1976, but only in the smaller amounts permitted by the new laws.

No comprehensive compilation of 1976 donors was made by the FEC or private organizations. The changes the 1974 Amendments required wealthy donors to make in their patterns of political giving may be illustrated, however, by examining the contributions of Stewart R. Mott in the 1972 and 1976 election campaigns. In 1972 Mott contributed $822,592 to a variety of candidates and political organizations. Most were candidates for federal office; George McGovern alone received $400,000 of Mott's contributions. In 1976, as Table 3-2 indicates, no candidate for federal office received more than $1,000 from Mott and the total of his contributions to federal candidates and multicandidate committees came to $25,000, nearly $800,000 less than his contributions in the previous presidential election year.

Other Sources of Funds

To make up for the revenue lost because of restrictions placed on large donors, candidates sought to fund the prenomination campaigns in a variety of ways. Some sought the volunteer services of rock music groups and other entertainers who held benefit concerts that netted the candidates the seed money they needed. Some used direct-mail appeals to solicit small contributions from large numbers of donors. The use of direct mail in presidential and other election campaigns is considered later in the chapter. Some candidates benefited from contributions by political action committees, though to a lesser extent than in 1972. Those contributions were not matchable under the public funding system used in the 1976 presidential election, and PAC money was directed mainly to Congress. The role of political action committees in 1976 as well as in previous years is considered in detail in Chapter 4.

Table 3-2 Federal Political Gifts of Stewart R. Mott, 1976 [a]

Recipient	Date	Amount		Recipient	Date	Amount		Total
President								
Bayh	12/75	$ 250		McCarthy	12/75	$ 250	+$750 on 2/76 + 200 on 9/76	
Brown	5/76	250						
Carter	12/75	250		Sanford	12/75	250		
Church	12/75	250	+$750 on 3/76	Shriver	12/75	250		
Harris	12/75	250		Udall	12/75	250	+$250 on 3/76	
Total president								$ 4,200
Senate								
Abzug	7/76	1,000	N.Y.	Mink	8/76	1,000	Hawaii	
DeConcini	10/76	200	Ariz.	Moss	2/76	150	Utah + $500 on 10/76	
Green	10/76	250	Pa.	Muskie	10/76	100	Maine	
Hayden	12/75	1,000	Calif.	Riegle	12/75	1,000	Mich. + $600 on 9/76	
Hayes	4/76	1,000	Ind.	Sarbanes	8/76	600	Md.	
Humphrey	10/76	150	Minn.	Sasser	10/76	200	Tenn.	
Kennedy	4/76	300	Mass.	Schaffer	8/76	1,000	Conn.	
Maloney	8/76	300	Del.	Tunney	10/76	150	Calif.	
Matsunaga	10/76	150	Hawaii	Tydings	12/75	1,000	Md.	
Melcher	8/76	300	Mont.	Warner	8/76	1,000	Ariz.	
Metzenbaum	8/76	600	Ohio					
Total Senate								12,550
House								
Badillo	8/76	500	N.Y. 21	Mankiewicz	4/76	200	Md. 3	
Baucus	8/76	100	Mont. 1	McCloskey	10/76	150	Calif. 12	
Carr	8/76	500	Mich. 6	Meyer	10/76	100	N.Y. 23	

Recipient	Date	Amount	District	Recipient	Date	Amount	District		
Clancy	8/76	200	Ill. 6	Meyner	8/76	200	N.J. 13		
Downey	8/76	500	N.Y. 2	Mezvinsky	10/76	100	Iowa 1		
Drinan	10/76	150	Mass. 4	Mikva	10/76	150	Ill. 10		
Fornos	4/76	200	Md. 4	Moffett	8/76	100	Conn. 6		
Fullinwider	8/76	200	Ariz. 1	Pattison	8/76	100	N.Y. 29		
Harkin	8/76	300	Iowa 5	Rapp	8/76	300	Iowa 3		
Hechler	10/76	150	W.Va. 4	Schroeder	10/76	200	Colo. 1		
Holtzman	6/76	200	N.Y. 16	Solarz	5/76	200	N.Y. 13		
Keys	10/76	150	Kan. 2	Spellman	8/76	200	Md. 5		
Kildee	7/76	500	Mich. 7	VanderVeen	10/76	150	Mich. 5		
Koch	5/76	200	N.Y. 18	Weiss	8/76	100	N.Y. 20		
Lowenstein	10/76	150	N.Y. 5	Wirth	8/76	200	Colo. 2		
Maguire	8/76	100	N.J. 7	Wolpe	8/76	200	Mich. 3		
Total House									6,750
Multicandidate Committees									
Democratic Study Group					8/76			500	
National Committee for an Effective Congress (NCEC)					8/76			1,000	
Total Multicandidate Committees									1,500
Total Federal Political Gifts 1976									$25,000

[a]As of October 27, 1976

Note: In December 1975 Mott gave $10,000 to NCEC and $6,000 to the Women's Campaign Fund — both for general operating activities, not included in the $25,000 ceiling.

As we saw in Chapter 2, the Supreme Court upheld the FECA ban on direct contributions to the major-party nominees after the conventions, if those candidates accepted public funding. Since both Carter and Ford did accept the federal grants, individuals and groups were barred from directly contributing to their campaigns in the general election. Unions as well as corporations, however, were free to spend unlimited amounts on political communications directed toward their own members or employees and their families. As will be pointed out in Chapter 5, unions reported spending more than $2 million on such communications to help Carter. In addition, it is estimated that unions spent $11 million on other political activity, such as general political communication, voter registration and get-out-the-vote activities, that also benefited the Democratic nominee. Corporations and other business-related groups, on the other hand, did little spending on political activity during the general election campaign.

AMBASSADORSHIPS FOR BIG DONORS

The common practice of rewarding large contributors with federal jobs became the focus of one set of investigations by the special Watergate prosecutor following the 1972 election. After his landslide reelection, President Nixon had appointed 319 persons to high-level federal positions (including ambassadorships) and all won Senate confirmation. Fifty-two of these appointees, or 17 percent, were recorded as having contributed $100 or more to the Republicans; their gifts totaled $772,224, with $703,654 of that going to the Nixon campaign.

The appointment of Ruth Farkas, the largest single donor in the group, as ambassador to Luxembourg generated by far the most controversy of any of Nixon's ambassadorial appointments. Farkas, a sociologist and a director of Alexander's, a New York department store, had given $300,000 to Nixon's campaign. According to testimony during the Watergate hearings, Farkas reportedly had balked at an offer of an ambassadorship to Costa Rica, saying, "Isn't $250,000 an awful lot of money for Costa Rica?" [29]

Several individuals felt the repercussions of the Farkas affair. Herbert W. Kalmbach, President Nixon's personal lawyer, was imprisoned for fund-raising activities relating in part to "ambassadorial auctions" — a promise of a federal job in return for financial support is a violation of federal law. Peter Flanigan, who as a White House aide had figured in the Farkas discussions, asked President Ford not to renew his nomination as ambassador to Spain.

Carter's Pledge

During his campaign, Carter had declared that he would take the selection of envoys out of the realm of politics. Carter's efforts as president to implement his announced policy brought a wide variety of reaction from informed commentators. But an analysis of the campaign contributions of the Carter-appointed ambassadors is not possible because the FEC has not compiled full lists of contributors for 1976, and limits on allowable donations make their analysis less revealing than in previous election years.

Some of Carter's nominations met with criticism. The American Foreign Service Association (AFSA) opposed the nominations of Anne Chambers Cox and Philip H. Alston, Jr., who were named ambassadors to Belgium and Australia, respectively. The AFSA charged that both had been major contributors to Carter's past political campaigns and that neither was qualified. The appointment of Marvin L. Warner, an Ohio real estate developer, to Switzerland also was controversial. Warner, a large contributor to Carter's campaign, also had been an Ohio fund-raiser for Carter, arranging one breakfast netting $20,000. Cleveland businessman Milton Wolfe, named ambassador to Austria, was a former Jackson supporter who switched to Carter and is credited with helping to raise $80,000 in one evening from Cleveland businessmen.

On the other hand, some observers complained that Carter's appointments to ambassadorial and other posts were not sufficiently political. These critics included the Democratic National Committee, which adopted a resolution opposing the new president's approach to patronage.

DIRECT-MAIL APPEALS

1972 Campaign

The direct-mail approach to raising campaign funds — essentially an appeal for a great many individual contributions, however modest — has been used in politics for a number of years, but it was raised to something of a high art form in the 1972 contests.

McGovern Campaign. The use of direct mail made a financial success of George McGovern's campaign, even though the Democratic senator from South Dakota lost badly to Nixon in the general election. Direct mail also contributed to McGovern's political success in the preconvention period.

The Democratic presidential nominee's campaign, launched with a reported $280,000 debt, was the party's first to end with a surplus since the campaigns of Franklin D. Roosevelt. In part, this was due to McGovern's appeal to a clear-cut segment of the voting population. Like Barry Goldwater in 1964 and George Wallace in 1968, McGovern was considered a fractional or fringe candidate. All three succeeded in getting financial support from large numbers of small contributors though, in the end, they failed to win the election.

McGovern attracted at least 600,000 donors. McGovern's massive direct-mail drive was begun more than a year before he won the nomination, in early 1971. During that year, when McGovern was the choice of fewer than 10 percent of Democrats responding to the national opinion polls, $600,000 was raised by this means. Between the New Hampshire primary in March 1972 and the convention in the summer, an additional $2.4 million was raised through direct mail; that spring, some three million pieces were mailed. Thus, McGovern raised some $3 million in the prenomination period, at a cost of more than $1 million. That sum was largely received in contributions of $100 or less. In the general election campaign, $12 million was brought in through direct mail, with 15 million pieces mailed, at a cost of about $3.5 million to the national headquarters alone.

McGovern's use of direct mail had its beginnings in South Dakota politics. A compulsive list-keeper as he crisscrossed the traditionally Republican state, he added to his lists when he moved into the national spotlight with anti-Vietnam War activities in 1970. He obtained still more names that year from a massive national direct-mail appeal for some of his fellow Democratic senators.

In January 1971, three days before McGovern formally announced he was seeking the presidency, 300,000 letters went into the mail, timed to arrive on the day he announced. The seven-page letter had been drafted in consultation with Morris Dees, a millionaire civil rights lawyer and direct-mail expert, and Thomas Collins of Rapp and Collins, a New York advertising firm. The letter discussed McGovern's reasons for seeking the nomination, and it appealed for funds to help. The strategy subsequently proved to be the most successful effort using this approach in American political history. It more than tripled the Goldwater results of 1964, which raised some $5.8 million from about 651,000 donors.

A major appeal of McGovern fund-raisers was for loans from wealthy persons to serve as "seed money" for the direct-mail drive. This money made it possible to reach out continually to the thousands of potential small contributors, whose gifts, in turn, helped repay the loans. This practice of lending large sums of money is no longer possible since the contribution limits of $1,000 per candidate per election include loans within the definition of contribution.

McGovern mailings averaged about 16 cents apiece, broken down as follows:

Postage	$0.080
Letter	0.015
Envelope	0.008
Return envelope	0.005
Mailing house fee	0.015
Lists and record keeping	0.030
Agency fee	0.010
Total	$0.163

McGovern invariably appealed for funds at the conclusion of his television broadcasts; some five-minute broadcasts were designed essentially as fund-raisers. Such appeals brought in an estimated $3 million. Broadcasts were timed to coincide with direct-mail appeals that were already on their way.

Nixon Direct Mail. Although direct mail did not have the importance in the 1972 Nixon campaign that it had in McGovern's campaign, the Nixon organization did make use of it. A gross of $9 million was realized from mailings of 30 million pieces. Before July 1972 the appeals to small contributors were conducted chiefly by the Republican National Committee (RNC). In the months before Nixon's renomination, the RNC raised $5.3 million through its sustaining membership program. The contributions averaged $20. A telephone drive during that period brought in more than $500,000. In that drive, the contributions averaged $30. Direct-mail drives conducted by the RNC alone and conducted jointly with the Committee for the Reelection of the President (CRP) after Nixon's renomination brought in $14.3 million. Combined telephone drives raised $2.5 million.

A number of claims were made regarding the number of Republican contributors in 1972. About 250,000 persons contributed to the RNC. About 600,000 contributors were claimed by national and state affiliates of the CRP. Eliminating duplications and repeat contributors, probably 600,000 gave some money to the RNC in its annual program, in response to its combined Nixon mailings after his nomination, or to some level of the CRP or of Democrats for Nixon.

1976 Primaries

Most major candidates who entered the presidential primary contests in 1976 used direct-mail fund raising, at least to some extent. When Morris Dees, who helped engineer McGovern's 1972 direct-mail fund drive, became Jimmy Carter's national finance chairman in 1975, the role of direct mail in Carter's campaign was assured. Dees felt that direct mail would not be so productive for a centrist candidate like Carter as it had been for the more liberal McGovern. Consequently Carter did not rely so heavily on direct mail as McGovern had. Nevertheless, by May 1976, according to Dees, about one-third of all private contributions — more than $2.5 million — came in response to direct mail.

Senator Henry Jackson's campaign mailed fund-raising appeals to selected groups, such as members of the Jewish segment of the population which significantly supported Jackson's candidacy largely because of his pro-Israel posture. Though the Jackson campaign relied more heavily on other fund-raising techniques, it achieved maximum income from a relatively small mailing list.

According to one of Representative Morris Udall's campaign managers, direct mail was the "heart and soul" of Udall's campaign finances. In all, about 62,000 people sent money to Udall. Of these, some 7,000 donated more than once.

As in previous election years, George Wallace was successful in his use of direct mail. By the end of the primary season, the Wallace campaign had received about $6.8 million, much of it coming in response to direct-mail appeals. However, at least $2.6 million went to the fund-raising firm Wallace had hired.

On the Republican side, both Gerald Ford and Ronald Reagan benefited from direct mail. In all, the President Ford Committee mailed nearly 2.6 million appeals and raised $2.5 million. Reagan also had some success with direct mail, but found televised pitches more effective.

(Since both Carter and Ford accepted public funding after they won the nominations, they were prohibited from soliciting private donations and direct mail was not used to raise funds for the 1976 presidential general election campaigns.)

Candidates for other offices as well as a variety of political action committees also have come to rely on direct mail to raise needed funds. In 1978, for example, Senator Jesse Helms, R-N.C., raised some $6.9 million for his reelection campaign. A large portion of that money was contributed in response to direct-mail appeals.

One outstanding example of the successful use of direct mail is the RNC's Republican National Sustaining Fund, which was organized in 1962. An annual sustaining membership costs $20 per contributor, with donations of up to $499 considered in the last two years in the following totals:

1962	$ 700,000	1970	$ 3,040,000
1963	1,100,000	1971	4,369,000
1964	2,369,000	1972	5,282,000
1965	1,700,000	1973	3,964,000
1966	3,300,000	1974	4,759,482
1967	3,500,000	1975	5,971,877
1968	2,400,000	1976	10,112,078
1969	2,125,000	1977	7,755,800*
		1978	9,730,000*

* *Includes contributions of up to $499.*

In 1978, there were 510,000 individual contributors.

PATTERNS IN POLITICAL GIVING

Recent elections have become known for disillusionment with candidates and the political process on the part of large segments of the electorate. At the same time, the techniques of fund raising — television, sophisticated direct-mail appeals and other means — have been used to seek out broader audiences. Indeed, while new fund-raising techniques are reaching more people, the proportion that is contributing seems not to be increasing.

Still, the probability that there is a reservoir of untapped potential for campaign funds is suggested by other survey findings. From time to time, the Gallup Poll has asked people whether they would contribute $5 to a party campaign fund if they were asked. Throughout the 1940s and 1950s, approximately one-third of those surveyed said that they would be willing to contribute; in the 1960s this segment increased to more than 40 percent. Even with the enormous costs of today's presidential elections, only a small portion of potential of this kind would have to be tapped to eliminate many of the financial problems of the parties.

In both the centimillionaire and new rich groups, the percentages of those contributing are very high — ranging from 46 percent to 72 percent — compared with the rest of the population. For example, surveys indicate that from 8 to 12 percent of the total adult population contributes to politics at some level in presidential election years. However, about 25 percent of federal income tax payers consistently show a willingness to

Table 3-3 Percentage of National Adult Population Solicited and Making Political Contributions, 1952-76

		Solicited by:			*Contributed to:*		
Year	*Polling Organization*	*Rep.*	*Dem.*	*Total*[a]	*Rep.*	*Dem.*	*Total*[a]
1952	SRC				3	1	4
1956	Gallup	8	11	19	3	6	9
1956	SRC				5	5	10
1960	Gallup	9	8	15	4	4	9
1960	Gallup						12
1960	SRC				7	4	11
1964	Gallup				6	4	12
1964	SRC	8	4	15	6	4	11
1968	SRC	9	7	23[b]	4	4	9[c]
1972	SRC				4	5	10[d]
1974	SRC				3	3	8[e]
1976	Gallup				3	3	8[f]
1976	SRC				4	4	9[g]

[a]The total percentage may add to a total different from the total of Democrats and Republicans because of individuals solicited by or contributing to both major parties, nonparty groups, or combinations of these.

[b]Includes 4 percent who were solicited by both major parties and 1.4 percent who were solicited by Wallace's American Independent Party (AIP).

[c]Includes .7 percent who contributed to Wallace's AIP.

[d]Includes contributors to American Independent Party.

[e]Includes .7 percent who contributed to both parties, and .8 percent who contributed to minor parties.

[f]Includes 1 percent to another party and 1 percent Do Not Know or No Answer.

[g]Republican and Democratic figures are rounded. The total includes .6 percent who gave to both parties, .4 percent to other, and .3 percent Do Not Know.

SOURCE: Survey Research Center (SRC), University of Michigan; data direct from center or from Angus Campbell, Philip E. Converse, Warren E. Miller, Donald E. Stokes, *The American Voter* (New York: John Wiley and Sons, 1960), p. 91; Gallup data direct or from Roper Opinion Research Center, Williams College, and from American Institute of Public Opinion (Gallup Poll).

earmark $1 of their payment to the presidential campaign fund through the checkoffs.

Survey results compiled by the Gallup Poll and the Survey Research Center of the University of Michigan over the last quarter-century show a large increase in the number of political contributors during the 1950s (Table 3-3). As shown below, the number remained relatively steady in 1960 and 1964, fell off in the 1968 election, and in 1972 climbed back to about the level of eight years earlier. Applying survey percentages to the adult, noninstitutionalized population suggests that there were:

3 million contributors in 1952,
8 million contributors in 1956,
10 million contributors in 1960,
12 million contributors in 1964,
8.7 million contributors in 1968,
11.7 million contributors in 1972, and
12.2 million contributors in 1976.

We have seen in this chapter that while federal law has inhibited the role of the wealthy individual giver, small donors in large numbers have become increasingly important — and have the potential to play an even bigger part in financing campaigns. Next we will look at another money source that has been given an enhanced role: business, labor and other special interest groups.

NOTES

1. Jasper B. Shannon, *Money in Politics* (New York: Random House, 1959), p. 14.
2. Louise Overacker, *Money in Elections* (New York: The Macmillan Co., 1932), p. 102.
3. Roy Franklin Nicholas, *The Democratic Machine 1850-1852,* as quoted in Shannon, *Money and Politics,* p. 21.
4. Wilfred E. Binkley, *American Political Parties* (4th ed.; New York: Alfred A. Knopf, 1962), p. 279.
5. Edwin P. Hoyt, Jr., *Jumbos and Jackasses, A Popular History of the Political Wars* (Garden City: Doubleday & Co. Inc., 1960), p. 77.
6. Alexander Heard, *The Costs of Democracy* (Chapel Hill, N.C.: University of North Carolina Press, 1960), p. 233.
7. John Bigelow, ed., *Letters and Literary Memorials of Samuel J. Tilden, 1908,* p. 245, as quoted in Shannon, *Money and Politics,* p. 26.
8. Eugene H. Roseboom, *A History of Presidential Elections* (New York: The Macmillan Company, 1957), p. 242,
9. Shannon, *Money and Politics,* p. 27.
10. Hoyt, *Jumbos and Jackasses,* p. 189.
11. Roseboom, *Presidential Elections,* p. 304.
12. Shannon, *Money and Politics,* p. 33.
13. Roseboom, *Presidential Elections,* p. 316.

14. M. R. Werner, *Bryan* (New York: Harcourt, Brace and Co., 1929), p. 101.
15. *Robert M. LaFollette, Autobiography* (Madison, Wis.: *LaFollette's Magazine,* 1913), pp. 23-24, as quoted in Shannon, *Money and Politics,* p. 35.
16. Shannon, *Money and Politics,* p. 35.
17. O. G. Villard, *Fighting Years, 1939,* pp. 179-181, as quoted in Shannon, *Money and Politics,* p. 35.
18. *Robert M. LaFollette, Autobiography,* pp. 23-24, as quoted in Shannon, *Money and Politics,* p. 35.
19. Overacker, *Money and Politics,* p. 180.
20. Arthur M. Schlesinger, Jr., *The Politics of Upheaval* ("The Age of Roosevelt," vol. III, 1960 [Boston: Houghton Mifflin Co.]), pp. 594-595.
21. CRF Listing of: *Political Contributors and Lenders of $10,000 or More in 1972* (Princeton, N.J.: Citizens' Research Foundation, 1975).
22. CRF Listing of: *Political Contributors of $500 or More Voluntarily Disclosed by 1972 Presidential Candidates* (Princeton, N.J.: Citizens' Research Foundation, 1972), Introduction, unpaged.
23. Christopher Lydon, "Big Donor Wants Nixon Impeached," *The New York Times,* May 15, 1974.
24. Stephen D. Isaacs, *Jews and American Politics* (Garden City, N.Y.: Doubleday & Co. Inc., 1974), pp. 1-6.
25. For the listing of centimillionaires see: Arthur M. Louis, "America's Centimillionaires," *Fortune,* May 1968, pp. 152-157; 192-196.
26. The analysis of the 1968 contribution patterns is contained in Herbert E. Alexander, *Financing the 1968 Election* (Lexington, Mass.: Lexington Books, D.C. Heath and Co., 1971), pp. 187-188. Other information on 1968 throughout this book is drawn from the same source.
27. Arthur M. Louis, "The Rich of the Seventies," *Fortune* (September 1973), pp. 170-175, 230, 232, 236, 238, 242.
28. CRF Listing of: *Political Contributors and Lenders of $10,000 or More in 1972* (Princeton, N.J.: Citizens' Research Foundation, 1975).
29. *Final Report of the Senate Select Committee on Presidential Campaign Activities,* 93rd Cong. 2d sess. (Washington, D.C.: U.S. Government Printing Office, 1974), p. 904.

4

Sources of Funds: Groups

An overriding purpose of the campaign financing reforms of the 1970s has been to relocate some political power, taking it from monied interests and scattering it to the grass roots. Thus the new laws include restrictions aimed at reducing the political power of large contributors and of large corporations, labor unions and other so-called "special-interest" groups in American society.

Public policy, however, seldom develops precisely the way reformers want it to evolve. The Federal Election Campaign Act Amendments of 1974 have effectively reduced the influence of large contributors by limiting to $1,000 the amount an individual may contribute to any federal candidate in one primary or election. But the 1974 Amendments also allow a committee of a business, a labor union or another organized group (usually called a political action committee, or PAC) to contribute, under the right conditions, as much as $5,000 per candidate per election.[1] This provision gives new emphasis to the roles of business, labor and other special interests in the electoral process.

Unlike individuals, who sometimes have to be cajoled to make political contributions, special interests often are eager to support candidates they feel would be friendly to their causes if they think they can win. Consequently, they often object to laws and regulations designed to prevent them from using their powerful resources to exert influence on elections.

CORPORATIONS

Even before the 1971 FECA provided that companies may spend their own funds on the administration of their own political action committees, the corporate role in the electoral process was considerable. It reached a new level in the 1972 election, chiefly in the interest of reelecting President Nixon and often in response to fund-raising appeals that some of those solicited thought bordered on extortion. In funneling their money into the campaign, as will be discussed in more detail later in this chapter, some companies "laundered" cash abroad, disguised it in Swiss bank transactions or purchased nonexistent equipment to move cash from where it was available to where it was needed for political purposes.

Partisan Political Spending

Although generally tamer than these subterfuges disclosed by the Senate Watergate Committee or the Watergate special prosecutor, there traditionally have been a number of ways by which corporate funds could percolate into partisan politics. One has been the use of expense accounts to reimburse employees for political spending. Federal law has prohibited corporate contributions since 1907. A few companies got around the prohibition by giving employees pay raises or bonuses with the understanding that the employee would make political contributions with the extra money. That was the device used by the American Ship Building Co. in 1972 to raise $25,000 as a Nixon gift (the company chairman, George Steinbrenner III, an owner of the New York Yankees, later was found guilty and fined for his role). The bonuses were scaled higher than the expected contributions so the employee could pay his taxes at no personal loss.

Another way to get around the federal prohibitions has been to provide free use of company goods, services and equipment, ranging from furniture and typewriters to airplanes or office suites or storefronts. Complimentary travel in company autos and airplanes has been common even when no campaigns were going on. Corporations also have kept executives and their secretaries on the payroll while they were working full-time in a campaign. In the aftermath of the abuses brought to light in Watergate-related investigations, the laws against such corporate practices are now being more vigorously enforced and corporations generally are far more cautious.

Payments to public relations firms, lawyers and advertising agencies have been used by companies to charge off to "business-as-usual" what are really political contributions. During the last year of the Johnson administration and the first year of the Nixon administration — 1968 and 1969 — there were a series of federal prosecutions of corporations for illegal practices. The Justice Department obtained 15 indictments and 14 convictions of businesses, many of them in Southern California, for deducting, as legitimate business expenses, payments that were in effect political contributions; the cases had been uncovered initially by the Internal Revenue Service.

Institutional advertising also can serve as a means of using corporate funds to convey a political message. For example, oil company ads in newspapers and news magazines, such as those placed by Mobil, Exxon and other corporations, frequently seek to influence public opinion and public policy on energy and rated issues.

Paying for Political Conventions

A fund-raising innovation in 1936 was aimed at circumventing the legal ban on direct contributions by corporations. At their national nominating convention that year, the Democrats produced a *Book of the Democratic Convention of 1936.* It contained pictures of the Democratic leaders, articles about various branches of the national government written by party figures and other information. Advertising space was sold to national corporations. The book itself was sold in various editions, ranging in price from $2.50 to a $100 deluxe edition that was bound in leather and autographed by President Roosevelt. Sales and advertising revenue from the book raised $250,000 for the campaign.[2]

Convention program books became more and more elaborate and the advertising rates went up accordingly, but after 1936 the money was used to pay for convention costs, not campaign costs. At the local level, however, program books often were used to raise money for party organizations.

The major parties continued to publish the convention books every four years, with ads costing about $5,000 a page, until 1964. That year, the Democrats published their convention book as a memorial to President Kennedy. Ads were $15,000 a page, and advertising produced an estimated profit of $1 million. The success prompted the Republicans to publish a program in 1965 called *Congress: The Heartbeat of Government,* which charged $10,000 a page for ads and raised about $250,000. Not to be outdone, the Democrats came back in late 1965 with *Toward an Age of Greatness.* Ads again cost $15,000 a page, and they produced a profit of at least $600,000. This edition had been prepared for distribution at fund-raising movie premieres for Democratic congressional candidates in 1966.

But now matters had gone too far; swift reaction in Congress and the press was hostile. The result was an amendment in 1966 that required the Internal Revenue Service to disallow corporate tax deductions for advertisements in political program books, which previously had been construed as legitimate business expenses. Congress backed off a bit in 1968, however, changing the law to permit such tax deductions, but only in connection with the national nominating conventions.

Besides buying ads in program books, business firms also directly helped host cities pay the costs of nominating conventions. For many years, hotels, restaurants and transportation lines servicing the host city made contributions, considered as legitimate business expenses, to nonpartisan committees established to guarantee bids for bringing the convention to the city. Such funds helped the host city provide the extra services required by a national political convention. The reported pledge of the International Telephone and Telegraph Co. (ITT) of $100,000 or more to help San Diego finance the 1972 Republican convention was one example of that practice. The subsequent uproar, which caused the

Republicans to relocate the convention, was not so much about the propriety of the pledge itself as about an alleged connection between the pledge and the terms of the government's settlement of an antitrust suit against ITT.

In addition to money for bid guarantees, many companies provided free goods or services, forms of indirect contributions, to the national conventions — car dealers provided fleets of autos, soft drink companies gave away drinks. Many such practices, however, became illegal for the 1976 and future national conventions under new guidelines set down by the Federal Election Commission in the process of administering the FECA. The 1974 Amendments established for the first time an option for public financing of party conventions. Both major parties exercised that option for their 1976 national conventions, though the Republicans did so with reluctance. Each party was entitled to $2,182,000 of convention money from the presidential checkoff fund. Neither party, however, used the full amount.

Ostensibly, public funding replaced the traditional mode of convention financing. The 1974 Amendments eliminated any income tax deduction for advertising in convention program books; neither the Republican nor Democratic program books contained paid ads. Also absent in 1976 were the contributions in kind provided by many companies in the past, such as free cars from the auto makers, liquor donated by distilling companies and the familiar delegates' lounges run by the airlines. Nevertheless, private and host city money still played a role in the 1976 convention, albeit a limited and newly regulated one.

Prompted by complaints from the Republican and Democratic National Committees that a narrowly defined subsidy of $2.2 million would be unrealistically low, the FEC ruled that state and local governments could provide certain services and facilities such as convention halls, transportation and security assistance, the cost of which would not count against the expenditure limits tied to the subsidy. But those same services, the committee decided, would be prohibited by the FECA if donated or leased by a corporation to state or local governments below the fair market value.

The FEC made two exceptions to the general prohibition of corporate contributions and free services. One of these allowed the parties to accept such items as free hotel rooms and conference facilities in return for booking a certain number of room reservations, so long as other conventions of similar size and duration received similar benefits. The second exception allowed nonprofit host committees to collect contributions, under specified conditions, from businesses based in the convention city and from national corporations having local operations there.

By sanctioning certain spending in addition to federal grants, the FEC facilitated a partial return to traditional convention finance. As in previous years, the parties engaged in complex site-selection processes and a type of competitive bidding with potential convention cities. The packages of facilities, goods and services offered by New York to the Democrats and Kansas City to the Republicans led to the selection of those cities for the respective national conventions. The new system of convention financing, then, may have curtailed the influence of private interests but it has enhanced the role of municipal interests.

The 1979 Amendments raised to $3 million, plus Consumer Price Index adjustments, the amount that each major political party may receive for the nominating conventions of 1980 and thereafter.

LABOR UNIONS

Labor union funds became significant in national politics in 1936 and ever since have provided an important resource to the Democratic Party. With a great infusion of labor support in 1968, Humphrey in the end nearly defeated Nixon. With labor badly divided in 1972, presidential nominee George McGovern went down to the worst Democratic defeat in history. With the help of significant labor expenditures on internal communication with members and their families on voter registration and on getting out the vote in 1976, Jimmy Carter defeated an incumbent Republican president.

In their early years, unions were not important political contributors. Union funds were used only for expenses such as postage, leaflets and speakers and were not contributed directly to candidates. In 1936, however, unions are estimated to have contributed $770,000 to help reelect Franklin D. Roosevelt. The biggest contributor was the United Mine Workers, which gave $469,000.[3] John L. Lewis, the union president, wanted to show up at the White House during the campaign with a check for $250,000 and a photographer, but Roosevelt vetoed the idea.[4]

In 1943, when resentment had mounted against wartime strikes and labor's successful organizing drives of the 1930s, the restrictions enacted in 1907 on corporate giving were extended temporarily to labor unions. Under the Smith-Connally Act, which Congress passed in 1943 by overriding the president's veto, labor contributions to federal election campaigns were barred for the duration of World War II. In 1947 the Taft-Hartley Act made the ban permanent and barred corporate and union contributions and expenditures for primary elections and nominating conventions as well.

Like corporations, unions learned ways to get around the law against direct contributions. They formed political auxiliaries, such as the AFL-CIO's Committee on Political Education (COPE), which collect voluntary contributions from union members for political purposes. In 1944, the first year in which there was a union-affiliated political committee, more than $1.4 million was raised.[5] That was the campaign in which the Republicans charged that everything the Democrats did had to be "cleared with Sidney" — referring to Sidney Hillman, then head of the CIO.[6]

Although the union members' contributions to these committees are not mandatory, a strong union may use various means, not the least of which is simple social pressure, to persuade members to "volunteer." The funds thus gathered can be used legally for direct assistance to candidates.

Besides these voluntary funds, there are three other channels by which labor money can flow into campaigns:

1. *Nonfederal Contributions.* These are sums spent where state laws permit contributions by labor unions to election campaigns for state and local office. As will be seen in Chapter 7, more states prohibit or limit corporate contributions than they do labor contributions. Studies have shown that labor consistently provides 10 to 20 percent of the funds of major Democratic candidates in some states and often is the largest single organized group in Democratic circles.

2. *'Educational' Expenditures.* Funds taken directly from union treasuries to be used for technically "nonpolitical" purposes such as registration drives, get-out-the-vote campaigns or the printing of voting records of legislators are considered "educational" expenditures. Labor's registration drives may be of more value to Democratic candidates than direct money contributions. In recent presidential election years, COPE has spent more than $1 million on registration drives, carried out selectively in heavily Democratic areas.

3. *Public Service Activities.* Union newspapers, radio programs and the like, financed directly from union treasuries, express a sharply partisan, prolabor point of view. Such expressions of opinion are, of course, constitutionally protected, but the law does restrain corporations and labor unions in circulating literature regarding candidate endorsements, except to employees, stockholders and members, and their families.

Spending in the 1970s

Although labor was badly split over the McGovern candidacy in 1972, the unions reported gross disbursements at the federal level of $8.5 million, which was $1.4 million more than in 1968. The increase, however, resulted almost entirely from the requirements for more comprehensive reporting. This disclosed: 1) previously unreported AFL-CIO spending from dues money for COPE staff and fixed operational costs, which was legal but never had been disclosed before; and 2) the first-time filings of scores of state and local union political committees whose activities fell under the FECA because they involved federal elections.

The 1972 campaigns were no exception to the rule that at the national level labor spends relatively less on presidential campaigns ($1.2 million) than on senatorial and House campaigns ($5 million).

Though the public funding provided to both presidential candidates in 1976 prevented labor from contributing directly to Jimmy Carter's general election campaign, labor is estimated to have spent some $11 million for nonreportable items such as registration, get-out-the-vote, candidate logistical support and general political education — all activities of great benefit to labor-backed candidates.[7] In addition, as is spelled out below, in 1976 labor unions reported spending $17.5 million, $8.6 million in direct contributions to candidates.

Many political observers contend that labor's true strength lies not in its campaign war chests but in the volunteers it can muster to handle the strenuous precinct work, with all the drudgery of registering voters and getting them to the polls. In 1968, when the labor effort almost put Humphrey over the top in the closing weeks of the campaign (he had been trailing Nixon in the polls), unions registered 4.6 million voters, and printed and distributed more than 100 million pamphlets and leaflets from Washington, D.C. Local chapters deployed nearly 100,000 telephone callers or house-to-house canvassers and, on election day, put 94,457 volunteers to work as poll watchers and telephone callers, and in other jobs designed to get "their people" to the polls.[8] Labor has concentrated the same sort of effort in many other campaigns as well.

The money limits set by the 1974 legislation work to place an even greater value on the ability of labor to mobilize large numbers of volunteers. There are no limitations on the use of "person power," and labor has an enormous pool of manpower when it can be motivated to help. A similar advantage accrues to any other organization that can draw on the services of large numbers of people.

ILLEGAL CONTRIBUTIONS

One of the disturbing aspects of election financing in 1972, brought to light by Watergate-related investigations, was the string of illegal contributions made by a number of the most prestigious U.S. companies. That some businesses had engaged in such practices in the past was suspected; what was particularly startling about the roster of illegal corporate contributors in 1972 was its "blue chip" quality and the amounts involved. Moreover, these disclosures opened the window on a multitude of unethical practices by American industry, both within the country and abroad.

The story began in the fall of 1973 when the Watergate special prosecutor filed suit in U.S. District Court in the District of Columbia against American Airlines Inc., Goodyear Tire & Rubber Co., and Minnesota Mining & Manufacturing Co., alleging violations of federal laws in making illegal contributions of corporate funds to Nixon and other presidential candidates in the 1972 campaign. Over the next two years, 21 companies pleaded guilty to this charge. The companies, their contributions and the disposition of the cases are shown in Table 4-1.

In all, the 21 companies were charged with contributing almost $968,000 illegally, with the bulk of it, $842,500, going to the Nixon cam-

Table 4-1 Illegal Corporate Contributions in the 1972 Presidential Campaigns

Corporation	*Campaign*	*Amount of Contribution*	*Plea (Date)*	*Court Action*
American Airlines	Nixon	$55,000 (refunded by FCRP)[a]	Guilty (10/17/73)	$5,000 fine
American Ship Building Co.	Nixon	$25,000	Guilty (8/23/74)	$20,000 fine
George M. Steinbrenner III, chrm.			Guilty (8/23/74)	$15,000 fine
John H. Melcher, Jr., exec. vice pres., counsel			Guilty (4/11/74)	$2,500 fine
Ashland Petroleum Gabon Inc.	Nixon	$100,000 (refunded by FCRP)	Guilty (11/13/73)	$5,000 fine
Orin E. Atkins, chrm. bd., Ashland Oil Inc.			No contest (11/13/73)	$1,000 fine
Associated Milk Producers Inc. (AMPI)	Nixon Mills Humphrey	$100,000 5,000 50,000	Guilty (8/1/74)	$35,000 fine
Harold S. Nelson, gen. mgr.			Guilty (7/31/74)	3 yr. sent. susp.-4 mo., $10,000
David E. Parr, spec. counsel			Guilty (7/23/74)	
Braniff Airways	Nixon	$40,000 (refunded by FCRP)	Guilty (11/12/73)	$5,000 fine
Harding L. Lawrence, chrm. bd.			Guilty (11/12/73)	$1,000 fine
Carnation Co.	Nixon	$7,900	Guilty (12/19/73)	$5,000 fine
H. Everett Olson, chrm. bd.			Guilty (12/19/73)	$1,000 fine

Table 4-1 Cont.

Corporation	Campaign	Amount of Contribution	Plea (Date)	Court Action
Diamond International Corp.	Nixon	$5,000	Guilty (3/7/74)	$5,000 fine
	Muskie	1,000		
Ray Dubrowin, vice pres.			Guilty (3/7/74)	$1,000 fine
Greyhound Corp.	Nixon McGovern	total $16,040 to both candidates' committees	Guilty (10/8/74)	$5,000 fine
Goodyear Tire & Rubber Co.	Nixon	$40,000 (refunded by FCRP)	Guilty (10/17/73)	$5,000 fine
Russell DeYoung, chrm. bd.			Guilty (10/17/73)	$1,000 fine
Gulf Oil Corp.	Nixon	$100,000 (refunded by FCRP)	Guilty (11/13/73)	$5,000 fine
	Mills	15,000 (refunded)		
	Jackson	10,000 (refunded)		
Claude C. Wild, Jr., vice pres.			Guilty (11/13/73)	$1,000 fine
HMS Electric Corp.				
Charles N. Huseman, pres.	Nixon	$5,000	Guilty (12/3/74)	$1,000 fine
LBC & W Inc. architecture firm	Nixon	$10,000	Guilty (9/17/74)	$5,000 fine
William G. Lyles, Sr., pres. & chrm.			Guilty (9/17/74)	$2,000 fine
Lehigh Valley Cooperative Farmers	Nixon	$50,000	Guilty (5/6/74)	$5,000 fine
Richard L. Allison, pres.			Guilty (5/17/74)	$1,000 susp.
Francis X. Carroll, lobbyist			Guilty (5/28/74)	$1,000 susp.
Minnesota Mining & Mfg. Co. (3M)	Nixon	$30,000 (refunded by FCRP)	Guilty (10/17/73)	$3,000 fine
Harry Heltzer, chrm. bd.	Humphrey	1,000	Guilty (10/17/73)	$500 fine
	Mills	1,000		
National By-Products Inc.	Nixon	$3,000	Guilty (6/24/74)	$1,000 fine

Table 4-1 Cont.

Corporation	*Campaign*	*Amount of Contribution*	*Plea (Date)*	*Court Action*
Northrop Corp.	Nixon	$150,000	Guilty (5/1/74)	$5,000 fine
Thomas V. Jones, chrm. bd.			Guilty (5/1/74)	$5,000 fine
James Allen, vice pres.			Guilty (5/1/74)	$1,000 fine
Phillips Petroleum Co.	Nixon	$100,000 (refunded by FCRP)	Guilty (12/4/73)	$5,000 fine
William W. Keeler, chrm. bd.			Guilty (12/4/73)	$1,000 fine
Ratrie, Robbins & Schweitzer Inc.	Nixon	$5,000	Guilty (1/28/75)	$2,500 fine
Harrie Ratrie, president			Guilty (1/28/75)	
Augustus Robbins III, exec. v.p.			Guilty (1/28/75)	
Singer Co.[b]	Nixon	$10,000	Guilty (6/11/75)	$2,500 fine
Raymond A. Long, M.A. leader				
Time Oil Co. (Seattle)	Nixon	$6,600	Guilty (10/23/74)	$5,000 fine
	Jackson	1,000		
Raymond Abendroth, pres.			Guilty (10/23/74)	$2,000 fine
Valentine, Sherman & Associates	Humphrey	$25,000 worth of computer		
Norman Sherman		services, paid by AMPI	Guilty (8/12/74)	$500 fine
John Valentine			Guilty (8/12/74)	$500 fine
TOTAL CONTRIBUTIONS:		$967,540		
Nixon		842,500 (excluding Greyhound amount)		
Others		109,000 (excluding Greyhound amount)		

[a] Finance Committee for the Reelection of the President.
[b] Prosecuted by the attorney general.

paign. Democrats receiving illegal corporate contributions included McGovern, Humphrey, Jackson, Wilbur D. Mills and Edmund S. Muskie.

'Laundered' Money

As mentioned earlier, the phrase "laundering" of money entered the American political lexicon in 1972. The phrase described the process by which corporations sought to hide the fact that the contributions had originated in their company treasuries and were thus illegal. The laundering took many forms. For example, American Airlines sent money from one U.S. bank to an agent in Lebanon for supposed purchase of aircraft; it came back to a second U.S. bank and then on to the Finance Committee for the Reelection of the President.

Other firms drew on secret slush funds, sold bogus airline tickets or created fictitious bonus schemes for employees. The employees then contributed the bonus to a campaign.

Although there had been sporadic federal prosecutions of corporate political practices in past elections, the picture that unfolded from 1973 to 1975 suggested illegal corporate giving on a scale unlike anything previously imagined. Many of the convicted corporate officials said they had contributed illegally because the fund raising had been carried on by high officials such as Maurice Stans, former secretary of commerce, and by persons close to the president, such as Herbert Kalmbach, Nixon's personal attorney. They claimed they gave not to obtain favors but to avoid possible government retaliation against them. Some said that the Nixon fund-raising effort differed from earlier campaign fund raising in the amounts of money involved and the unquestioning acceptance of cash. In the words of the Senate Select Watergate Committee, " ... there is no evidence that any fund raiser who was involved in these contributions sought or obtained assurances that the contribution was legal at the time it was made."[9]

Certain companies reportedly flatly refused when they were asked for large amounts. Among them were American Motors Corp.[10], Union Oil Co. and Allied Chemical Corp.[11]

Most of the prime defense contractors, a *New York Times* survey disclosed, had been solicited by fund-raisers from the Finance Committee for the Reelection of the President. The customary amount suggested for the major corporations was $100,000; requests were scaled down for the smaller firms. A distinct pattern of high-pressure solicitation was discerned by some.[12] Ironically, the image of the greedy businessman as the corrupter, seeking favors from the politician, underwent change in the minds of some observers as reports of the kind of pressures applied came to light. Instead, the businessman became the victim, not the perpetrator, of what some saw as extortion. American Airlines' chief executive officer, George Spater, told the Senate Watergate Committee that he was motivated by "fear of the unknown," likening his state of mind to "those medieval maps that show the known world and then around it, Terra Incognita, with fierce animals." Gulf's Claude Wild said he decided to arrange the contribution so that his company "would not be on a blacklist or at the bottom of the totem pole" and so that somebody in Washington would answer his telephone calls.[13] How much of this was rationalization on the part of corporate executives, remains for the reader to determine.

Stans' Finance Committee for the Reelection of the President maintained that it never solicited corporate contributions — that it only asked corporate executives to take responsibility to raise money from among other executives. Target amounts were proposed, it was admitted, but no quotas imposed. Yet targets by their very nature suggest quotas that, if unmet, pose problems for those not complying. And because the Nixon campaign represented an incumbent administration, requests for funds were taken seriously. The pattern of pressure was reported by so many corporate executives that the abuses could not be attributed merely to the overzealousness of some fund-raisers operating on behalf of an incumbent with his implied power.

The uncovered illegal practices led to a widening circle of investigations which, by mid-1975, were being conducted by four government agencies and one Senate subcommittee. The focus shifted from the relatively limited area of illegal contributions to U.S. politicians, to the issue of multimillion-dollar efforts practiced by corporations seeking to obtain contracts or influence abroad. In perspective, $100,000 to a presidential campaign is not much compared with millions of dollars given in Italy, Korea and other countries by certain American multinational corporations.

Dairy Contributions

A classic illustration of how money may "talk" when special interests deal with the government was provided by the alleged "milk deal" of March 1971, in which President Nixon played a leading role. The question was whether he had raised milk price supports in return for campaign contributions already received from and pledged by the nation's three largest milk co-ops.

Two weeks after an initial announcement that price supports would not be raised, the dairy industry put on a lobbying campaign that climaxed on March 23, 1971, with an "audience" at the White House for 16 dairy executives. Although Nixon made no reference to any pledges of campaign contributions — the three co-ops had offered $2 million to the Nixon reelection effort — he agreed in a follow-up meeting with administration officials to support higher parity. Later that day, the White House passed word to the dairy officials that it expected a reaffirmation of their $2 million campaign commitment in light of the forthcoming hike in price supports. The next day, March 24, the dairymen renewed their pledge and made a contribution of $25,000 as evidence of their intentions. The price support boost was announced by the Department of Agriculture on March 25. The boost meant a windfall variously estimated at $300 million to $700 million for dairy farmers. The bill was paid by consumers in higher milk prices and by taxpayers in the larger subsidies.

Actual donations by the dairy co-ops fell short of the pledged $2 million. Altogether, they contributed $682,500 to Nixon's 1972 reelection. Most of the money came from the three biggest co-ops.

Some Case Histories

There were a number of instances relating to campaign contributions in 1972 in which the questions raised were often a matter of the ethics as well as of the legality of gifts. Moreover, with respect to these contributions, it was conjecture as to whether the subsequent treatment accorded the giver resulted from the gift. These cases represent a problem area that troubles many observers of political finance. The problem arises from the fact that it is difficult to draw the line between the contributions given to candidates as a signal of support for their positions and that given in expectation of influencing or changing their positions. The former has been found "entirely proper and legal" in a court of law[14] and is indeed to be encouraged as a desirable aspect of citizen participation, whereas the latter either is, or verges on, bribery.

Howard Hughes. Perhaps the most widely publicized case in this category — one of Watergate's remaining mysteries — was the matter of a $100,000 gift from Howard Hughes to the Nixon campaign, which Bebe Rebozo, Nixon's close friend, said he kept intact in $100 bills and returned in 1973 to the millionaire recluse.

The mystery is replete with conflicting evidence as to when the $100,000 was delivered to Rebozo, where it was delivered and for what purpose. Hughes' death in 1976 virtually assured that the purpose of the gift may never be known. It may have helped gain Hughes a number of things, among them federal approval to purchase the airline, Air West, a new reading on a Justice Department prohibition against a Las Vegas casino purchase, or even a CIA contract for his ship, *The Glomar Explorer,* in an attempt to salvage a sunken Russian submarine. Such is the degree of mystery about the Hughes-Nixon involvement that Watergate investigators have speculated that somewhere in the relationship may be hidden the real reason for the break-in at the Democratic National Committee headquarters in the Watergate building on June 17, 1972.

Lawrence O'Brien, Democratic national chairman, once handled publicity for Hughes. In addition, Robert Oliver, father of R. Spencer Oliver, Jr., chairman of the Association of Democratic State Chairmen, represented Hughes interests for a Washington public relations firm.

Both O'Brien and the younger Oliver had offices at the Democratic headquarters. Investigators have postulated that the team of Cuban-Americans that broke into the headquarters may have been hunting for evidence thought to be in the Democrats' possession relating to the Hughes $100,000.

Foreign Money. Watergate investigators studied foreign money given to the Committee for the Reelection of the President, an ironic twist in light of the fact that one early "cover story" of the Watergate burglars was that they were looking for evidence of money from Fidel Castro's government allegedly given to support the Democrats. Brought to light were sizable gifts to the Nixon campaign from representatives of Philippine interests.[15] One contribution for $25,000 came from Raymon Nolan, a roving representative for Philippine sugar interests. The Philippines had the largest foreign share of the U.S. sugar market in 1972, a quota set by the American government at twice the level allocated to any other nation.

A number of Greek nationals were contributors to the Nixon campaign in 1972. The late Nikos J. Vardinoyiannis contributed $27,500. Of that amount, $12,500 was donated after a Greek company he headed was chosen to supply fuel to the U.S. Sixth Fleet.[16] Thomas A. Pappas, a Greek-born industrialist from Boston, gave the Nixon reelection campaign $101,673. Pappas' name came up in March 1973 when the White House was looking for cash to pay the Watergate defendants. In the round of phone calls and meetings that followed E. Howard Hunt's demand for $130,000 and the possibility of having to find an eventual sum of $1 million, the president, former Attorney General John N. Mitchell and White House aides John Dean, John Ehrlichman and H. R. Haldeman all made references to Pappas as a possible source of funds.

There were also allegations, though no proof, that money from the Swiss bank account of the now-deposed shah of Iran, Mohammed Reza Pahlavi, perhaps amounting to $1 million or more, found its way to the Nixon campaign after being transferred to a bank in Mexico.[17]

Under federal law in 1972,[18] it was a felony to solicit, accept or receive a political contribution from a foreign principal or an agent of a foreign principal. The law also prohibited an agent of a foreign principal from making a political contribution on behalf of his principal or in his capacity as agent of the principal. The legality of political contributions by foreign nationals hinged on the definition of the term "foreign principal." A direct contribution from a foreign national, without an agent or other connection with a "foreign principal," was considered legal — even though that had the effect of permitting political contributions from individuals who neither resided in the United States nor had the right to vote in U.S. elections. The FECA Amendments of 1974, however, revised the law to apply directly to foreign nationals. Under the 1974 Amendments, any individual who is not a U.S. citizen and who is not lawfully admitted for permanent residence (as defined in the Foreign Agents Registration Act of 1938) is prohibited from contributing.

CORPORATE AND LABOR PACs

The reforms of the 1970s sought, among other things, to further restrict the kind of illegal contributions uncovered by Watergate-related investigations and to diminish the influence of special interest groups and wealthy contributors in the electoral process. While reducing the role of the large individual contributor, the changes, particularly the 1974 Amendments, have served to increase — or at least to make more visible — the roles played by special interests by sanctioning the establishment of political action committees.

A PAC normally is organized by a business, labor, professional, agrarian, ideological or issue group to raise political funds on a voluntary basis from members, stockholders or employees, for the purpose of aggregating numerous smaller contributions into larger, more meaningful amounts that are then contributed to favored candidates or political party committees. A PAC can contribute up to $5,000 per candidate per election (i.e., $5,000 in a primary and another $5,000 in the general election) provided that the committee has been registered with the Federal Election Commission for at least six months, has more than 50 contributors and has supported five or more candidates for federal office.

As noted, by the time the reform legislation was passed, labor unions already had significant experience in the formation and use of political action committees. Though unions had long been prohibited from using treasury funds to administer such committees, and though the committees had been barred from making direct contributions to federal candidates, for many years their prowess in organizing political activity was envied by business. In the reforms of the 1970s, labor unions, ironically, supported the legislation that triggered establishment of many corporate and business PACs that now rival the labor committees in political influence. Now, business-oriented PACs use the techniques pioneered by labor, and the labor movement is wary of the large potential that business PACs pose in terms of their increasing numbers and the amounts of money they raise.

1971 Legislation

For years labor officials pushed for legislation allowing unions and corporations to establish and operate PACs, finally succeeding with passage of the 1971 FECA. The new legislation did not change the longstanding — but heretofore ill-enforced — prohibitions against the use of corporate or union funds in federal elections. But it did permit treasury funds of corporations and unions to be used to set up and administer PACs and solicit voluntary contributions to them.

Labor included corporations in the proposed legislation to gain Republican support for it. Labor officials, however, were confident that business could not fully exercise its rights in this area, since the old law barring federal contractors from "directly or indirectly" contributing remained intact. Using corporate funds to administer a PAC could be considered an indirect contribution, thus precluding direct political activity by companies that were government contractors, which included most of the nation's largest corporations.

Although the restrictions on government contractors did somewhat inhibit the growth of corporate-related PACs, the 1971 law's main effect was that it sanctioned direct and open participation by labor and corporate organizations wanting to play a prominent role in partisan politics. Even with the restrictions, almost 90 corporate-related PACs were in existence during the 1972 election, many sprouting after enactment of the 1971 law. (Corporate PACs were permissible before that law was passed, but the use of corporate money to support them was not legally sanctioned.)

1974 Legislation

The 1972 elections brought new pressures for more election reforms, culminating in the 1974 Amendments. One provision had a significant impact on the use of PACs by corporations as a main vehicle for political giving. The 1974 Amendments changed the definition of "government contractor" to permit corporations and labor unions that were contractors to create PACs. Again, ironically, it was labor that successfully worked to have the prohibition amended. Having secured government manpower training contracts, a few labor unions were concerned that their maintenance of PACs otherwise might be challenged because they held government contracts. Thus, the 1974 Amendments permitted the large defense and other contractors to use corporate funds for establishing and administering their PACs and for fund-raising purposes. Many of the largest corporations in the United States have since done so.

1976 Legislation

Having recognized its strategic errors in supporting changes in the original FECA and concerned about the rapid growth of corporate PACs, labor sought legislative remedies. The 1976 Amendments placed new restrictions on the range of corporate, trade association and labor PAC solicitation. Corporate PACs can seek contributions only from stockholders and executive or administrative personnel and their families. Labor union PACs can solicit contributions only from union members and their families. Twice a year, however, corporate and union PACs are permitted to seek contributions, by mail only, from all employees not otherwise available to them for solicitation. A trade association or its PAC can solicit contributions from stockholders and executive or administrative personnel of any of the association's member corporations if such solicitation is separately and specifically approved by the corporation. No corporation, however, can approve any such solicitation by more than one trade association in any calendar year.

Corporations, unions and membership organizations must report expenditures that are directly attributable to a communication expressly advocating the election or defeat of a clearly identified candidate if the costs exceed $2,000 an election. This provision does not apply if the communication, such as a union or company magazine or newspaper, is devoted to general news of interest to the employees or membership and was not sent primarily to help elect or defeat a clearly identified candidate.

The law imposed a $5,000 ceiling on individual contributions to a political committee in a calendar year.

The 1976 Amendments also restricted the proliferation of membership organizations and corporate and union political action committees. All PACs established by a company or an international union are treated as a single committee for contribution purposes. Finally, and most important, the 1976 legislation allowed corporate, union and association officials to determine, within the limitations of the law, how the money collected should be used.

Republicans and the business community generally were unhappy with the 1976 law but have managed to use it to their advantage. Despite the added restrictions, corporate and trade association committees have demonstrated their ability to increase the number of PACs they sponsor and the amounts raised and contributed to candidates.

How PACs Operate

Few corporate PACs take advantage of the right to solicit stockholders. In 1977 a survey by the Chamber of Commerce of the United States found that only 2 percent of the corporate PACs asked stockholders for contributions. "Stockholders are a broad and very diverse group," commented Frank S. Farrell, chairman of the Burlington Northern Employees Good Government Fund. "Many of them have differing political complexions and points of view. It's a question of whether it's worth the time and effort." [19]

Corporate PACs mainly solicit management personnel, but they differ in how far down into the management ranks they reach and how often they ask the executives for contributions. General Electric's PAC solicits its 540 top executives and about two-thirds participate, contributing about $70,000 a year. On the other hand, the Lockheed Good Government Program solicits its full management group and approximately 600 — about 5 percent of the number solicited — contribute.

Many of the larger corporations use payroll withholding plans for their executives to make contributions. The methods of solicitation are mail, personal contacts, group presentations and combinations of all three.

Some corporations permit a PAC contributor to designate which party is to receive his money or to allow the PAC to use it at its discretion. Decisions about which candidates will receive contributions usually are made by special committees of the PAC. But in some cases a PAC may leave the decision to the PAC chairman, who consults informally with colleagues.

There is less variation in solicitation practices among labor PACs. Generally a business agent or steward will solicit members in person or in a group on an annual basis. Few unions use payroll withholding for voluntary political contributions. If a company uses payroll withholding to collect contributions from its executives, it must make the same service available for a union to collect contributions from its members who work for the company.

To receive a contribution from the AFL-CIO Committee on Political Education (COPE) in each state, a candidate must receive a two-thirds vote at a state labor convention or from a body designated by the convention.

Growth of PACs

With each passing election, recognition of the potential of PACs by business executives has grown significantly. Contributions by corporate and business-related trade association PACs increased dramatically in 1976, almost tripling 1974 totals.[20] Federal Election Commission records show that the 450 corporate-related PACs registered for the 1976 campaign reported receiving $6,782,322 and spending $5,803,415 during 1975 and 1976. Most of the corporate PAC direct contributions went to candidates for the Senate and the House. Corporate and business-related trade association PACs together spent $12,587,000 during the 1975-76 period, more than $7 million of it in direct contributions to congressional campaigns. Labor, by way of contrast, spent $17,489,000 during the same period. Of that amount, $8.6 million was given to candidates and another two million or more was spent in communications costs on behalf of federal candidates. Like corporate and business money, labor money was focused on the Senate and the House. But while nearly 95 percent of labor's money went to Democratic candidates, corporate committees split their spending about 57/43 between Republican and Democratic candidates.

According to FEC reports, 1,938 PACs were active during the 1977-78 election cycle.[21] Of that number, 81 were corporate PACs, almost twice the number operating during the 1975-76 period. Labor union PACs, however, decreased from 303 in 1975-76 to 281. Most of the remaining PACs were classified as trade/membership/health PACs or no-connected PACs — ideological, issue-oriented or functional groups.

According to the FEC, PACs raised $80.5 million and spent $77.8 million during the 1977-78 period. Of the total amount they spent, $35 million was contributed to federal candidates. According to Common Cause, that figure represents a 60 percent increase over the $22.6 million PACs gave House and Senate candidates in 1976 and is almost three times the $12.5 million they gave in 1974 (Figure 4-1).[22] But, as Michael Malbin points out, although the amount of money PACs contributed to congres-

SOURCE: Common Cause, How Money Talks in Congress: A Common Cause Study of the Impact of Money on Congressional Decision-Making (1979), p. 6.

sional candidates in 1978 represented a significant increase over their 1976 contributions, PACs were responsible for approximately the same percentage of all congressional campaign contributions in 1978 as in 1976 — about 25 percent.[23]

In 1978 House candidates received more than $24.9 million from PACs, Senate candidates more than $10.1 million and presidential candidates $.05 million. Trade/membership/health PACs received $25.2 million and spent $24.2 million, $11.5 million in direct contributions to federal candidates. Labor PACs received $19.8 million and spent $18.9 million, $1.3 million in contributions to federal candidates. Corporate PACs received $17.7 million and spent $15.3 million, contributing $9.8 million to federal candidates. For the 1977-78 period more than 60 percent of corporate PAC money went to Republican candidates. In contrast, 95 percent of labor money went to Democrats.

Though labor union PACs have steadily increased the amounts of money they have raised and spent on behalf of favored candidates, the percentage of increase (tripled from 1974 to 1976) by the corporate and business-related (including trade association) groups far outstrips that of labor groups (up 30 percent in the same period). The growth in spending by business-related PACs however, does not wholly represent an influx of new money into the political process. Rather, the amounts now contributed by corporations and other business interests openly through their PACs in part replace what some few corporations and businesses formerly contributed under the table. Even so, while labor PACs are not likely to increase much, there is still room for growth in the number and influence of corporate PACs. As late as September 1978, only 196 of *Fortune* magazine's top 500 companies had registered PACs with the FEC. Seven of the top 25 and 29 of the top 100 companies had no PACs.

Table 4-2 shows the 10 leading spenders among political action committees in the 1977-78 election cycle. The list includes PACs of the type described above, as well as the ideological and presidential-hopeful committees described below.

Labor Union Reaction

The mushrooming of corporate and other business-related PACs as well as their potential for continued growth has spurred action by organized labor to counter their influence. Unions, along with election reform groups such as Common Cause, are in the forefront of efforts to extend public financing to congressional campaigns. Labor officials see public funding as a means of forestalling the perceived threat of financial dominance of election campaigns by corporate and business interests. So far, however, their efforts have been unsuccessful; the extension of public funding to congressional races has met with strong opposition.

Alternatively, some labor union representatives have suggested that the contribution limits on PACs be reduced to $2,500 from $5,000, and

Table 4-2 Ten Leading PAC Spenders in 1978

Political Action Committee	*Receipts*[a]	*Disbursements*[b]
Citizens for the Republic	$3,114,514	$4,509,074
National Conservative Political Action Committee	2,989,923	3,030,193
Committee for the Survival of a Free Congress	2,010,260	2,029,122
American Medical Association Political Action Committee	1,656,265	1,879,164
Realtors Political Action Committee	1,853,774	1,805,390
Gun Owners of America Political Action Committee	1,449,118	1,548,075
Automobile and Truck Dealers Election Action Committee	1,461,493	1,541,761
AFL-CIO COPE Political Contributions Committee	1,443,385	1,340,404
UAW-V-CAP (UAW Voluntary Community Action Program)	1,432,855	1,158,673
National Committee for an Effective Congress	1,051,663	1,052,137

[a] Gross receipts minus transfers from affiliated committees.
[b] Gross disbursements minus transfers to affiliated committees.

SOURCE: Federal Election Commission news release, May 10, 1979.

that partial public funding of House general election campaigns be enacted. Though union PACs gave more $2,500-and-over contributions in 1976 than did business or corporate PACs, labor apparently is looking warily to the future when business and corporate PACs might well surpass them in that category.[24]

Labor Union Influence

Even though labor might appear to be on the defensive, it remains a powerful force in electoral politics. Its influence cannot be measured simply in terms of the amount of money labor PACs contribute directly to candidates. Labor's greater strength remains its ability to generate manpower for registration and get-out-the-vote activity as well as to generate large amounts of communication expenses in dealing with its members and their families on electoral issues and candidates. Expenses for some of those activities go unreported under existing law.

Just as business and corporate influence in the election process is not going unchallenged, so labor's influence faces obstacles, including opposition in the courts. A series of complaints was filed with the FEC by a Virginia voter contending that the AFL-CIO's COPE and PACs established by AFL-CIO member unions are affiliated, rather than independent of each other, and thus are limited to an aggregate contribution of $5,000 per candidate per election under terms of the 1974 Amendments. The FEC dismissed the complaint without an investigation. The National Right to Work Committee subsequently filed suit against the FEC and on April 17, 1979, a federal judge ruled the dismissal improper because the FEC had not stated a cause of action. Since it did not deal with the substantive question raised by the complaints, the decision cast a pall of uncertainty over union political fund-raising efforts. The judge later upheld the FEC decision and dismissed 17 cases, representing a consolidation of related cases and three similar ones previously dismissed, alleging the same violation. These cases exemplify continuing challenges to labor's political activity.

OTHER SPECIAL INTERESTS

Like corporate, labor union and trade/membership/health PACs, those designated by the FEC as "no-connected" PACs have shown growth in the amounts of money raised and spent. Among no-connected PACs, two types are particularly notable: ideological committees and committees recently formed by Republican presidential hopefuls.

Ideological Committees

Committees in the ideological spectrum range from extreme right-wing to liberal left and include issue-oriented groups such as gun interests, environmentalists and women's groups. Some of the ideological committees represent a broad range of interests, while others, such as anti-abortion groups, are single-issue committees. In the 1975-76 election cycle, an explosion of spending occurred in this category — the most dramatic increase of all nonparty spending. The total adjusted ideological spending in 1972 was $2,650,000; the total contributions to candidates were less than $1 million. In 1975-76 the total adjusted ideological spending was $12 million with gifts to candidates of $2.1 million.

Organizations of long standing, such as the American Conservative Union (ACU) and the National Committee for an Effective Congress (NCEC), were among the leading money-raisers and spenders in the ideological-group category in 1975-76. But newcomers to the group accounted for much of the additional spending. Chief among these were two conservative units: the Committee for the Survival of a Free Congress (CSFC) and the National Conservative Political Action Committee (NCPAC); three gun-lobby groups: the Gun Owners of America Political Action Committee, the National Rifle Association Political Action Committee and the Right to Keep and Bear Arms; and three women's committees: the National Women's Political Caucus, Women For: and the Women's Campaign Fund.

The trends evident in ideological committee spending continued in the 1977-78 election cycle. According to the FEC, no-connected organizations, including the committees established by presidential hopefuls that are described below, reported adjusted receipts of $15.4 million and adjusted disbursements of $16.8 million. Of the money spent, $2.5 million represented direct contributions to candidates for the House and the Senate. Organizations such as the NCPAC, the CSFC and the NCEC remained among the leading money-raisers and spenders in 1977-78.[25]

'Presidential Hopeful' PACs

A new type of PAC, with budgets comparable to those of other traditional special interest groups, emerged as a force in American politics in 1978. Established by Republican presidential contenders to solicit funds for GOP candidates, these organizations actually served more as shadow presidential committees for their founders. They enabled presidential hopefuls to cement ties early by traveling around the country making speeches and by providing financial help to other candidates. They also provided a way around the contribution and expenditure limits. Foremost among these groups was the Citizens for the Republic, established in January 1977 by Ronald Reagan with $1 million left over from his unsuccessful presidential bid. By the end of 1978 the Reagan PAC had built a mailing list of more than 300,000 contributors and spent $4.5 million. The success of Reagan's operation led three other presidential hopefuls — George Bush, John Connally and Robert Dole — to establish their own PACs.

Most of the $5.6 million spent by these four independent PACs during the 1978 election went mainly to pay operating costs and travel expenses. Reagan visited 86 cities in 26 states on behalf of GOP candidates. Dole paid for eight trips to New Hampshire, and Bush paid $40,203 in air travel. According to FEC reports, the four PACs collectively spent $809,330 in direct or in-kind contributions to federal, state and local candidates and various party organizations across the country. The bulk of this sum, some $615,385, came from Reagan's Citizens for the Republic and went to 400 Republicans: 25 Senate candidates, 234 House candidates, 19 gubernatorial candidates and 122 candidates running for other offices.[26]

The fact that such small percentages of their budgets went to political contributions for candidates has raised questions about the legitimacy of the independent nonparty PACs. By establishing qualified committees, the Republican presidential hopefuls and their supporters obviously were able to avoid the individual contribution limits. As a multicandidate PAC, each organization could solicit and contribute up to $5,000 per individual instead of the $1,000 limit. Moreover, the presidential hopeful could raise and spend without consideration for the maximum spending limits. It was for these reasons that in April 1979 the

National Committee for an Effective Congress filed a complaint with the FEC against the PACs of Reagan, Connally and Bush for alleged violations of the FECA.[27] The NCEC argued that the PACs and the separate presidential committees for these individuals should be considered one and the same, simply because in each case they were established by and are maintained and controlled by the same people. According to the NCEC, the fact that a substantial portion of the contributors to the presidential committees gave to the PACs as well also indicated that the PACs and the presidential committees were affiliated and thus subject to a single contribution limit.

THE POTENTIAL OF POLITICAL ACTION COMMITTEES

As we will see in the next chapter, business PACs did not reach their potential in the 1976 election. But with the new laws conditions have become favorable for a corporate PAC movement and labor is worried about the possibility of this happening. A COPE newsletter of January 16, 1978, raised the specter of corporate PACs creating "a giant money funnel mostly to conservative candidates, perhaps accounting for $20-$25 million." Labor is especially fearful of the growth of "ideological" PACs organized in support of right-wing causes, as they foresee an alliance between these groups and corporate PACs, "giving them a combined potential wallop in the $40-$50 million range."[28]

While labor's fears have not been realized, the growth of corporate PACs will continue to be significant. On the other hand, the business PACs are not likely any time soon to match organized labor's superior ability to mobilize large numbers of volunteers to get voters to the polls.

NOTES

1. The conditions under which PACs may contribute up to $5,000 are described later in this chapter in the section on corporate and labor PACs.
2. Louise Overacker, *Presidential Campaign Funds* (Boston: Boston University Press, 1946), p. 29.
3. Overacker, *Presidential Campaign Funds,* p. 50.
4. Jasper B. Shannon, *Money and Politics* (New York: Random House, 1959), p. 54.
5. Eugene H. Roseboom, *A History of Presidential Elections* (New York: The Macmillan Co., 1957), p. 487.
6. Overacker, *Presidential Campaign Funds,* p. 49.
7. Michael J. Malbin, "Neither a Mountain nor a Molehill," *Regulation,* May/June 1979, p. 43.
8. Theodore H. White, *The Making of the President 1968* (New York: Atheneum, 1969), p. 365.
9. *Final Report of the Senate Select Committee on Presidential Campaign Activities,* 93rd Cong., 2d sess. (Washington, D.C.: U.S. Government Printing Office, 1974), pp. 446-447.

10. Morton Mintz and Nick Kotz, "Automen Rejected Nixon Fund Bid," *The Washington Post,* November 17, 1972.
11. Michael C. Jensen, "The Corporate Political Squeeze," *The New York Times,* September 16, 1973.
12. Ben A. Franklin, "Inquiries Into Nixon's Re-election Funds Turning Up a Pattern of High Pressure," *The New York Times,* July 15, 1973.
13. *Final Report,* p. 470.
14. U.S. District Judge George L. Hart, Jr., in his instructions to the jury in the bribery case against Sen. Daniel B. Brewster of Maryland in 1972. For a discussion of this, see Lawrence Meyer, "The Fine Line Between Contributions and Bribes," *The Washington Post,* March 17, 1973; and Brooks Jackson, "Bribery and Contributions," *The New Republic,* December 21, 1974. On the question of political temptation Lincoln Steffens once observed that Adam blames Eve who in turn blamed the Serpent, whereas the real fault, in Steffens' view, was and continued to be with the apple.
15. James R. Polk, "Philippine Cash Surfaces," "Sugar Envoy Mum on Donation" and "Nixon Donation From Second Filipino Revealed," *The Washington Star,* June 11, 12 and 13, 1973.
16. Rowland Evans and Robert Novak, "Greek Gifts for President," *The Washington Post,* July 20, 1972; and Seth Kantor, "Jaworski Eyes Probing Foreign '72 Gifts," *The Washington Post,* January 25, 1974.
17. Columnist Jack Anderson made the allegations, which he said came from the report of a former Justice Department official to Watergate investigators. See Anderson, "Kissinger to Press Shah on Oil Costs," *The Washington Post,* November 1, 1974. The story later was denied by the Committee for the Reelection of the President.
18. 18 U.S.C. § 613.
19. The section on how PACs operate is based on Charles W. Hucker, "PACs: Major New Weapons for Lobbies," in *The Washington Lobby, Third Edition* (Washington, D.C.: Congressional Quarterly Inc., 1979), p. 76.
20. All receipt, expenditure and contribution figures for the 1975-76 election cycle are derived from Herbert E. Alexander, *Financing the 1976 Election* (Washington, D.C.: Congressional Quarterly Press, 1979).
21. FEC news release, May 10, 1979. All 1977-78 receipt, expenditure and contribution figures are taken from this release.
22. "Interest Group PACs Contributed Heavily to House Newcomers," Common Cause news release, May 15, 1979.
23. Michael J. Malbin, "Campaign Financing and the 'Special Interests,' " *The Public Interest*, 56 (Summer 1979), p. 26.
24. Michael Malbin doubts that reducing the contribution limits would serve labor's purposes. He writes: "Reducing the contribution limits would not hurt corporate PACs at all. The organizations that would be hurt would be labor unions and the incumbent-leaning associations, both of which gave larger contributions than the corporate PACs. Moreover, a reduction in the limits probably would not hurt the ideological PACs, for they would most likely respond by increasing their constitutionally protected 'independent expenditures,' which so far only they, the American Medical Association, and a few other highly organized groups have exploited." Malbin, "Special Interests," p. 32.
25. Michael Malbin stresses the influence that conservative ideological PACs had in the 1978 election. According to Malbin, "the top conservative ideological PACs, by concentrating their resources even more narrowly than business and labor were able in 1978 to become almost as important a factor in the House races they entered as either business or labor." Malbin, "Special Interests," p. 30.

26. Rhodes Cook, "GOP Presidential Hopefuls Gave Plenty to Party Candidates in 1978," Congressional Quarterly *Weekly Report,* February 17, 1979, p. 307.
27. National Committee for an Effective Congress news release, April 10, 1979.
28. Memo from COPE, "The Radical New Right and Corporate PACs," January 16, 1978, p. 5.

5

The 1976 Election: Public Funding for President

The 1976 presidential election was unusual in several respects. For the first time, public funding was provided in different forms by the federal government in both the prenomination and postnomination campaigns. A new law, the Federal Election Campaign Act (FECA), limited the amount of money that could be contributed or spent. A new agency, the Federal Election Commission (FEC), administered the law and disbursed the public funds. At least partly because of public funding, a Southerner, an outsider not attuned to Washington politics and without access to traditional sources of money, won the Democratic Party's nomination and subsequently the election. He defeated an incumbent president who had not been on the ballot four years earlier.

TYPES OF AID

Three kinds of government funding were available for different phases of the 1976 presidential campaigns:

Prenomination Period — Matching funds of up to about $5.5 million (adjusted for inflation) were provided for qualifying candidates seeking the nominations for president.

National Conventions — Grants of about $2.2 million (adjusted for inflation) were provided to each of the major parties to arrange for and run the national nominating conventions. Lesser amounts would have been provided for qualifying minor-party conventions, but none were eligible in 1976.

General Election — A flat grant of $21.8 million (the amount was adjusted from $20 million, again according to movements of the Consumer Price Index) was provided for each of the candidates of the major parties in the general election period. Smaller amounts were available for qualifying minor-party candidates, though none qualified in 1976.

We will explain briefly the formulas for distributing the funds and then show how the public funding system worked in the 1976 election. (The new method of financing the national conventions was described in Chapter 4.)

Prenomination Campaigns

The 1974 Amendments provided that candidates for the presidential nomination could spend up to $10 million, receiving up to about $5 million each in tax-generated funds for preconvention campaign expenses. To qualify, a candidate must show to the satisfaction of the FEC that he or she has raised $5,000 in individual contributions of $250 or less in each of 20 states. Thus candidates vying for the presidential nomination need to raise individual funds, which then are matched on a limited basis. Accordingly, they are allowed to spend 20 percent beyond the expenditure limit for fund raising. Adjusted for inflation, the spending limit in 1976 was $10.9 million, plus the fund-raising overage, for a grand total of $13.1 million permitted to be spent by a candidate to achieve nomination.

A candidate theoretically could raise up to $5.5 million (half the $10.9 million limit) in private funds, plus almost $2.2 million for fund-raising purposes, or a total of about $7.6 million, with the government matching up to $5.5 million. (These amounts are indexed according to cost-of-living adjustments, and were higher in the 1980 campaigns.) Of course, the government matches only up to $250 per individual contribution, or only 25 percent of the $1,000 that each candidate may legally accept from an individual. The purpose of matching only up to that level is to encourage candidates to broaden their fund-raising base. But its effect is that few if any candidates will ever receive as much as half their money in matching funds.

General Election

Unlike the prenomination period, there is no matching-fund requirement after the conventions. In fact, major-party presidential nominees who accept the government funds are limited to spending the amount of the grant, which in 1976 amounted to $21.8 million for each of the two candidates. Presidential candidates who do not accept government funds may spend as much as they can raise, possibly making the private funding route attractive for candidates who are wealthy and willing to spend their own money for their own campaigns or who are confident of their ability to raise more money than that provided by the federal government. But, as mentioned earlier, this is more difficult than in the past because the $1,000 limit on individual contributions to a candidate applies even if he or she forgoes public funds.

Presidential nominees who accept the government funds cannot raise private money in addition. Their parties, however, can spend up to two cents per voting-age citizen, or about $3.2 million more, on their behalf. Spending by the party depends, of course, upon the party's ability to raise sufficient money to cover its operating expenses and its costs on behalf of other candidates, apart from the presidential and vice presidential candidates.

In addition, the *Buckley v. Valeo* decision allows independent spending in unlimited amounts by individuals and groups, so long as it is not controlled by the candidates or coordinated with them or their campaigns. Since such spending is outside the candidate's control, it may be wasted, helpful or harmful.

While candidates limit their spending by accepting public funds, they save fund-raising expenses since they cannot raise money privately. In 1972, for example, the McGovern campaign spent about $3.5 million for direct-mail fund raising, $1 million for newspaper ads and additional sums for appeals tagged on at the end of paid broadcasts.

Hence, with party help up to the limit and no fund-raising costs, the public money available in 1976 was adequate — but certainly not generous.

Tax Checkoff

The money for each of the three phases of federal funding is provided by the so-called tax checkoff. The arrangement provides that every individual whose federal tax liability for any taxable year is $1 or more can designate on his or her federal income tax form that $1 of his or her tax money be paid to the Presidential Election Campaign Fund. Those filing joint returns can designate $2 of their tax money. Major-party candidates are defined as those nominated by political parties whose presidential candidates received 25 percent or more of the popular vote in the preceding general election.

Minor-Party Candidates. A minor-party nominee may receive payments before the general election if he or another candidate of such a party received between 5 and 25 percent of the previous presidential vote. If a new party emerges that was not on the ballot four years earlier, or an older minor-party is newly successful, the candidate of such a party can qualify retroactively after the November election for a share of the funds if he or she receives 5 percent or more of the presidential vote in the current election. The amount of money a minor-party candidate may receive in public funds is determined by his or her share of the popular vote in relation to the average popular vote received by the major-party candidates.

Presidential Year Payout. The federal checkoff program operates on a four-year cycle, accumulating money in each tax year with the payout all in the presidential election year. Over the four-year period, 1972-75, $94.1 million was accumulated for the 1976 payout. The 1976 payout was:

Prenomination matching funds	$24.1 million
National nominating conventions	4.4 million
General election flat grants	43.6 million
Total (approximate)	$72.1 million

The excess of about $20 million was available in case any minor-party nominee qualified for general election funding. Since none did, part of the surplus was returned to the Treasury and part was held for the next election. A fund for the 1980 campaigns began to build through checkoffs on 1977 federal income tax returns and continued through the next three years for the 1980 payout. As will be shown in more detail in Chapter 8 (Table 8-1), more than 25 percent of the taxpayers use the checkoff, generating about $36 million a year for the Presidential Election Campaign Fund.

PRENOMINATION CAMPAIGNS

Public financing was the center of attention for the 1976 election because it had an enormous effect on how candidates campaigned. With the lengthy cutoff of public funds while the FEC was being reconstituted under the *Buckley* decision, the law even had some effect on who could afford to campaign. The combination of severely restricted contribution levels and the availability of public funds shaped the nature and direction of the 1976 race for the presidency.

The advent of public financing brought to the competition new faces as well as novel fund-raising methods, and bookkeeping practices hitherto unknown in politics. A rise in the number of state primaries and changes in election rules continued a process, begun after 1968, through which the national party organizations found their control over the choice of their nominees significantly reduced. Thus, the reforms, both financial and electoral, set the stage for an open and competitive nominating procedure.

New Sources of Funds

Probably the single greatest change effected by the new fund-raising laws was the elimination of the prominent role played by wealthy donors. Many individuals who had poured hundreds of thousands of dollars into the campaigns of favored candidates in earlier years continued to contribute in 1976, but only in the reduced permissible amounts. Some were hostile to the new restrictions; others approved them. One commentator suggested that corporations should seize the occasion to reduce the tension between business and government. Another observer commented that the role formerly filled by donors such as Stewart Mott, the wealthy General Motors heir and longstanding contributor to political campaigns, had now been assumed by rock stars,[1] a number of whom gave their time and talents to raising money for various candidates, thus helping to provide the seed money needed for effective campaigns. The new laws placed no restrictions on entertainers' contribution of their personal services to help candidates.

With the individual gift limits in effect, contributions from political action committees assumed some importance, even though they were not matchable. New attention also focused on modest donations from large numbers of blue-collar workers, small farmers and middle-income groups, whom direct-mail specialists now sought out with renewed force.[2] Campaign managers also were acutely aware of the value of volunteer workers and of the financial potential afforded by certain donations of time that were not restricted by the law.

Changes in Fund Raising

The legislation obliged finance managers to develop new fund-raising strategies. The law placed a premium on those who, no longer able to give $50,000 themselves, could attract from among their social contacts, business associates and political acquaintances 50 donors of $1,000 each. Emphasis was placed on fund-raisers who could organize and solicit interest groups or tap into existing networks of persons. For example, groups of individuals who had been involved in the McGovern campaign of 1972 used their contacts and fund-raising lists first for one, then for another, candidate for presidential nomination. Emphasis also was placed on direct-mail fund-raising specialists possessing the mailing lists and expertise to produce needed dollars.

Several campaign managers felt that by making it more difficult to raise money, the FECA forced their candidates to curtail traditional forms of grass-roots campaigning. They also felt that the law required them to spend too much time and resources on fund raising, bookkeeping and budgeting. Several managers thought the candidates could have campaigned more effectively had the contribution limit been higher.[3]

Compliance Requirements

Compliance with the new campaign finance laws and pursuant regulations demanded considerable attention from candidate committees. The campaigns displayed varying forms of workable compliance systems, with an essential element being standardized records for contribution and contributor information. In addition, most organizations drew up form letters that were sent to contributors who had not supplied the proper data, and most top finance officials personally inspected all contribution checks in an effort to detect any illegal donations.

Financial Problems

Most of the 15 presidential candidates who became eligible for federal subsidies had no elaborate system for raising $5,000 in each of 20 states in contributions of $250 or less. Rather, they qualified quickly because their organizations simply raised as much money as possible and used personal networks of contacts to meet the threshold where necessary. Eligibility was made even easier when, as allowed by law, a donor split a $500 contribution with a spouse.

The major financial problem facing candidates in the primaries, however, was a cutoff of matching funds brought on by the *Buckley* decision. Candidates had begun their campaigns using as guidelines laws that were being tested in the courts. The court decision upheld much of the law but, by invalidating the manner in which the FEC was constituted, disrupted the flow of government money. The cutoff hurt many of the prenomination campaigns. Some candidates filed suit to renew the supply of matching funds.

By the time Congress reconstituted the FEC and matching funds were released, irreparable damage had been done to some candidates. For instance, Senator Frank Church detailed in court substantial cutbacks in his orders of campaign materials. Fred Harris revealed that he had been forced to halt all campaign activity toward the April 27 Pennsylvania primary. The two-month cutoff forced some candidates to rely wholly on private funds and loans during crucial primaries, and caused others to miss opportunities they otherwise might have utilized.

Results of Public Funding

As with any reform, public financing brought about both intended and unintended results. Among the intended results was a new emphasis on money management and accountability on the part of each campaign; gone were the days of secret contributions and undue influence disguised by purposely sloppy bookkeeping. Moreover, federal subsidization greatly improved access to the presidential contest by supplementing the treasuries of candidates who attained a modest degree of private funding. Public funding also helped free each candidate's personal organization from the party hierarchy. The latter lost control of the primary process, thereby making the nomination more responsive to the electorate at large, at least in theory. Evidence of the wide-open nature of the competition is found in the victorious campaign of little-known Jimmy Carter and the nearly successful insurgency of Ronald Reagan.

The chief unintended result of campaign finance reform in the 1976 prenomination period was a fragmented field of candidates on the Democratic side. Campaigns that experienced financial trouble from the outset undoubtedly were prolonged by federal subsidies and this may have affected certain outcomes at the polls. For example, if liberal Representative Morris Udall of Arizona had received the votes given to floundering liberal candidates in a few states, he would have had an edge over Carter.

By mid-primary season, even though government funding prolonged some campaigns, seven candidates had dropped out (Senators Birch Bayh of Indiana, Lloyd Bentsen of Texas and Henry M. Jackson of Washington, former Senator Fred Harris of Oklahoma, Governor Milton Shapp of Pennsylvania, former Governor Terry Sanford of North Carolina and Sargent Shriver, the 1972 Democratic nominee for vice president). Several of these candidates formally remained in the race as long as they did because they were in debt and needed to raise matchable contributions and draw additional public funds. To restrict such a practice in the future, the 1976 Amendments cut off matching funds 30 days after a candidate obtains less than 10 percent of the votes in two consecutive primaries.

PRESIDENTIAL SPENDING

More than 100 presidential candidates filed reports of spending for the 1976 nomination or election, but fewer than one-fourth were serious candidates.[4] The only serious Republican contenders were Ford and Reagan, with two other Republicans filing in 1975. The remaining serious contenders were Democrats. Four of them made exploratory forays but were not in serious contention in the heat of the prenomination campaigns (Bentsen, Sanford and Senators Robert C. Byrd of West Virginia and Walter F. Mondale of Minnesota). The rest of the Democratic field comprised 11 contenders (Bayh, Carter, Harris, Jackson, Shapp, Shriver, Udall, Senator Frank Church of Idaho, Governors Jerry Brown of California and George C. Wallace of Alabama, and Ellen McCormack of New York, an antiabortion candidate).

The 1976 presidential primaries saw relatively little spending on network television advertising. In fact, the networks refused to sell prime-time slots to some presidential candidates, largely because of an FECA requirement that broadcasters charge political candidates the lowest unit cost for the same advertising time available to commercial advertisers.

The biggest spenders for broadcasting during the primary season were Ronald Reagan, who spent about $200,000 for two prime-time half-hour programs, and Jimmy Carter, who spent $800,000 in two weeks near the end of the primary season.

The Democrats

Presidential hopefuls in the Democratic Party began preparing for the 1976 nomination as early as 1973, when the unfolding of the Watergate affair increased the possibility that the party soon would return to the White House. During 1974 several candidates had formed campaign committees that were not subject to the 1974 Amendments until January 1975. Although they were not bound legally by any individual contribution limit, three candidates voluntarily imposed one of $3,000. Senators Jackson and Bentsen adopted this maximum because it appeared in an early version of the FECA Amendments. Also observing a $3,000 ceiling was Senator Mondale, who scrapped his presidential bid later in 1974.

As the 1976 contest unfolded, the well-funded candidates (Wallace, Bentsen, Jackson) tended to be weak at the polls, while the financially strapped, dark-horse candidates (Carter, Church, Brown) showed more popularity with the voters. In all, 13 Democrats qualified for matching funds. In addition, Senator Byrd ran a notable favorite-son campaign in West Virginia, and Senator Hubert H. Humphrey of Minnesota almost entered the race at several points. Out of the crowded field, Jimmy Carter soon emerged to foster a surprising degree of unity for the "outparty."

To win the Democratic presidential nomination, Jimmy Carter spent $12.4 million. Other Democratic contenders spent a combined total of more than $33.9 million. Of the 13 Democratic candidates qualifying for matching funds from the U.S. Treasury, three of them — McCormack, Sanford and Shapp — spent less than $1 million each; Bayh, Bentsen, Brown, Church, Harris and Shriver spent less than $3 million each; Jackson, Udall and Wallace together accounted for more than $21 million.

Carter's financial support mounted steadily as he won primaries and endorsements. Only Brown, starting from a zero base in early spring, demonstrated a greater momentum at the end. Table 5-1 covers the Carter and other Democratic presidential campaigns, including independent expenditures, communication costs and DNC operations.

Carter. Jimmy Carter commenced a quiet campaign to gain national recognition shortly after the 1972 election. The Committee for Jimmy Carter began raising funds in 1974. Carter officially announced his candidacy on December 12, 1974, shortly before the end of his term as governor of Georgia. Seventeen primary victories and $12.4 million later, the man from Plains claimed the Democratic nomination.

The Carter financial drive, while always sound, was unspectacular until the candidate demonstrated his popularity at the polls. After Carter's early victories, both fund raising and spending accelerated rapidly.

The Committee for Jimmy Carter benefited from a remarkably steady inflow of money, building up in an unbroken pattern from the earliest days in 1974. The orderly development of the three-year campaign permitted its finance chairman to put in place an effective system of cost control that was one of the strengths of the Carter campaign. During the March 25-May 23 period, when federal funds were withheld from all candidates, loans were required to finance the final, crucial primary effort in a number of key states. Like the political aspect of Carter's bid, the financial operation, under the direction of Treasurer Rob-

Table 5-1 Democratic Spending in 1976 Presidential Campaigns

Carter		
Primaries		$12,400,000
General election		
by candidate committee	$21,800,000	
by national committee (DNC)	2,800,000	
		$24,600,000
Independent expenditures and communications costs — primaries and general election		1,200,000
Total Carter		$38,200,000
Other Democratic candidates		
Primaries		
by candidate committees	$33,700,000[a]	
Independent expenditures and communications costs	200,000	
Total other candidates		$33,900,000
Total, Democratic primaries		$46,300,000
Total, Democratic general election		24,600,000
Independent expenditures (Carter) not allocated between primaries and general elections		1,200,000
Democratic National Committee and affiliates[b]		9,700,000
Democratic National Convention committees		2,300,000
Democratic total		$84,100,000

[a]Includes $3.6 million spent (by Bentsen, Jackson, Wallace, *et al.*) in 1973 and 1974, and $600,000 in spending by a number of other Democratic candidates not included in *FEC Disclosure Series No. 7.*
[b]Direct expenditures only, not including the authorized party spending on behalf of Carter noted above.

SOURCE: Citizens' Research Foundation

ert J. Lipshutz, displayed an extraordinary degree of foresight and daring. Although the campaign went deep into debt during the period when matching funds were not available, the committee closed its books with a surplus and transferred $300,000 to the 1976 Democratic Presidential Campaign Committee's compliance fund.

A vital part of the Carter success story is the FECA. Without stringent contribution limits, better known candidates who had connections with wealthy contributors might have swamped Carter early in the primary season. Without federal subsidies, Carter would have lacked the money to consolidate his initial lead. As mentioned earlier, this combination had an equalizing effect because it lowered the advantage large contributors could provide while enhancing the value of small contributions. Public funding allowed a Washington outsider, a regional candidate, to break into the field and establish his candidacy.

The Republicans

Before President Nixon resigned, the Republican nomination appeared to be an open contest. The most active potential candidate was Senator Charles Percy of Illinois, who struck a note of reform by accepting no individual contributions greater than $5,000 during 1973 and 1974. Although the presidential opportunities narrowed when Gerald Ford became president, Ronald Reagan's challenge had grown by 1976 into a major threat, deadlocking the nominating contest of the "in-party." As a result, rumblings, but not serious candidacies, emanated from the camps of former Governor John Connally of Texas and Senator James Buckley of New York. Only at the Republican convention did President Ford gain a certain hold on the nomination.

One of many ironies of the Republicans' nominating process in 1976 was that the party philosophically opposed public financing, yet their two prospective standard-bearers received the most money in federal subsidies. The total money spent by Republicans in the 1976 presidential campaign is detailed in Table 5-2.

Ford. As the first unelected president, Gerald R. Ford sought the Republican nomination without many of the usual advantages of incumbency. Ford failed to appear unchallengeable despite his extensive campaigning for Republican congressional candidates, successful fund raising for Republican organizations and an early lead in opinion polls. When behind-the-scenes efforts could not dissuade Ronald Reagan from running, the president began a long campaign for which he was woefully unprepared. Organizational work finally began in June 1975 with formation of the President Ford Committee (PFC). The president formally announced his candidacy on July 6, pledging "an open and above-board campaign."[5] Although the Ford committee overcame initial fund-raising difficulties, it never developed a consistent political strategy. Ford vacillated between demonstrating his presidential qualities, by working visibly in Washington, and going out on the stump to attack opponent Reagan.

The disorganized campaign won narrow victories in early primaries, but was incapable of crushing the Reagan challenge, which started anew after Ford's unexpected loss in the North Carolina primary on March 23. At the Republican National Convention in Kansas City, President Ford captured the nomination by a margin of 117 votes. His triumph cost $13.6 million, the most expensive of all 1976 campaigns. Yet Ford's nomination proved to be a Pyrrhic victory, for the battle with Reagan had tarnished the president's image and weakened the party, paving the way for defeat in November.

Table 5-2 Republican Spending in 1976 Presidential Campaigns

Ford		
Primaries		$13,600,000
General election		
by candidate committee	$21,786,641	
by national committee (RNC)	1,400,000	
		$23,186,641
Independent expenditures and communications costs — primaries and general election		200,000
Total Ford		$37,000,000[a]
Reagan		
Primaries		
by candidate committee	$12,600,000	
Independent expenditures and communications costs[b]	500,000	
Total Reagan		$13,100,000
Total, Republican primaries		$26,700,000
Total, Republican general election[a]		23,200,000
Independent expenditures (Ford) not allocated between primaries and general elections		200,000
Republican National Committee and affiliates[c]		22,800,000
Republican National Convention committees		1,600,000
Republican total		$74,500,000

[a]Rounded figure.
[b]$300,000 by individuals and unauthorized delegates, $200,000 by political committees.
[c]Authorized party spending on behalf of Ford noted above not included here.

SOURCE: Citizens' Research Foundation

Reagan. Former California Governor Ronald Reagan challenged incumbent President Ford for the Republican nomination, but fell narrowly short of victory. The Reagan candidacy originated in the growing disappointment with Gerald Ford's moderate policies by the party's right wing. While deciding whether to lead an insurgent attack, Reagan disseminated his conservative ideology by way of the after-dinner circuit, a syndicated newspaper column and a radio commentary program. These lucrative endeavors functioned as a testing ground for his presidential bid. He took the first affirmative step in mid-July 1975 when he authorized formation of the Citizens for Reagan Committee. The committee had fund raising and strategy planning well under way when Reagan officially declared his candidacy on November 20.

Reagan intended to knock Ford out of the race in the early primaries, but he failed to score a win until the North Carolina election on

March 23. Unprepared for a campaign of attrition, the Reagan campaign experienced financial woes, intensified by the cutoff of matching funds. The candidate's adept use of television brought enough funds for survival until the primaries of the South and West, where Reagan demonstrated formidable electoral strength. The damage, however, already was done, for the funding squeeze had prevented effective drives in key Northeastern and Midwestern states. To no avail, the challenger fought the incumbent down to the last few uncommitted delegates at the Kansas City convention. Reagan's narrow loss cost $12.6 million.

GENERAL ELECTION CAMPAIGNS

Both major-party nominees, Jimmy Carter and Gerald Ford, accepted the public grants of $21.8 million for their general election campaigns and therefore were ineligible to accept additional private money. The national committees of the parties could spend an additional $3.2 million on behalf of the presidential candidates. Although the system worked smoothly, it was apparent that the grants (and consequent expenditure limits) were set at a low level. By way of contrast, the 1972 McGovern and Nixon general election campaigns had spent $30 million and $61 million, respectively. In addition, there was a 33 percent inflation factor between 1972 and 1976. The 1976 campaigns responded to the low-level subsidies by channeling a large proportion of their money into mass-media advertising (Table 5-3), the most cost-effective way to reach large audiences, and very little into the kinds of field operations and campaign activities that touch voters directly. The tight budgeting resulted in a substantial decrease in campaign activity and lower campaign exposure. Press reports throughout the campaign period described public apathy and accurately predicted record-low voter turnouts, which the reduced spending levels may have helped to bring about.

The Carter Campaign

For general election spending, Carter held one important advantage over his Republican opponent. With the nomination virtually assured some weeks before the Democratic National Convention, which preceded its Republican counterpart by one month, the Carter for President Committee had ample lead time to lay orderly plans for the fall campaign. The Carter campaign made maximum use of both the party and the federal funds made available to it.

The 1976 Democratic Presidential Committee fashioned its financial system with two goals in mind: first, to facilitate reporting to the FEC; and second, to give the national staff in Atlanta tight control over the spending of limited funds. The Carter staff sought a more efficient system than the one used in the prenomination period. The 1976 Presidential Campaign Committee was incorporated on July 15, 1976, and

Table 5-3 National Level Ford and Carter Advertising Expenditures for the 1976 General Election

	Carter	*Ford*
Time and Space		
TV	$ 7,819,091	$ 6,385,000
(Network	NA	2,500,000)
(Regional spot	NA	3,885,000)
Radio	1,262,230	1,490,000
Print	541,049	1,290,000
Other	153,365	NA
TOTAL TIME AND SPACE	$ 9,775,735	$ 9,165,000
Production		
TV	$ 464,055	NA
Radio	19,767	NA
Print	14,953	NA
Other	33,884	NA
TOTAL PRODUCTION	$ 532,659	$ 1,655,000
TOTALS	$10,308,394	$10,820,000[a]

[a]Does not include an additional $675,000 for campaign materials.

began spending for the general election at that time. Lines of financial authority extended from the Budget Committee to the Finance and Budget Center to the Responsibility Center directors. There were Responsibility Centers in each of the states and 39 others that were charged with various functions and contacts with interest groups. Some of these were based in Washington, D.C., but most had offices in Atlanta. The national headquarters consisted of three floors of offices in midtown Atlanta.

Gaining Exposure. The Democratic campaign saw the need to establish Carter's identity as a national candidate. The campaign budget thus emphasized TV time in target states and ads in newspapers and magazines to present Carter's views at length and contrast them with Ford's positions.

Carter's general election campaign budgeted $7,553,166 for TV time, using 30-minute programs, five-minute ads, two-minute ads and 60-second spots. Forty-three percent of the television budget was allocated for network commercial broadcasting, a cost of $3,277,699. An additional $12,000 was allocated for "non-wired" black networks. The remaining $4,263,466, including $71,258 for Spanish language broadcasting, went to local stations.

Carter perhaps more than Ford also benefited from free time provided by the networks for three presidential debates featuring the two major-party nominees. Thus each received more exposure to voters than he otherwise could have purchased.

Democratic National Committee. As mentioned earlier, the national committees of the political parties were permitted to spend two cents per the voting-age population, or $3.2 million, to help elect their nominees. The parties themselves were permitted to raise this money from private sources, with a limit of $20,000 on individual contributors. (Party contributions are included in the $25,000 aggregate contribution limit for individuals to all federal campaigns in a single calendar year. An individual who already had given $6,000 to congressional and presidential-primary candidates, for example, could then contribute $19,000 to a political party.)

At the Democratic convention in July, Finance Chairman S. Lee Kling announced that the national committee had committed itself to raising $10 million between the convention and election day.[6] In fact, the DNC fell short of its goal. For the entire year of 1976, it raised $7.5 million after spending $1.5 million on fund raising, for a net revenue of $6 million.[7] The DNC devoted $2.6 million from these revenues to the presidential campaign. Of this, $180,000 was spent on the "Carter Radio" program, by which the campaign maintained a phone hookup with radio stations to supply them with campaign news and quotes. More than $500,000 was spent on get-out-the-vote drives. Although these drives benefited the entire party slate, the fact that they were listed under "Presidential Election" in the DNC's annual audit indicates that they were designed by the party primarily to benefit Carter and Mondale.

In addition, the DNC obtained a ruling from the FEC allowing it to authorize state or local party committees to assume a portion of the DNC's $3.2 million presidential campaign expenditure limit. Under such authorizations, known as "agency agreements," the state and local committees spent $228,157 acting as agents of the national committee.[8] If this amount is added to the $2.6 million spent directly by the DNC, then the DNC's contribution to the Carter-Mondale campaign can be figured at $2.8 million, about $400,000 short of the permissible limit.

The Ford Campaign

Although President Ford's unelected incumbency had not deterred other Republicans from challenging him for the nomination, his general election strategy sought to make the most of the fact that he occupied the White House. At an informal June meeting, campaign advisers concluded that Ford would achieve the best results with a "no-campaign campaign." They suggested that the president, after securing the nomination, ought to announce at the convention that he would not campaign actively, but would stick to his job and let the people vote on the basis of his performance. They suggested further that he reject the

$21.8 million in public funds available to him and offer to debate Carter on a series of substantive issues.[9] Ford did not go that far; he accepted the subsidy to finance his campaign, and he challenged Carter to debate.

After the convention, tight headquarters control and strict budgeting marked a departure from most previous presidential campaigns with the exception of Nixon's 1972 campaign. State units were allotted minimal discretionary funds; payroll, telephone, rent and other operations were budgeted by headquarters. The Washington office decided when a local headquarters could open and when it must close down. As will be seen below, the Republican National Committee worked closely with the Ford campaign committee, enabling it to cope efficiently with the FEC's reporting requirements.

'Rose Garden Strategy.' Until the final weeks before the election, Ford tried to maintain what one campaign official called "a low political profile and a high Presidential profile."[10] This strategy entailed remaining in the White House and creating televised public ceremonies out of normally routine bill-signings and messages to Congress, thereby dramatizing Ford's incumbency and projecting the image of a purposeful, hardworking chief executive.

Early in the campaign, for example, the president created a televised ceremony in the White House Rose Garden out of his signing of a bill setting standards for day-care centers. He used the occasion to defend his veto of an earlier version of the bill. That veto, he said, as well as the 54 others he had made since assuming the presidency, had been made "with one concern in mind — to protect the American people from unrealistic responses to their very real needs, to see that the federal government does not merely serve the people but serves them well."[11] It was an effective — and free — campaign speech.

By giving the president valuable publicity, the "Rose Garden Strategy," as it came to be called, saved the Ford campaign considerable money. It also precluded Ford from making a major mistake, or simply appearing dull or clumsy on the campaign trail. The strategy was consistent with a blunt warning Ford's campaign staff had given him: "Your national approval rating declined when you were perceived as partisan, particularly when we campaign."[12]

But the Ford committee did not rely wholly on free air time. It spent $4 million on TV and radio broadcasting in the final 10 days prior to the election. This nationwide "saturation" was comprised primarily of the "Joe and Jerry Show," a series of 30-minute television commercials with former baseball player Joe Garagiola asking the president prerehearsed questions. Each program cost about $75,000 — $30,000 for air time, $30,000 for production and $5,000 for promotion and other expenses.

Republican National Committee. The Republican National Committee was determined to play an active role in the 1976 presidential campaign. The Republicans had learned a bitter lesson from Watergate, which they attributed in part to the complete independence from party supervision of the campaign waged by Richard Nixon's Committee for the Reelection of the President (CRP). The 1976 National Convention therefore adopted a new rule directing the chairman of the RNC to appoint a seven-member Select Committee on Presidential Campaign Affairs to "coordinate closely" with the nominee on his or her "full plan of financial expenditures" and to "review and monitor" such campaign spending.[13] Without mentioning Watergate, Richard Nixon or the CRP by name, the RNC's Rules Committee had recommended the creation of such a committee "to insure that no candidate's personal campaign shall conduct itself in a manner not in the best interest of the Republican Party" and "to insure that all expenditures are in full accordance not only with the law, but with established ethical practices for political campaigns."[14]

The President Ford Committee finance team relied on the RNC to implement its cost control system, utilizing the computer facilities in place at party headquarters. The coding format proved too sophisticated to be an effective campaign management tool, but the RNC operation smoothly handled the function it was essentially designed for: grinding out the massive campaign finance reports required to be filed with the FEC. This operation offered a marked contrast to a number of other presidential campaigns, in this and previous years, that struggled with reporting requirements long after the campaigns had been completed.

Yet, despite its attempts at coordination, the RNC failed to spend the full $3.2 million allowed by law on the presidential campaign, as it had planned. To accomplish this, the committee hoped to raise $23 million in 1976,[15] later revising the goal to $18 million.[16] In fact, it exceeded this target by raising more than $20 million. But an apparent failure of communication between the Ford committee and the RNC prevented the latter from playing a full role on Ford's behalf. The RNC spent only $1.4 million for the presidential campaign, which Ford finance chairman Jeremiah Milbank later told the RNC was "hard to comprehend in view of the closeness of the election and the fact that it was also expected to be close well before it took place."[17]

But there is little reason to speculate that the expenditure of another $1.8 million on Ford's behalf would have changed the outcome of the election. Since public funding eliminated the lopsided financial disparities that characterized some past presidential contests, analysts must look to other reasons for Carter's victory over an incumbent president.

CONGRESSIONAL SPENDING AND RECEIPTS

Patterns of spending and contributions followed customary lines in the 1976 congressional elections. When it came to raising money, as shown in detail below, Democrats did better than Republicans in the House but worse in the Senate, incumbents did better than challengers and winners did better than losers. Democratic candidates contributed more to their own campaigns in House races, while the opposite was true in Senate races. The results of some recent analyses of the impact of federal campaign laws on the 1976 elections will be found in Chapter 8.

Spending on House Races

In the 1975-76 election cycle, 860 House general election candidates — Republicans, Democrats, independents and minor-party candidates — received $65,740,937 for and spent $60,907,960 on their primary and general election campaigns. Together, the Democratic candidates raised $35,058,032 or 53.3 percent of total receipts, while the Republicans raised $30,201,691 or 46 percent. The remaining 0.7 percent — less than $500,000 — went to minor-party and independent candidates. Democrats also did better than Republicans on a per-candidate basis. The average amount received by Democratic candidates was $80,965 compared with $77,440 for Republicans. The average amount received by independent and minor-party candidates was only $13,006.

These averages, however, conceal sizable differences across individual House campaigns. Eighteen candidates, for example, (one Democrat, 11 Republicans, four independents, one People's Party and one Conservative) raised and spent no money; all of these individuals lost in the general election. At the other extreme, a number of candidates raised and spent upwards of $500,000. The biggest spender was Democrat Gary Familian, who raised $637,800 and spent $637,080 only to lose in a hotly contested open-seat race in California. The largest Republican spender was incumbent Ron Paul of Texas, who raised and spent just over $500,000 but also lost to a Democratic challenger who raised and spent about half that amount.

Republicans received slightly more funds from small contributors, while Democrats did somewhat better among the larger donors. Democratic candidates contributed more than twice as much to their own campaigns as did their Republican counterparts. They also had more than twice the amount of loans outstanding. Republicans received more ($3,658,310) than did the Democrats ($1,465,629) from party-related political committees. The Democrats, however, did much better from nonparty-related political committees. The Democrats were given $9,406,732 or 26.8 percent of their total receipts, while the Republicans received only $5,312,969 or 17.6 percent of their receipts from such sources.

Just over 53 percent of all funds ($35,071,334) went to incumbent candidates. Challengers were able to raise only $18,352,022 or 27.9 percent of total receipts. Almost 19 percent of total receipts — more than $12 million — went to candidates competing in contests in which there was no incumbent. On a per-candidate basis, the average incumbent raised $91,094, the average challenger raised $49,600 and the average open-seat contestant raised $117,310.

Incumbents and challengers received nearly the same amount of money — just in excess of $2 million — from political party committees. Incumbents, however, did much better from nonparty or special interest political committees; while challengers received only $2,808,106 from such sources, incumbents received about $11.9 million.

Almost two-thirds of all funds ($42,490,774) went to winning House candidates. Losers were able to raise only $23,250,163. Winners did better than losers at each level of individual contributions. Losing candidates contributed more than $2 million to their own campaigns and had personal loans outstanding of $2,116,784, while winning candidates spent only $369,844 of their own money and had loans outstanding of $1,937,877. Losing candidates did slightly better than winners from party-related political committees but winners raised almost three times as much from nonparty committees. Winners received almost $11 million while losers received only $3,810,598 from such sources.

Spending on Senate Races

In the 1975-76 election cycle, 63 major-party candidates and one independent Senate general election candidate received $39,129,660 for and spent $38,104,745 on their primary and general election campaigns. Democratic and Republican candidates received approximately equal portions of the total receipts. Together, the Democrats received $19,479,884 or 50 percent of the receipts. The Republicans received $18,840,430 or 48 percent. Senator Harry F. Byrd, Jr., of Virginia, the lone independent, received $807,346 or approximately 2 percent of the total receipts. On a per-candidate basis, the average Democrat received $590,300 while the average Republican received $628,014.

There were, of course, large variations in amounts received and spent in individual campaigns. At the one extreme, incumbent Democrat William Proxmire of Wisconsin found it necessary to spend less than $700 to protect his Senate seat from Republican challenger Stanley Work, who raised and spent more than $60,000. By far the biggest spender was Republican John Heinz, who spent more than $3 million to win an open-seat contest in Pennsylvania. The Democrat spending the most was incumbent John Tunney of California, who raised and spent almost $2 million only to lose to Republican challenger S. I. Hayakawa.

Republicans received more funds from small individual contributors, while Democrats did better among the large donors. Republican candidates contributed more than twice as much to their own campaigns as did their Democratic counterparts. Republicans also made more than twice as much in personal loans to their own campaigns; a comparison that is distorted, however, by the large loans Republican

John Heinz made to his own campaign, amounting to $2,465,500. Republicans received more ($930,034) than did the Democrats ($468,795) from party-related political committees. The Democrats, however, did much better from nonparty-related or special interest political committees. The Democrats were given $3,727,006 while the Republicans received only $1,977,977 from such sources.

Forty-two percent of all funds ($16,254,674) went to incumbent candidates. Challengers were able to raise only $10,571,058 or 27 percent of the total receipts. More than $12 million — 31 percent of total receipts — went to candidates competing in contests where there was no incumbent. On a per-candidate basis, the average incumbent raised $677,278, the average challenger raised $440,461 and the average open-seat contestant raised $768,995.

Challengers received more ($607,562) from political party committees than did incumbents ($349,702). Incumbents, however, did much better from nonparty political committees. Incumbents received $2,875,988 from nonparty or special interest political committees while challengers received less than half that amount from such sources.

Fifty-four percent of all funds ($21,052,900) went to winning candidates. Losing candidates received $18,076,760. On a per-candidate basis, the average winning candidate raised $637,967 and the average losing candidate raised $583,121. Losers received slightly more funds from small individual contributors while winners did better among the larger individual donors. Losers contributed $731,695 to their own campaigns while winners contributed only $160,244. Winners, however, had outstanding almost $3 million in loans to their own campaigns while the comparable figure for losers was less than $1 million — again a comparison distorted by the large loans that John Heinz made to his own campaign. Winning and losing candidates received approximately equal amounts from party-related political committees but winners did significantly better than losers from nonparty-related political committees, receiving $3,137,479 or 54 percent of the funds from such sources.

LABOR AND BUSINESS IN THE 1976 ELECTION

The acceptance of public funding by Ford and Carter barred individuals and organizations from making direct contributions to their general election campaigns. But unions, as well as corporations, were free to spend unlimited amounts on political "internal communications" directed toward their own members and their families.

We outlined these new rules in detail in Chapter 4. Here we will examine briefly how they were applied during the Ford-Carter contest, when unions in particular took advantage of the internal communications provisions.

Unions

Jimmy Carter had not been the first choice of most labor leaders. Once the Democratic convention made its choice, however, the labor movement was virtually unanimous in its support of the nominee and of the party's platform, which the movement saw as a repudiation of four years of Republican-inspired stagnation and unemployment. The AFL-CIO Executive Council met shortly after the close of the Democratic convention and unanimously pledged the federation's "all-out support" for the Democratic ticket.

Carter's standing in the labor movement was enhanced by his selection of Walter Mondale as his running mate. Mondale, unlike Carter, was a familiar face to union members. In his 12 years in the Senate, he had earned a reputation as a staunch friend of labor in the Democratic-New Deal tradition. This connection proved very productive during the campaign.

The $2,014,326 that labor organizations reported spending in 1976 on internal political communications did not count against Carter's spending limit. Since this spending was not considered an independent expenditure, labor leaders were free to consult with Carter-Mondale campaign officials and to coordinate their efforts to benefit the campaign. Most of the union communication was done by direct mail, which accounted for 87.1 percent of the expenditures.[18]

Carter and Mondale were the beneficiaries of $1,160,584 of the reported union communications expenditures, with virtually all of the rest going to Democratic House and Senate candidates.[19] The largest expenditures on communications in behalf of the presidential ticket were made by the AFL-CIO's COPE ($316,000) and the United Auto Workers ($306,000). In addition, the Communications Workers of America spent $107,000 and the Retail Clerks International Union spent $68,000 on such internal communications.

The reported figures do not tell the whole story of labor outlays for Carter. Unions that spent less than $2,000 on political communications were not required to file with the FEC, and many union locals probably tailored their spending to fit this limit. Furthermore, reportable spending included only communications whose main purpose was to advocate directly the election or defeat of a specific candidate. More general admonitions to "vote Democratic" were not reported. Nor were appeals for the election or defeat of a specific candidate if they were part of a communication whose basic purpose was not political, such as a regularly published union newsletter. According to one survey, "Virtually every [union] newsletter mailed to members in September and October included material praising Carter or criticizing Ford, usually with a picture of Carter on the cover. Almost none of this was reported to the FEC."[20] Michael Malbin has estimated that in the general election labor spent some $11 million on internal communications with its members, on voter registration and on getting out the vote. Most of that spending was not required to be reported, even though, according to Malbin, it was carefully coordinated with the Carter-Mondale campaign.[21]

Corporations

Unlike labor unions, corporations did not take full advantage of the FECA provision permitting them to spend unlimited amounts on advocating the support or defeat of particular candidates in communications to their stockholders, managerial personnel and members. While labor reported spending more than $2 million on such internal communications, only four corporations reported spending a total of $31,000.[22] Further, in general, business and corporations did very little spending for voter registration and on getting out the vote. Thus, corporations and other business-related groups, many of which might have been expected to support Gerald Ford in the general election campaign, did not approach the level of support for Ford that labor gave to Jimmy Carter.

In summary, Carter probably owed his election as much to the new campaign finance laws as to any other single factor. His determination, his organization, his image as an outsider "untainted" by Washington connections, his personal wealth — none of these likely would have gained him the White House without the additional advantages he derived from the new financing system. Public funding provided the money he needed to survive the primaries and to compete on an equal footing, at least from a financial standpoint, with Gerald Ford in the general election. And the reforms gave labor and business freedom to boost candidates among their own constituencies — an opportunity that unions seized to Carter's advantage, while corporations passed up their chance to do the same for Ford.

NOTES

1. Edgar F. Bronfman, "Which Alley for 'Fat Cats' Now?" *The New York Times,* September 21, 1976; "The New Kingmakers," Editorial, *The Wall Street Journal,* June 23, 1976.
2. Conservatives were particularly successful at tapping new segments of the population. Lou Cannon, "Tapping the Little Guy: Conservatives Broaden Financial Base," *The Washington Post,* March 6, 1977.
3. Jonathan Moore and Janet Fraser, eds., *Campaign for President: The Managers Look at '76* (Cambridge, Mass.: Ballinger Publishing Co., 1977) pp. 151-154.
4. All 1976 receipt, expenditure and contribution figures are derived from Herbert E. Alexander, *Financing the 1976 Election* (Washington, D.C.: Congressional Quarterly Press, 1979).
5. James M. Naughton, "Ford Announces Candidacy for '76 'To Finish the Job,'" *The New York Times,* July 9, 1975.
6. Text of a speech by Kling to the Democratic National Convention.

7. Democratic National Committee and Affiliated Organizations, "Statement of Combined Revenues and Expenses for the Years Ended December 31, 1976 and 1975."
8. Democratic National Committee and Affiliated Organizations, "Notes to Financial Statements, December 31, 1976 and 1975," p. 5.
9. Jules Witcover, *Marathon: The Pursuit of the Presidency, 1972-1976* (New York: The Viking Press, 1977), p. 537.
10. James M. Naughton, "Ford Putting Off Campaign's Start," *The New York Times,* September 3, 1976.
11. Witcover, *Marathon,* p. 546.
12. R. W. Apple, Jr., "The Election Outcome: One Week Later, the Politicians Tell How It Happened," *The New York Times,* November 10, 1976.
13. "RNC Role in Campaign Set by Rules," *First Monday,* September 1976, p. 7.
14. "Final Report of Rule 29 Committee — Additional Recommendations and Related Commentary," sent to RNC members December 20, 1974, p. 7.
15. "Byers Names Deputy to Finance Chief," *First Monday,* April 1976, p. 5.
16. "RNC Waging Biggest Effort," *First Monday,* October 1976, p. 6.
17. "Jeremiah Milbank's Remarks to the Republican National Committee — January 14, 1977, p. 3.
18. Federal Election Commission, *FEC Disclosure Series No. 5: Index of Communication Costs by Corporations, Labor Organizations, Membership Organizations, Trade Associations — 1976 Campaign,* Washington, D.C., April 1977, pp. 19-41.
19. *FEC Disclosure Series No. 5.*
20. Michael J. Malbin, "Labor, Business, and Money — A Post-Election Analysis," *National Journal,* March 19, 1977, p. 415.
21. Michael J. Malbin, "Neither a Mountain nor a Molehill," *Regulation,* May/June 1979, p. 43.
22. Edwin M. Epstein, "An Irony of Electoral Reform," *Regulation,* May/June 1979, p. 38.

6

The 1978 Election: Some Gains for Conservatism

The news media proclaimed 1978 as the year of the American taxpayers' revolt. Lacking a presidential race as an outlet for their frustrations, voters used state and congressional elections throughout the country to express their demands for slowing the rapid growth of inflation and reducing government spending.

Although fiscal conservatives wound up making only slight gains, candidates had gone into the fall elections feeling pressures to promise relief from high taxes. The overwhelming passage in June of California's Proposition 13, which drastically cut the state's property taxes, prompted many candidates to moderate their previous stances in favor of expensive government programs.

The antispending mood likely contributed to modest gains by the Republican Party. Although the Republicans were not so successful in their comeback as they had hoped, they did manage to decrease the size of the Democratic majority at the national level and to develop a stronger base at the state level. The Republicans gained 12 seats from the Democrats in the House of Representatives, while achieving a net gain of three seats in the Senate. In the state elections, the GOP added six new governorships to the 12 they already held and tripled their representation in the state legislatures.

MONEY AND POLITICS IN 1978

Political money was a significant factor in determining the outcome of the 1978 elections, particularly in congressional races. Congress had discussed the idea of extending the public funding of presidential elections to Senate and House campaigns, but it had not approved the legislation, so candidates were dependent on traditional sources of political money. Some states, however, provided public subsidies in 1978 for candidates for state office. (The states' experience with campaign finance regulation is discussed in the next chapter.)

As usual, the Republican Party was much better off financially than the Democratic Party in the congressional elections. According to the FEC's 1978 report, together the major parties contributed $6.4 million to federal candidates and spent an additional $4.4 million backing them in the general election.[1] Of that total, 326 Democratic party-related committees contributed $1.8 million and spent an additional $300,000 on the candidates' behalf in the general election. In comparison, 359 Republican party-related committees contributed $4.5 million and made additional expenditures of $4.1 million on the candidates' behalf.

At the national party committee level, the Republicans, who received most funds in contributions of less than $100, collected primarily by direct-mail solicitation, were able to give more financial help to their candidates than were the Democrats, who remained heavily burdened by old debts. Two national Republican senatorial committees contributed $500,000 directly to Republican Senate candidates in 1978 and spent an additional $2.6 million on their behalf. The Democratic Senatorial Campaign Committee, on the other hand, contributed $400,000 directly to its Senate candidates but made no expenditures on their behalf. Two national Republican congressional committees contributed $1.8 million to House candidates and spent $800,000 on their behalf, while five national Democratic congressional committees contributed $500,000 to the party's House candidates but made no expenditures on their behalf.

Although outspent at the national party committee level by Republicans three to one, the Democratic Party maintained its traditional majority at all levels. After the 1978 elections, the Democrats still controlled more than three-fifths of the seats in the House, just under three-fifths in the Senate and nearly two-thirds of the governorships and state legislatures.

GOP Gains

Although its efforts to achieve greater numerical balance in two-party politics at the national level were not very successful, the GOP did make important gains in the states. Fearing that the Democrats would gerrymander them into an even weaker position when congressional and state legislative lines are redrawn after the 1980 census, the Republican National Committee made an unprecedented effort to support state legislative candidates. Working with state party organizations, the RNC spent $2 million, including $1 million in direct contributions, for state campaigns. The heavily indebted Democratic Party, however, was financially unable to assist any of its state legislative candidates. Though their gains were somewhat modest, the Republicans captured 300 of the 800 targeted Democratic seats. After the 1978 elections, the

GOP controlled 12 state legislatures (Iowa, Colorado, Idaho, South Dakota, Wyoming, New Hampshire, Arizona, Indiana, Kansas, North Dakota and Vermont) and one legislative chamber in 11 other states.

1978 Newcomers

As in the past, incumbents did well in 1978 congressional races, with 95 percent returning to the House. Many newcomers, however, entered the scene. The House gained 77 new members, which represents 18 percent of the total, while the Senate got 20 new members, 20 percent of the total. Significantly, nearly one-half of the House and one-third of the Senate members have been elected since 1974. In the statehouses, 19 new governors took office.

Many of 1978's newcomers, who had been elected in the open-seat category, were lacking in political experience and were not closely tied to the state or local parties. The success of many of these candidates depended greatly on money that came from either personal funds or special-interest groups.

The Supreme Court's 1976 removal of the FECA restrictions on candidates' use of personal monies for political campaign purposes made a significant impact in 1978. Several wealthy candidates were able to dip into their own funds to support their campaigns. Among successful partially self-subsidized candidates were new Senators Bill Bradley, D-N.J., John W. Warner, R-Va., Alan K. Simpson, R-Wyo., and Nancy Landon Kassebaum, R-Kan. Not all wealthy candidates who contributed or loaned money to their own campaigns, however, were victorious. Among those who lost in Senate primaries or general election campaigns were Robert Short of Minnesota, Alex Seith of Illinois, Jane Eskind of Tennessee, Luther H. Hodges, Jr., of North Carolina, Phil Power of Michigan and Clive DuVal, Carrington Williams and Rufus C. Phillips, all of Virginia. All of the losing self-investors were Democrats.[2]

In addition, many newcomers received substantial contributions from special-interest groups. According to a Common Cause study, the 77 House newcomers, 54 of whom ran in open races not involving an incumbent, received $3.3 million from interest group PACs during the 1978 campaign — an average of $43,000 per representative.[3]

CONGRESSIONAL SPENDING AND RECEIPTS

All political financing records for congressional campaigns were broken in 1978. Approximately $158 million was raised by Senate and House general election candidates, significantly more than the $105 million raised by their 1976 counterparts and more than twice the $77 million available to general election candidates in 1974, the previous nonpresidential election year.[4]

Most of the increase can be attributed to inflation. Television advertising costs skyrocketed. For example, Senators Howard Baker and Charles Percy found that compared with the costs in their 1972 campaigns the rates had jumped 300 percent in Tennessee and 600 percent in Illinois, respectively.

Fund-raising costs also shot up. Republican Senator Jesse Helms of North Carolina, who raised a record $7.5 million, spent about $2 million to pay direct-mail fund-raising costs. That amount, however, included money Helms spent on issue development for future political and fund-raising purposes. Adding to the campaign costs, too, were federal reporting requirements. Most candidates had to hire separate staffs to handle the bookkeeping records and the filing of financial statements with the FEC.

Incumbents' Spending

As in previous years, in 1978 incumbents were better financed than challengers. Among House and Senate general election candidates, 401 incumbents spent $71.7 million compared with $45.7 million spent by their challengers. The 161 candidates running for open seats spent $36.1 million.

Of the 377 House incumbents who ran in the 1978 general election, only 19 lost.[5] In 1974, 40 of the 323 House incumbents were defeated by challengers, but that was an unusual Republican loss following Watergate.

In the Senate, 22 of the 35 seats contested in the 1978 general election were defended by incumbents. Seven were defeated, including the only three incumbents who spent less than their challengers — Wendell Anderson, D-Minn., Floyd Haskell, D-Colo., and William Hathaway, D-Maine.

The four who lost despite spending more than their challengers were Thomas McIntyre, D-N.H., Dick Clark, D-Iowa, Edward Brooke, R-Mass., and Robert Griffin, R-Mich.

Spending on House Races

In 1978, 810 major-party House general election candidates spent $87.3 million on their campaigns. The average expenditure of $108,000 represents a notable increase from the $73,000 average figure for 1976. This amount, however, does not present an accurate picture of political financing in 1978 House campaigns, since approximately 80 percent of all House candidates who filed with the FEC spent less than the average.[6] The large sums raised and spent by a small minority of candidates raised the average considerably. In fact, 1978 saw the first recorded million-dollar House campaign. In New York City, Carter Burden, a Democrat, spent $1.1 million in his losing race; in Louisiana, Democrat Claude Leach spent $771,000 to win.

The national Republican Party contributed $3.1 million to its House candidates, or more than three dollars for each one the Democrats gave to theirs. In a few cases the big spending by the GOP paid off at the ballot box. Seven Democratic House members who had taken over Republican seats in 1974 and won second terms in 1976 were defeated in 1978. In 1976 the seven Democrats and their Republican challengers had almost equal spending totals, but in 1978 the winning Republicans greatly outspent the losing Democrats, $1,325,000 to $790,000.[7]

Spending on Senate Races

In 1978, 70 major-party Senate general election candidates spent $65 million on their campaigns. The average expenditure was $928,571. The GOP candidates outspent the Democrats; Republicans spent $38 million, while Democrats spent $27 million. In 1976, 63 major-party candidates and one independent Senate general election candidate spent $38,104,745, an average of $595,387.

The number of million-dollar Senate campaigns continued to increase in 1978. There were four such campaigns in 1972, seven in 1974, 10 in 1976 and approximately 14 in 1978. In 1976, John Heinz, R-Pa., set the record for the single most expensive Senate campaign. Heinz spent more than $3 million to win his seat. That amount, however, was far surpassed in 1978 by Senator Helms' $7.5 million campaign in North Carolina.

Special-Interest Groups

Special-interest spending in the 1978 congressional races was considered in detail in Chapter 4. Separate consideration, however, should be given to the pronounced impact of special-interest funding on the 1978 senatorial campaigns. A number of Senate candidates sought financial support from out-of-state contributors, many of whom had a special interest in federal legislation. In South Carolina, for example, both candidates, Republican Strom Thurmond and Democratic Charles Ravenel, received about two-thirds of their campaign funds from contributors outside the state. Other candidates who received significant out-of-state contributions were Senators Jesse Helms, R-N.C., Jennings Randolph, D-W.Va., and Claiborne Pell, D-R.I., all reelected, and Robert Griffin, R-Mich., and Edward Brooke, R-Mass., both defeated. Except for Helms, a relative newcomer, all had served several terms in the Senate and had established reputations and power positions that enabled them to attract donations from persons and groups across the country.

With more candidates turning to sources outside their constituencies, some political observers have expressed concern that the idea of federalism may be replaced by a "nationalization" of the Senate.[8] As illustrated below in the case of Helms' reelection campaign in North

Carolina, a candidate with a sharp ideological image — in Helms' case strongly conservative — can draw financial support nationally from individuals and organizations who agree with the candidate's political philosophy and would like to see him or her in Congress. And modern computerized direct-mail techniques, which the so-called New Right has been especially adept at using, enable such candidates to seek funds from potential supporters far outside their states' borders.

A variety of groups organized around single issues also made their presence felt in congressional races. Through the use of computerized mailing lists, these organizations were able to identify supporters and to solicit their money. In the past such single-issue organizations have not been taken too seriously, but in 1978 several of these groups played an important role in the election of some House and Senate candidates. The grass-roots activity of the antiabortion organizations, for example, helped to prevent the reelection of Democratic Senators Clark in Iowa and McIntyre in New Hampshire.

THE 1978 ELECTION IN THE STATES

As in the federal elections, money played a decisive role in the outcome of a number of important statewide elections. In California, New York and Texas, for example, candidates spent record amounts in pursuit of the governorships. In addition, ballot issues commanded a good deal of the voters' attention as well as a significant amount of political money.

The brief accounts that follow describe political spending for elective office in selected states. A concluding section considers the significance of the ballot issues that confronted voters in a number of states.

California

In 1974 California voters overwhelmingly passed Proposition 9, which imposed spending limits in statewide and legislative elections; but the spending limits were invalidated by the U.S. Supreme Court in the *Buckley v. Valeo* decision. Four years later, candidates for statewide and legislative offices and supporters and opponents of various ballot measures spent a record-breaking $58.2 million in campaign contributions. Approximately $26.4 million was expended in the June primary, and $31.8 million more was spent for the November general election.[9]

Reliable records of political campaign financing in California were not kept until 1958 and, in the five gubernatorial elections since then, the Republican nominee outspent the Democratic nominee. This was not the case in 1978. Edmund G. Brown, Jr., the Democratic incumbent, outspent his Republican opponent, State Attorney General Evelle J. Younger, $3.4 million to $2.3 million. In addition, Brown spent $1.3 million in his campaign against eight political unknowns in the primary, while Younger spent slightly more than $1 million to capture the GOP nomination.

In the lieutenant governor's race, music company executive Mike Curb became the first candidate to spend more than $1 million for that office. Republican Curb, the winner, outspent his Democratic opponent, incumbent Mervyn M. Dymally, by more than a 3-to-1 margin, $1.5 million to $500,000.

Minnesota

For the first time in more than 30 years the Republicans captured the three major statewide offices in Minnesota — governor and the two U.S. Senate seats. Much of the GOP success can be attributed to the disorganized condition of the Democratic-Farmer-Labor party. The decline of the DFL began when Minnesotans reacted negatively to former Governor Wendell Anderson's stepping down in 1976 so that his successor, Rudy Perpich, could appoint him to Walter F. Mondale's vacated Senate seat. The death of Senator Hubert Humphrey, one of the founders of the DFL, also weakened the party's position.

In the gubernatorial election, Republican Albert Quie forced Perpich out of the position he inherited in 1976 from Anderson. An 11-term veteran of Congress, Quie had promised Minnesotans to cut taxes — or not seek reelection. In one of the Senate races, Anderson was unseated by Republican Rudy Boschwitz, who spent $1.9 million to Anderson's $1.2 million.[10]

In the other Senate contest, attorney David Durenberger, a Republican moderate, defeated DFL nominee Robert Short, a conservative millionaire businessman. Short outspent Durenberger $2 million to $1.1 million.[11] But Short's expenditures could not make up for his lack of support from the moderate-to-liberal wing of the DFL. In the primary, Short had defeated the party favorite, liberal Congressman Donald M. Fraser, by spending nearly $1 million of his own money on an anti-Fraser media campaign. Short also contributed $40,000 to a right-to-life political committee that distributed anti-Fraser materials at Catholic churches. Short's attacks on big government, taxes and the federal bureaucracy appealed to conservative Democrats, but he also sought support from Minnesota Republicans. In the final week of the primary campaign, Short mailed a half-million pamphlets to Republicans instructing them how to cross over in Minnesota's open primary. It is estimated that some 100,000 Independent Republicans switched over in an election won by fewer than 4,000 votes.

New York

New York passed a law in 1974 that set limits on contributions to state election campaigns. The limitations, based on a formula tied to voter registration, covered contributions to the primary and general election campaigns, but contributions made before the beginning of the primary were not covered. The law also stipulated that large loans not paid by election day automatically would be counted as contributions. These limitations, however, seemed to have had little effect on the role of big money in the 1978 gubernatorial race. Both candidates, Democratic incumbent Hugh Carey and Republican challenger Perry Duryea, spent about $5 million each.

As in 1974, Carey's victorious campaign depended heavily on large contributors; a significant number gave $20,000 or more. A total of 76 persons or organizations gave more than half of the funds spent by Carey. Approximately $1.7 million came from loans of up to $75,000 from big contributors and unpaid bills, all of which became contributions on election day, according to New York election law. Carey's major expenditures were for television and radio advertising, which cost more than $2.8 million. Another major expenditure amounted to $174,973 for last-minute mailings to special interests.[12]

In contrast to Carey's generously financed campaign, Duryea's losing bid was broader based, depending more on contributions of smaller amounts. Some 39 persons or groups gave nearly one-fourth of Duryea's total, and, denied financial support from Nelson Rockefeller and his friends, Duryea had to borrow approximately $600,000. Television advertising costs of $1.8 million were Duryea's largest single expense.[13]

North Carolina

Incumbent Republican Jesse Helms became the biggest spender in any U.S. Senate campaign in history. With his $7.5 million war chest, Helms outraised and outspent the Democratic challenger, State Insurance Commissioner John Ingram, by a margin of at least 32 to 1. Ingram managed to capture 46 percent of the vote, even though his populist positions alienated many traditional party loyalists and despite Helms' heavy spending.

The key to Helms' financial success was the direct-mail fund-raising effort put together by conservative Richard A. Viguerie, whose computerized operation was paid approximately half the amount raised through direct-mail appeals. Viguerie, based in the northern Virginia suburbs of Washington, D.C., by 1978 had compiled a list of more than five million contributors to conservative causes or candidates. This list could be "prospected" by computer for selected lists of potential but unproven donors for other candidates. But the process was expensive and Viguerie has been criticized over the years for passing on to candidates too small a share of the money he raised for them. Some of his New Right and gun owners' client groups also have been involved in controversy for sending out mailings over the signatures of conservative members of Congress, including Helms.[14]

Besides Viguerie's help, another important factor in Helms' success in 1978 was the loyal national following he had established by taking a notably conservative stance in the Senate. Contributing heavily to Helms were traditional conservative groups from across the country, such as members of the National Rifle Association and the American Conservative Union. The PACs of major oil companies (Ashland, Conoco, Texaco, Gulf, Getty, Amoco, Shell and Sun) and large corporations (Alcoa, Sears, Monsanto, J. P. Stevens, Republic Steel and Kemper Insurance) gave generously. Donations from these groups, however, amounted to less than 10 percent of Helms' total funding. The rest came from small contributors, more than half of whom lived outside North Carolina.

Texas

Money is often a decisive factor in Texas statewide elections, primarily because of the state's size. That was certainly the case in 1978, when nearly $18 million was spent by general election candidates in the two top races alone, the races for governor and U.S. senator. The vastness of the state makes for heavy costs for travel, organization and communication. Texas has 54 television stations and nearly 500 radio stations in 17 separate media markets. Buying air time in each takes a major portion of a candidate's campaign finances. In large cities such as Dallas, a single 30-second spot can cost as much as $8,000.

In one of the most significant upsets in Texas political history, William Perry Clements, a multimillionaire oil-driller from Dallas, became the state's first Republican governor in 105 years. A former deputy secretary of defense in the Nixon-Ford administrations, Clements spent $7.2 million to defeat John Hill, the state attorney general. Although Clements spent more than twice as much as Hill, he won the election by less than 1 percent out of 2.3 million votes cast. More than $4.5 million of Clements' funds came from personally guaranteed loans from several Dallas banks. Clements planned to hold several fund-raisers to pay off the loans.

In the Senate race, Republican John Tower, with 17 years' incumbency, spent $4.3 million to defeat challenger Robert Krueger, a Democratic congressman who spent $2.9 million.

Ballot Issues

Voters in the individual states were confronted by a notable number of ballot propositions in 1978. The general election ballots in 37 states included some 350 statewide proposals, 40 of which were initiatives placed on the ballots by voter petition.[15] In addition, the 1978 primary election ballots in some states included important ballot propositions, such as California's tax-cutting Proposition 13 initiative.

The results of the initiative elections were mixed.[16] Tax restraint and spending limit measures — notably Proposition 13 — were greeted favorably. Voters, however, turned down initiatives dealing with other types of issues, including some that were fought by affected businesses.

A study of 1978 ballot issues conducted by the Council on Economic Priorities lends substance to the criticism that initiatives can be dominated by well-financed special interests.[17] The CEP study surveyed 16 initiatives and referenda that directly affected corporate interests. Study findings showed that almost $14 million was spent in the 16 campaigns, which took place in 11 states. Corporations spent $9.7 million of that amount, including about $6.1 million spent by four out-of-state tobacco companies to defeat California's Proposition 5, an initiative to prohibit smoking in certain public places. Unions spent another $2.4 million against a Missouri right-to-work initiative. Other noncorporate interests accounted for the remaining $1.7 million disbursed.

According to the study, the corporate-backed position won in eight of the 12 campaigns where corporations were financially dominant. In the four campaigns where corporations did not dominate, the corporate-backed position lost. The study did not conclude that financial dominance in an election guarantees victory — but it did point out that in 11 of the 15 elections drawing heavy expenditures the side spending the greatest amount won.

The CEP study confirms a trend uncovered in an earlier study conducted by John Shockley.[18] Shockley examined contributions in eight antinuclear and four bottle-deposit initiatives from the 1976 campaigns. He found that corporate-backed opponents of the eight antinuclear measures outspent proponents $11.1 million to $3.8 million. Seven were voted down. Corporate-backed opponents of the bottle-deposit initiatives outspent proponents $3.9 million to $200,000. Two of the four were defeated.

Following the U.S. Supreme Court's 1978 ruling in the case of the *First National Bank of Boston et al. v. Bellotti,* we can expect corporations to continue their contributions for or against ballot propositions perceived as affecting their interests.[19] In a 5 to 4 ruling, the court in effect held that a state cannot prohibit such corporations from spending money to influence the outcomes of public referenda. The majority found for the first time that corporate spending is a type of political speech and that as such it comes under First Amendment protection broadly defined as affecting corporate interests.

In summary, the 1978 elections provided numerous examples of individuals and groups using the election process to protect their own financial interests. The party associated with fiscal conservativism, the Republican Party, attracted more money and was able to outspend Democratic candidates by substantial margins. But the heavier GOP spending resulted in relatively few seats being picked up in Congress, where the Democrats retained their majorities.

In congressional and state elections throughout the country, politicians campaigned mindful of the warning that the success of Proposition 13 had sounded at midyear. When the 1978 elections were over, repercussions of the "taxpayer revolt" were still being felt, and future candidates and framers of ballot questions were likely to consider in advance how the voters might react to the positions being tested at the ballot box.

NOTES

1. Federal Election Commission news release, May 10, 1979.
2. David S. Broder, "Should a Rich Candidate Be Allowed to 'Buy' Public Office?" *Los Angeles Times,* November 20, 1978.
3. "Interest Group PACs Contributed Heavily to House Newcomers," Common Cause news release, May 15, 1979.
4. All figures for receipts and expenditures of 1978 congressional general election candidates are taken from Federal Election Commission news release, June 29, 1979, unless otherwise indicated. Figures for 1976 candidates are derived from Herbert E. Alexander, *Financing the 1976 Election* (Washington, D.C.: Congressional Quarterly Press, 1979), and for 1974 from Herbert E. Alexander, *Financing Politics* (Washington, D.C.: Congressional Quarterly Press, 1976).
5. Common Cause news release, May 15, 1979.
6. David S. Broder, "Political Cash — Too Little, Not Too Much," *Los Angeles Times,* November 28, 1978.
7. "7 Class of '74 Dems Fall to $$ Barrage," *Memo from COPE,* December 25, 1978.
8. Edward Roeder, "Masters of Receipt: A Look at Senatorial War Chests," *Los Angeles Times,* November 19, 1978.
9. Jerry Gillam, "Spending Pattern Broken in Brown-Younger Race," *Los Angeles Times,* May 16, 1979.
10. Richard E. Cohen, "Public Financing for House Races — Will It Make a Difference?" *National Journal,* May 12, 1979, p. 786.
11. Cohen, "Public Financing," p. 786.
12. Frank Lynn, "Carey Campaign Cost Over $5 Million," *The New York Times,* December 7, 1978.
13. Frank Lynn, " 'Big Money' Influences Race Waged by Carey and Duryea," *The New York Times,* December 26, 1978.
14. Alexander, *Financing the 1976 Election,* pp. 717-721.
15. John Herbers, "Deciding by Referendum Is a Popular Proposition," *The New York Times,* November 12, 1978.
16. Larry L. Berg, "Study of Initiative Measures Reveals: Voters Seizing the Reins in the Seventies," *USC Chronicle,* March 26, 1979.
17. Steven D. Lydenberg, *Bankrolling Ballots: The Role of Business in Financing State Ballot Question Campaigns* (New York: Council on Economic Priorities, 1979), 89 pp.
18. John S. Shockley, "The Initiative, Democracy, and Money: The Case of Colorado, 1976," Statement Submitted to Subcommittee on the Constitution of the Committee on the Judiciary, U.S. Senate, 95th Congress, first session, pp. 172-189; and John S. Shockley, "The Initiative Process as Issue Voting," unpublished manuscript.
19. 435 U.S. 765 (1978).

7

Regulation of Political Finance: The States' Experience

While the new federal laws governing campaign financing were being conceived and enacted, some noteworthy experimentation in election reform was taking place in many of the states. In the 1970s almost every state changed its election laws in significant ways. These laws imposed on candidates for state offices restrictions similar to those governing congressional and presidential elections. Many states that had adopted campaign laws subsequently had to change them to conform to the 1976 U.S. Supreme Court ruling in *Buckley v. Valeo.* In general, that ruling left intact the public disclosure, contribution limitation and public financing provisions of existing federal (and, by implication, state) election laws. The decision, however, prohibited spending limitations unless they were tied to public financing.

STATE RESTRICTIONS

Disclosure

Forty-nine states have disclosure requirements. Forty-seven of them require both pre- and postelection reporting of contributions and expenditures. Two states, Alabama and Wyoming, require only postelection disclosure. North Dakota is the only state that does not require any disclosure of campaign contributions and expenditures (Table 7-1).

Reports. The reporting requirements vary by state, but the disclosure laws usually require identification of contributors by name, address, occupation and principal place of business, plus the amount and date of the contribution. The laws also usually require a report of total expenditures and itemization of certain of them including the amount, date and particulars of each payment. The states differ as to the threshold amount at which reporting requirements take effect. For example, Kansas requires itemization of contributions amounting to $10 or more.

Louisiana has a reporting requirement for contributions of $1,000 or more. The states also vary as to when the reports must be filed. Alabama requires one postelection report 30 days after the election. California law calls for filing of two preelection reports, 40 days and 12 days before the election, and one postelection report 65 days after the election. Alaska requires two preelection reports, one month and one week prior to the election, and two postelection reports, one 10 days after the election and the final report on December 31.

Socialist Workers' Lawsuits. Challenges to disclosure laws have come in the form of a series of suits by the Socialist Workers Party (SWP) supported by the American Civil Liberties Union at the federal level and in several states.[1] Suits were brought in California, New Jersey, Ohio, Texas and the District of Columbia, among others. Where the lawsuits have been successful, the states have provided exceptions for minor-party disclosure insofar as the listing of contributors is concerned. They have based their actions on the Supreme Court's decision in *Buckley v. Valeo,* which stated that case-by-case exemptions for minor parties may be permitted if there is a "reasonable probability that the compelled disclosure of a party's contributors' names will subject them to threats, harassment, or reprisals from either government officials or private parties."[2]

In 1977 a U.S. District Court ordered the FEC to develop a full factual record within six months and make specific findings of fact concerning the "present nature and extent of harassment suffered" by the SWP as a result of the disclosure provisions of the act.[3] The FEC's appeal was dismissed. In 1979 the court approved a consent decree to exempt the Socialist Workers Party from certain FECA disclosure requirements through the 1984 elections.

Contribution Limits

Contribution limits, sanctioned in the *Buckley* decision, vary by state and by level of candidacy. Approximately 25 states place no limits on donations. Eighteen states have relatively simple restrictions; seven states have rather detailed limitations. Contribution limits for gubernatorial elections range downward from unlimited contributions to as low as $800 per individual in New Jersey's publicly funded general election campaigns for the governorship. Most statewide individual contribution limits range from $1,000 to $3,000 per election or per calendar year. In New York they are based on a specified number of cents per registered voter. Cash contributions usually are prohibited or restricted to $100 or under.

Some states limit contributions for each calendar year, others for each election year and still others for each two-year period. Some limits apply overall to all state campaigns, others only to contributions by individuals (Table 7-1), some others to contributions to candidates and still others to contributions by or to political committees or party committees.

Four states — Florida, Kansas, North Carolina and Wyoming — seek to strengthen the political parties by permitting unlimited contributions to and by party committees while restricting contributions by individuals and other political committees. In addition, Maine permits political party committees to distribute slate cards listing three or more candidates and exempts their costs from the contribution limits.

One innovative approach is that used in Connecticut, New York and Minnesota, where stratified contribution ceilings are imposed, depending upon specific races. Some states allow appropriate officials to recommend adjustments in restrictions, or charge a dependent minor's contribution against the parent's limit. Still other approaches provide for exemption of volunteer services, property use and travel expenses of $500 and under. Others permit unlimited individual contributions to political committees, even though these committees may be restricted in the amount they can contribute to a candidate.

Restrictions on Business and Labor. Numerous states prohibit direct corporate contributions, but fewer ban direct labor contributions. Twenty-four states restrict contributions by corporations. Some states restrict campaign contributions by government contractors. West Virginia, for example, prohibits state contractors from contributing to political candidates, committees or parties during the contract negotiation period. Oregon bars contributions from most public businesses such as banks, utilities and common carriers, as well as companies that can condemn or take land. Other states exclude heavily regulated industries, such as public utilities, banks and insurance companies.

Seven states — Delaware, Florida, Indiana, Maine, Maryland, Mississippi and New York — and the District of Columbia permit corporations to contribute but set limits on amounts they can give. Even though federal law treats corporations and unions alike by prohibiting contributions from either, only 10 states restrict labor union contributions to campaigns. The 10 states are Arizona, Connecticut, New Hampshire, North Carolina, North Dakota, Pennsylvania, South Dakota, Texas, Wisconsin and Wyoming. [4]

But most states, including those that prohibit direct corporate contributions, now permit corporations and unions to form political action committees that can seek voluntary contributions from employees, stockholders and members. In recent years, business, industry and trade association PACs have proliferated at the state level as they have at the federal level.

In the past, corporate and union contributions-in-kind, such as the free provision of office space or furniture, or the lending of a car to a candidate, often were not accounted for. Now, federal law and most state disclosure provisions consider contributions-in-kind and loans as gifts

Table 7-1 Regulation of Political Finance by the States

State	Election Commission	Disclosure Before and After[a]	Individual Contribution Limits	Expenditure Limits[b]	Public Subsidy	Credit	Tax Provisions Deduction[e]	Tax Provisions Checkoff
Ala.								
Alaska	✓	✓	✓			✓		
Ariz.		✓					✓	
Ark.		✓	✓				✓	
Calif.	✓	✓					✓	
Colo.		✓						
Conn.	✓	✓	✓					
Del.		✓	✓	✓				
Fla.	✓	✓	✓					
Ga.	✓	✓						
Hawaii	✓	✓	✓	✓	✓		✓	✓
Idaho		✓			✓	✓		✓
Ill.	✓	✓						
Ind.	✓	✓						
Iowa	✓	✓			✓		✓	✓
Kan.	✓	✓	✓					
Ky.	✓	✓	✓		✓		✓	✓
La.	✓	✓						
Maine	✓	✓	✓		✓			✓[c]

Md.	✓	✓	✓	✓	✓			✓[c]
Mass.		✓	✓		✓			✓[c]
Mich.		✓	✓	✓	✓		✓	✓
Minn.	✓	✓	✓	✓	✓	✓	✓	✓
Miss.		✓						
Mo.	✓	✓						
Mont.		✓	✓		✓			✓[c]
Neb.	✓	✓						
Nev.		✓						
N.H.		✓	✓					
N.J.	✓	✓	✓	✓	✓			✓[d]
N.M.		✓						
N.Y.	✓	✓	✓					
N.C.	✓	✓	✓	✓	✓			✓
N.D.				✓				
Ohio	✓	✓						
Okla.	✓	✓	✓		✓		✓	✓
Ore.		✓			✓	✓		✓
Pa.		✓						
R.I.	✓	✓			✓			✓
S.C.	✓	✓						
S.D.		✓	✓					
Tenn.		✓						
Texas		✓						
Utah		✓		✓	✓		✓	✓

Table 7-1 Regulation of Political Finance by the States (Cont'd)

State	Election Commission	Disclosure Before and After[a]	Individual Contribution Limits	Expenditure Limits[b]	Public Subsidy	Tax Provisions: Credit	Tax Provisions: Deduction[e]	Tax Provisions: Checkoff
Vt.		✓	✓			✓		
Va.	✓	✓						
Wash.	✓	✓						
W.Va.	✓	✓	✓					
Wis.	✓	✓	✓	✓	✓			✓
Wyo.			✓					
D.C.	✓	✓	✓			✓		

[a] Only one state, North Dakota, requires no disclosure. Two states, Alabama and Wyoming, require disclosure only after an election. In some states, disclosure requirements are not identical for primary and general elections.

[b] Expenditure limits were declared unconstitutional by the U.S. Supreme Court on January 30, 1976, in *Buckley v. Valeo* unless the candidate accepts public financing. Four states, Michigan, Minnesota, New Jersey and Wisconsin, have expenditure limits that apply only to candidates who accept public financing. In another four states, Delaware, North Carolina, North Dakota and Utah, expenditure limits have not yet been repealed by the state legislatures. In 1979 Hawaii enacted a public financing system that ties a contributor's income tax deduction to a candidate's acceptance of spending limits.

[c] Maine, Maryland, Massachusetts and Montana have surcharge provisions.

[d] New Jersey enacted a state income tax after the subsidy program, which was applicable to the 1977 gubernatorial elections, became law. The new income tax system included a checkoff, but the 1977 funding was appropriated by the legislature.

[e] Some additional states that used to allow indirect tax deductions tied to the federal tax deduction no longer can do so because the tax deduction under federal law was repealed as of January 1, 1979. The federal tax credit for political contributions remains in force, but there is no indirect benefit for a taxpayer paying state income tax based on the federal system.

SOURCES: Based on data as of July 1979, combined from: *Analysis of Federal and State Campaign Finance Law: Summaries and Quick Reference Charts,* prepared for the Federal Election Commission by the American Law Division of the Congressional Research Service, Library of Congress, Washington, D.C. (December 1977); *The Book of the States, 1976-1977,* XXI (Lexington, Ky.: The Council of State Governments, 1976), pp. 223-226; Karen Fling, ed. "A Summary of Campaign Practices Laws of the 50 States," *Campaign Practices Reports, Report 4* (Washington, D.C.: Plus Publications Inc., October 1978); *Federal-State Election Law Updates: An Analysis of State and Federal Legislation,* prepared for the Federal Election Commission by the American Law Division of the Congressional Research Service, Library of Congress, Washington, D.C. (December 1978).

that must be reported with reasonable estimates of value received, and the value must be within contribution limits where they exist.

In several states, corporations and unions were prohibited from contributing to ballot initiative campaigns, a logical extension of the restrictions on such contributions to candidates. But, as noted in Chapter 6, the U.S. Supreme Court in 1978 declared unconstitutional a Massachusetts law prohibiting corporations from spending money to influence the outcomes of tax referenda. This decision in *First National Bank of Boston v. Bellotti* was followed by a U.S. District Court action ruling unconstitutional Florida's state law preventing corporations from spending more than $3,000 on ballot initiatives. One result of these decisions may be greater business involvement in ballot referendum and initiative elections.[5]

Improper Influence. The extent to which campaign contributions are received with expressed or tacit obligations in terms of policy, jobs or contracts cannot be measured, but it undoubtedly is greater at the state and local levels that at the federal level. In many places, systematic solicitation of those who benefit from the system occurs.

In Indiana, for example, the Two Percent Club, composed of certain government employees who are assessed 2 percent of their salaries, is a formal basis of financing the party in power.[6] There also have been clear cases of extortion or conspiracy to obtain campaign money in return for favors or preferment. In New Jersey, a former Democratic secretary of state was convicted in May 1972 on federal charges of bribery and extortion in seeking $10,000 in political contributions from a company that sought a contract to build a bridge. His successor, a Republican, similarly was indicted and convicted in October of the same year for extorting $10,000 for the state Republican Party in return for attempting to fix the awarding of a state highway construction contract. Clearly, corruption crosses party lines.[7]

Another example of the malignant links that can develop between money and politics is the case of former Vice President Spiro Agnew. Routine investigations of corruption in Baltimore County, where Agnew had been county executive, led to the grand jury indictment of Agnew for alleged bribery, extortion and tax fraud. According to witnesses, Agnew allegedly had pocketed well over $100,000 by using his political office to hand out county and state contracts in exchange for personal payoffs from seven engineering firms and one financial institution. Agnew's resignation from the vice presidency in 1973 was one of the conditions of a plea bargaining agreement, under which he pleaded no contest to a single count of tax evasion.[8]

Criminal Funds. The amount of political money supplied by criminal elements is a subject on which there are few facts. Part of the problem is the difficulty in distinguishing campaign gifts from other exchanges of money.

More than two decades ago, the Second Interim Report of the Special Senate Committee to Investigate Organized Crime in Interstate Commerce (the so-called Kefauver committee) concluded that one form of "corruption and connivance with organized crime in state and local government" consisted of: "contributions to the campaign funds of candidates for political office at various levels by organized criminals. . . ." Such criminal influence is bipartisan. According to the Kefauver committee, "not infrequently, contributions are made to both major political parties, gangsters operate on both sides of the street."[9] Little has changed to revise this description.

Unfortunately, the extent of such activity is still unknown. Some scholars have estimated that perhaps 15 percent of the money for state and local campaigns is derived from the underworld.[10] Excluding the federal level where the incidence of such behavior is presumed to be low, this would mean that almost $36 million might have come from criminal elements in 1976. If such money is indeed concentrated in nonfederal campaigns, there is special reason to study legislation at the state and local levels designed to regulate such behavior.

BIPARTISAN ELECTION COMMISSIONS

The states vary in their systems of election administration. Twenty-nine states have bipartisan, independent commissions that oversee elections. In most states, the governor appoints the commission members. In other states, such as Michigan, the secretary of state has that responsibility. In Delaware, Massachusetts and Montana, a single officer is appointed instead of a commission.

The commissions represent an attempt to isolate from political pressures the functions of receiving, auditing, tabulating, publicizing and preserving the reports of political candidates and campaign receipts and expenditures required by law. The commissions usually have replaced partisan election officials, such as secretaries of state, who traditionally were repositories of campaign fund reports but whose partisanship as elected or appointed officials did not make them ideal administrators or enforcers of election law. Some commissions have strong powers including the right to issue subpoenas and to assess penalties, powers that also are available for the administration and enforcement of contribution limits and of public funding in states providing it.

Budget and Legal Problems

Generally, the commissions receive and audit campaign contribution and expenditure reports, compile data, write and implement regulations and give advisory opinions. They also conduct investigations that include auditing records. Because of the amount of paperwork handled and because of understaffing and underfinancing, most commissions must rely on complaints filed and on investigative newspaper reporting to detect violations. For example, the Election Board in North Carolina had in 1978 one director, two full-time clerks and a budget of approximately $70,000. During election years, two part-time clerks are hired. In these circumstances, the director stresses administration and processing rather than monitoring of reports.[11]

While independent bipartisan election commissions theoretically are insulated from political pressures, they face many constitutional and enforcement problems. The original method of choosing the Federal Election Commission was challenged successfully in *Buckley v. Valeo* on the ground that congressional appointments violated the constitutional separation of powers. Similarly, an Illinois court ruled that the manner of selection of the bipartisan State Board of Elections contravened the state constitutional prohibition against the legislative appointment of officers of the executive branch.[12] Members of the Illinois board were nominated by the majority and minority leaders of each house of the legislature; each leader nominated two persons, and the governor selected one of the two. But an Alaska court threw out a suit that contended the Democratic and Republican parties derived unwarranted statutory protection from a law requiring appointment to the state election board from lists submitted by the two parties.[13]

Enforcement

The line between outright bribery and campaign contributions may often be a thin one, but where there is no accounting whatever of campaign funds or of sources of income it is easy to rationalize that one was meant to be the other. Statutory disclosure brings at least some discipline to transactions involving money and elected public officials, and if laws are enforced, even more discipline will result.

Some 30 states require candidates or public officials to disclose their personal finances, but definitions of ethics and conflict of interest are elusive and laws regulating them can be as difficult to enforce as are campaign laws. In some states, such as California, the same commission enforces both areas. Gray areas between compliance and noncompliance sometimes result in antagonisms on the part of state legislators who may work to undercut the administration of such laws. As a result, the responsible offices often exist under severe budget restrictions.

Since the state election commissions have only civil prosecutorial power, they must refer apparent criminal violations to appropriate enforcement officers — normally an attorney general or district attorney, who is a partisan official with discretion on whether to pursue the referrals. While these officials may be less equipped than the commissions to deal with election violations, there is no alternative to referring criminal violations to them.

STATE PUBLIC FUNDING

Seventeen states provide for public financing of state election campaigns (Table 7-2). The states' approaches to collecting and distributing the money vary widely. Funds are collected by either an income tax checkoff or an income tax surcharge procedure. The latter permits a taxpayer to add a dollar or two onto one's tax liability, while the former lets the taxpayer earmark for a special political fund a dollar or two that he or she would have to pay anyway. Funds are distributed either to parties or to candidates, or to a combination of both.

Tax Checkoff

Thirteen states use an income tax checkoff provision similar to that of the federal government. Taxpayer participation in using the income tax checkoff varies by state. Although the checkoff system does not increase tax liability or decrease the amount of the tax refund, participation is relatively low; it ranges from 38 percent in New Jersey to 8.8

Table 7-2 Public Finance of State Elections

Year First Bill on Public Financing Was Passed	*States*	*Years in Which Public Monies Have Been Allocated to Parties/Candidates*
1973	Iowa	1974-78
1973	Maine[a]	1974-78
1973	Rhode Island	1974-78
1974	Minnesota	1976-78
1975	Montana[a]	1976
1974	Maryland[a]	—
1974	New Jersey	1977
1973	Utah	1975-78
1975	Idaho	1976-78
1975	Massachusetts[a]	1978
1975	North Carolina	1977-78
1976	Kentucky	1977-78
1976	Michigan	1978
1977	Oregon	1978
1977	Wisconsin	1978
1978	Hawaii	—
1978	Oklahoma	—

[a]States with tax surcharges; all others have tax checkoffs.

SOURCE: Ruth S. Jones, "State Public Financing and the State Parties," in Michael J. Malbin, ed., *Parties, Interest Groups, and Campaign Finance Laws* (Washington, D.C.: American Enterprise Institute, 1980).

percent in North Carolina. The average participation rate is 22 percent, somewhat below the rate for participation in the federal system.

Tax Surcharge

Four states — Maine, Maryland, Massachusetts and Montana — have an income tax surcharge provision. The surcharge in Maine adds to the tax liability a $1 contribution to the party designated; alternatively, one dollar of the tax refund may be stipulated for a specific political party.

In Massachusetts, the $1 contribution goes into a general fund for statewide candidates to be distributed on a matching basis. In Maryland, a $2 contribution may be designated to a general campaign fund that also is distributed on a matching basis. Montana, in 1979, switched from a checkoff to a surcharge system and other states also are considering changes.

The surcharge participation rate is considerably lower than that of the checkoff system. For the tax year 1977, in Maine, only .5 percent of the taxpayers participated; in Maryland, 3.2 percent; in Massachusetts, 4.1 percent. In Maryland, the payout to candidates had been planned for 1978 but was postponed until 1982 because the available funds were inadequate.

Distribution of Funds: To Political Parties

Eleven states distribute public funds to political parties.[14] In five states, the money is allocated to the parties and to a general campaign fund designated for candidates. In two states, Idaho and Rhode Island, the money raised is distributed to political parties without restrictions as to how the money can be used other than to prohibit primary election use. In five others, the money goes to parties but with restrictions: In Minnesota, the money must be distributed by parties to selected categories of candidates according to formula; in North Carolina, the money goes from the parties to specified general election candidates only; in Oregon, the money cannot be used to reduce a postelection campaign deficit and half the money received by the party must go to the county central committees; in Iowa, the money cannot go to federal candidates if they receive federal public subsidy; in Utah, the money must be proportionately divided between state and county central committees.

In the nine states where the taxpayer may designate the recipient political party, the Democrats have received far more funds than the Republicans (Table 7-3). Utah is the only state where the Republican Party has been designated more often than the Democratic Party. In Rhode Island and North Carolina, the ratio is approximately 3-to-1 in favor of the Democrats; in Oregon, it is almost 2-to-1. The Democratic edge has led some observers to be concerned that the system could lead

Table 7-3 Distribution of State Checkoff Funds to Political Parties, 1978

	Taxpayer[a] Participation Rate	*Democrats*	*Republicans*	*Other*
Idaho	18.4%	$ 12,992	$ 10,701	$ 411[b]
Iowa	15.2	121,528	94,418	
Kentucky	16.7	180,127	64,738	
Maine (surcharge)	.5	2,132	1,260	
Minnesota	19.8	187,812	132,913	12,013[c]
North Carolina	8.8	146,847	50,501	[d]
Oregon	25.7	167,031	89,444	12,426[e]
Rhode Island	23.1	82,393[f]	30,706[f]	
Utah	25.6	53,958	55,827	7,820

[a] The states differ in the base used to determine the percentage of taxpayer participation — Iowa, Kentucky, Maine, Minnesota, North Carolina and Rhode Island use percentage of total number of individual taxpayers, whereas Idaho, Oregon and Utah figures are based on the total number of tax returns.

[b] Idaho's general campaign fund had $38,183.

[c] Minnesota also allocates money to a general campaign fund designated for candidates. In 1977 the general campaign fund had $118,774.

[d] North Carolina's general campaign fund had $62,341.

[e] In Oregon, only the Republican and Democratic parties were eligible to receive funds.

[f] Rhode Island's general campaign fund had $82,576, which was disbursed among the political parties. The party checkoff designations were $22,973 for the Democrats and $7,550 for the Republicans.

to a "strong-get-stronger, weak-get-weaker" situation. Since the difficulties of forming a new party are great, such a situation could lead to one party dominating a state, with a fractionalized multiparty minority. In Rhode Island, Minnesota and Idaho, suits against the checkoffs claimed that the distributions were discriminatory and unconstitutional. In Idaho, the suit was dismissed; in Minnesota, the court upheld the constitutionality of the checkoff law but required some changes that were made. In Rhode Island, the court determined that the party could not use checkoff funds in favor of an endorsed primary candidate, but refused the requested injunction.[15]

How a party may spend public funds varies from state to state. For example, in Minnesota, though taxpayers can check off a party designation if they wish, the distribution requirements are such that the money goes directly to candidates — whether from the party designations or the general fund — with no flexibility provided the party and no funds available for general party use. Thirty percent of the money must be used in the five statewide campaigns, with a fixed percentage designated for each of the five races. The remaining funds are apportioned to the candidates for the state legislature. Within these quotas, the funds are divided equally among candidates. All the candidates of one party for the legislature share equally in funds allocated to their respective offices from the party account. Some candidates have rejected public funds.

Iowa, by contrast, allows a great deal of flexibility in the way the parties distribute the funds. Other than requiring that candidates at the same level receive the same amount of money — for example, all six congressional candidates of one party must get the identical amount — the Iowa law allows the parties to allocate the money as they wish so long as it is spent for legitimate campaign purposes. Particularly among the Democrats, the money has been used in some instances for strengthening the party effort; in others, the money has aided candidates.

Several states have both a party fund and a general campaign fund whereby the money goes to the former for distribution to parties and to the latter for distribution to candidates. An Oklahoma law provides that the checkoff money be divided equally between parties and candidates. Of the party fund, 10 percent goes to each party while the remainder is distributed according to the number of registered voters per party. The parties may not use the money for primaries or conventions. The other half of the checkoff fund is allocated to statewide candidates in the general election. Twenty percent goes to gubernatorial candidates, 15 percent apiece to candidates for lieutenant governor and attorney general, 10 percent to candidates for state treasurer, and the remainder is divided among the candidates for other offices.

This new source of political money becomes more and more necessary as the recipients begin to depend on it. Ruth S. Jones, in one of the first studies of the effects of state public financing on parties, found that in several states where parties used subsidies to hire staff and pay rent "public funds have apparently had a great impact. ...[S]taff is viewed by most party leaders as the key to expanding the influence and status of the party." [16]

Noting that the concept was still too novel for a complete assessment, Jones concluded that 1) states are definitely influenced by state public financing policies and that 2) the methods of raising, allocating and overseeing public financing determine the impact of these policies on state parties. Those states that distribute public funds to political parties tend to strengthen the party, while those states that disburse public money to candidates tend to weaken the party. Ironically, the states with strong party systems tend to give public funds to candidates, whereas the weak-party states tend to channel public money to the parties.[17]

The implications of public financing for political parties are discussed below.

Distribution of Funds: To Candidates

Seven states — Hawaii, Maryland, Massachusetts, Michigan, New Jersey, Oklahoma and Wisconsin — distribute money from the public fund directly to candidates. The states that offer public support of state campaigns usually do so on a matching incentive basis. Michigan and New Jersey provide for public financing of the gubernatorial race. Michigan finances both primary and general election gubernatorial campaigns, allocating up to two-thirds of the $1 million spending limit. New Jersey was one of the first states to provide public financing of campaigns without spending limits. It has a matching program under which a gubernatorial candidate in the primary and general election, after reaching a threshold of $50,000 in private contributions not exceeding $800 each, can be eligible for matching funds of two dollars for each dollar raised in contributions up to $600.

As will be noted in Chapter 8, in 1978 the New Jersey Election Law Enforcement Commission recommended that spending limits, which had been in effect in the 1977 election, be repealed so long as there are provisions for limits on contributions, on candidates' use of personal funds, on loans and on amounts of public funding for candidates. In 1979 Oklahoma adopted a public financing system with no spending limits. In contrast, Hawaii recently enacted a program whereby income tax deductions are recognized only if the candidate receiving the contribution agrees to accept overall expenditure limits.

IMPLICATIONS OF PUBLIC FUNDING

Although public subsidies in campaigns provoke many arguments, scant attention has been paid to the implications that the various state plans have for the political system in general and the two-party system in particular. Questions of fairness, cost, administration and enforcement need to be asked, assumptions challenged and an understanding developed of the conditions that ought to be met if subsidies are to be provided. Public financing is not a panacea, and it will bring fundamental changes in the political structure and electoral processes.

Criteria

The main questions raised about public funding are who should receive the subsidy and how and when it should be made. The goal of government subsidization is to help serious candidates. A subsidy system should be flexible enough to permit those in power to be challenged. However, it should not support candidates who are merely seeking free publicity, and it should not attract so many candidates that the electoral process is degraded. Accordingly, the most difficult policy problems in working out fair subsidies are definitional: How does one define major and minor parties and distinguish between serious and frivolous candidates without doing violence to equality of opportunity or to "equal protection" under the federal or state constitutions? Any standard must be arbitrary, and certain screening devices must be used, based upon past votes, numbers of petitions, numbers of smaller contributions to achieve qualifying levels or other means.

While it is desirable to increase competition in the electoral arena, there are certain related considerations. One is whether the provisions of government funding can induce two-party competition in predominantly one-party areas by means of providing funding to candidates of the minority party; competition may be extremely hard to stimulate. Another is whether public funding of the political parties will serve to strengthen them and, if so, whether that is desirable. Still another is whether government domination of the electoral process will follow government funding.

As the states establish systems of public financing, the cost of electing large numbers of elected officials — a hallmark of this country's political system — will become obvious. In the United States, more than 500,000 public officials are elected over a four-year cycle. Long ballots require candidates to spend money in the mere quest for visibility, and the long ballot and frequent elections combined bring both voter fatigue and low turnout. In New Jersey, there are statewide elections at least every six months because the gubernatorial and state legislative campaigns are held in odd-numbered years. New Jersey, however, elects only one statewide public official — the governor — and then lets him appoint the rest. As financial pressures mount, other states may want to give increasing consideration to reducing the number of elective offices, thus diminishing the amounts of money (whether public or private) needed to sustain the electoral system.

Impact on Parties

Public funding of political campaigns, when the money is given directly to candidates, could accelerate the trend toward candidate independence and further diminish the role of the two major parties. With government funding available and made doubly attractive by limits on private contributions, the candidate's need to rely on party identification is greatly lessened. Supported even partially with government funds, the candidate is less beholden to his party. While traditionally the parties have not provided much money to candidates, they have eased fund raising by opening access to party workers for volunteer help and to contributors for money. Thus as their obligations to the party are reduced, candidates may become even more independent.

At the least, one can speculate that subsidies to candidates without reference to parties will lead to more independence in legislatures and an erosion of party loyalty. A legislator who ignored the demands of the leadership would not be fearful of being frozen out of a reelection bid or denied adequate funds because government would provide at least partial funding. To avoid splintering legislatures and maintain party strength, if policy makers decide that strengthening political parties is desirable, candidate funding — at least in the general election period — could be channeled through the parties.[18]

STATE TAX INCENTIVES

To the extent that campaigns are funded with public funds, the role of large contributors and special interests is reduced. Where there is less emphasis on private money, there is theoretically less chance for corruption or favoritism. But it is also desirable to encourage people to contribute money to politics in small sums, so the federal government and 15 states provide some form of indirect public support. Of the 41 states that impose an income tax, 10 offer a tax deduction for political donations, usually a deduction from gross income for contributions up to $100. Five states, Alaska, Idaho, Minnesota, Oregon and Vermont, plus the District of Columbia offer tax credits, most of them for one half the amount of contributions up to a maximum credit of $10. The tax credit provides greater incentive to contribute because it visibly reduces the amount of taxes paid, while the deduction simply reduces the amount of income subject to taxation.

Other forms of direct or indirect government assistance can be suggested. Rather than provide money, governments can supply services that relieve parties and candidates of the need for certain expenditures. For example, some state governments provide campaign help through the assumption of greater responsibilities for registration of voters, distribution of voter information pamphlets and election day activities. Moreover, public funding can help meet the transition costs between election day and inauguration day.[19]

Among the most important of such services would be government-sponsored universal voter registration. This would vastly reduce the cost to political parties and candidates of performing an essentially public function and would also reduce dependence on special interests for their registration activities. Such assistance would, furthermore, be likely to increase voting participation in a nation having complex registration requirements and a highly mobile population.

TESTING NEW CONCEPTS

Some states have been more experimental than the federal government in dealing with public funding, and the results of their pioneering may affect development of federal electoral regulation policy in the future. Until recent years it has been mostly the other way around, with the evolution of federal reforms influencing the adoption of similar changes in the states.

Eleven states distribute public funds to political parties and, like the federal government, seven states distribute the money directly to candidates. In the nine states where taxpayers can specify which party they want to help, the Democrats have received far more money than the Republicans. But preliminary studies indicate that, Democrat or Republican, the parties are strengthened where public funds are channeled through them — a development that some electoral reformers feel is needed to restore some of the vitality that parties have lost as an intended or unintended result of the vast changes in the American political system. We will discuss this subject at more length in the next, concluding chapter.

NOTES

1. *Socialist Workers Party v. Jennings,* Civ. No. 74-1328 (D.D.C.).
2. *Buckley v. Valeo,* 424 U.S. at 68.
3. *FEC Record,* March 1977, p. 6.
4. Wisconsin permits contributions from unions incorporated prior to January 1, 1978.
5. See Karen J. Fling, "The States as Laboratories of Reform," in *Political Finance,* Herbert E. Alexander, ed. (Beverly Hills: Sage Publications Inc., 1979).
6. Robert J. McNeill, *Democratic Campaign Financing in Indiana, 1964* (Bloomington, Ind., and Princeton, N.J.: Institute of Public Administration at Indiana University and Citizens' Research Foundation, 1966) pp. 15-19, 35-40.
7. For a discussion of these New Jersey and other state cases, see George Amick, *The American Way of Graft* (Princeton, N.J.: The Center for Analysis of Public Issues, 1976).
8. See *United States v. Spiro T. Agnew,* Crim. A. No. 73-0535, U.S. District Court, District of Maryland, October 10, 1973.
9. *Second Interim Report of the Special Senate Committee to Investigate Organized Crime in Interstate Commerce,* 82nd Cong., 1st session, Report No. 141, p. 1.
10. According to Alexander Heard, this estimate "embraces funds given in small towns and rural areas by individuals operating on the borders of the law who want a sympathetic sheriff and prosecutor, but who are not linked to crime syndicates. The estimate applies chiefly to persons engaged in illegal gambling and racketeering. It does not extend, for example, to otherwise reputable businessmen who hope for understanding treatment from building inspectors and tax assessors." Alexander Heard, *The Costs of Democracy* (Chapel Hill, N.C.: University of North Carolina Press, 1960) p. 164, fn 73; also pp. 154-168; also see Harold Lasswell and Arnold A. Rogow, *Power, Corruption and Rectitude* (Englewood Cliffs, N.J.: Prentice-Hall, 1963) pp. 79-80; and Donald R. Cressey, *Theft of the Nation: The Structure and Operations of Organized Crime in America* (New York: Harper & Row, 1969) p. 253.
11. Martin Donsky, "Undisclosed Disclosures? A Passive Approach to Campaign Finance Reporting," *NC Insight* Vol. 1, No. 4 (Fall, 1978) North Carolina Center for Public Policy Research Inc., Raleigh, N.C., pp. 12-13.

12. *Walker v. State Board of Elections,* Illinois Circuit Court, 7th Judicial Circuit, No. 364-75 (1975).
13. *Abramczyk v. State of Alaska,* Superior Court, 3rd Judicial Circuit, No. 72-6426 (1975).
14. Some authorities consider Minnesota and Montana to be "candidate" states since the designated parties have no control over the allocation of funds to the candidates. Another state, Oklahoma, will distribute money to both parties and candidates.
15. See unpublished paper by James R. Klonoski and Ann Aiken, "The Constitutional Law of Political Parties and the Emergent Dollar Checkoff," University of Oregon School of Law.
16. Ruth S. Jones, "State Public Financing and the State Parties," prepared for the Conference on Parties, Interest Groups and Campaign Finance Laws, September 4-5, 1979, in *Parties, Interest Groups, and Campaign Finance Laws,* Michael J. Malbin, ed. (Washington, D.C.: American Enterprise Institute for Public Policy Research, 1979), p. 296.
17. Jones, *State Public Financing,* p. 303.
18. There is extensive literature on party responsibility. Among the more recent books and articles see, for example: Austin Ranney, *Curing the Mischief of Faction: Party Reform in America* (Berkeley: University of California Press, 1975); and Herbert E. Alexander, "The Impact of Election Reform Legislation on the Political Party System," an unpublished paper prepared for the 1975 annual meeting of the American Political Science Association, San Francisco, California, September 5, 1975. For earlier literature, see Herbert E. Alexander, *Responsibility in Party Finance* (Princeton, N.J.: Citizens' Research Foundation, 1963).
19. For a complete discussion of proposals, see Herbert E. Alexander, *Regulation of Political Finance* (Berkeley and Princeton: Institute of Governmental Studies, University of California, and Citizens' Research Foundation, 1966), pp. 16-36.

8

Past Reform And Future Directions

Now that public financing of presidential elections is a reality, many election reformers continue to be dissatisfied with the state of campaign financing — particularly in connection with congressional elections. At the heart of their dissatisfaction are two problems that persist despite the reforms of the 1970s. First, some candidates, especially incumbents, attract more money than others, creating imbalances in candidate spending. And, second, the system as it exists allows special interests to influence public policy to a degree that reformers feel is unwarranted and dangerous.

In this concluding chapter we will examine some of the proposals being put forth to address these problems, review some of the studies of the reforms already in place and try to discern where campaign finance regulation might be headed in the 1980s.

THE POWER OF INCUMBENCY

The public affairs lobby Common Cause contends that the two-party system as it now functions really means two classes of candidates — the incumbents and the challengers — instead of just one class of candidates ideally competing on an equal footing on the basis of their qualifications. The lobby's proposal for creating a better balance is to limit contributions as well as expenditures, and provide public funds. The idea is to hold the advantaged (incumbent) down and help the disadvantaged (challenger) up, presumably making elections more competitive. In the process, the influence of large contributors and special interests is diminished through the contributions limits. As will be explained below, Common Cause and other advocates of electoral reform feel that special-interest contributors' preference for incumbents, besides giving officeholders an unfair edge over challengers, adversely affects their ability to judge legislation on its merits.

Monetary Advantage

In general, the candidate who already holds the office has an overwhelming financial edge over the candidate trying to attain it. In an effort to identify the monetary value of incumbency, the Americans for Democratic Action has reported that an incumbent House candidate, by way of benefits and special privileges, has more than a half-million-dollar advantage over nonincumbent candidates, a margin that has risen 16 percent since 1975 and more than 50 percent since 1973. The ADA found that these benefits, which include a representative's salary, staff allowances, the franking (postage) privilege, office space and communications and travel expenses, amounted to $567,191 as of 1977.

The ADA concluded that these benefits have contributed to the notable staying power of congressional incumbents. With the exception of 1974, when the post-Watergate reaction led to the defeat of many representatives, at least 95 percent of incumbents have won in every House election in the 1970s. In the Senate, the turnover rate was unusually high in 1976 and 1978 — 64 percent in 1976, 68.1 percent in 1978. In many parts of the country, incumbents are so deeply entrenched that voters do not even have the choice of two major-party candidates running in the general election. There were 64 such unopposed House candidates in 1978 and 42 in 1976.[1] In 1974 the figures were 60 and in 1972, 52. Most were lacking a Republican challenger.[2]

Communications

The most advantageous political benefits for an incumbent may be those dealing with communications with the constituency, particularly the franking privilege, which allows members of Congress free use of the mails. According to a March 1977 report in *The Washington Monthly*, the average congressman was mailing four newsletters a year to his constituency at a cost of $88,400. On the other hand, at the time the article was written, the average challenger for a House seat was spending about $75,000 on his entire campaign. In addition, Congress has given each of its members $12,000 a year to pay for computer services, which greatly facilitate the compilation of selective mailing lists of wealthy or politically active constituents for subsequent campaigns.[3] Common Cause has had litigation in progress regarding congressional use of the franking privilege. In addition to the mailing privileges, incumbents also benefit from their access to congressional radio and television studios on Capitol Hill.

SPECIAL-INTEREST INFLUENCE

Common Cause contends that the integrity of our political system is being eroded by conditions that force members of Congress into financially dependent relationships with powerful, narrowly focused special-interest groups. Under the existing system, election reformers claim, legislative actions too often are dominated by political money. According to them, the size of campaign contributions, not the issues involved, sometimes determines whether a bill passes or dies.

Not able to contribute to the presidential general election campaigns, interest groups now are channeling their money into the campaigns of House and Senate candidates. In so doing, reformers maintain, the interest groups have gained a dominant grip on the decision-making process in Congress.

Such influence, according to Common Cause's reform proposals, would be diminished by the combination of contribution limits, which reduce the candidate's dependence on special interests or large individual contributors, and partial public funding. The latter is designed to provide candidates with money to obtain minimal access to the electorate. Public funding seeks to minimize financial pressures, thus providing candidates with alternative funds and permitting them to refuse contributions offered with strings attached.

Two Lobbying Battles

To substantiate its claim that interest groups in effect make legislative policy through their campaign contributions, Common Cause has cited action by Congress on two pieces of legislation — the cargo preference bill and the Hospital Cost Containment Act of 1977.[4]

Cargo Preference. On December 30, 1974, President Ford vetoed a cargo preference bill Congress passed to require an increased percentage of imported oil to be carried by U.S. ships. In 1977 Representative John M. Murphy, D-N.Y., chairman of the Merchant Marine and Fisheries Committee, introduced basically the same legislation, proposing that 30 percent of oil imports be carried on U.S. ships. After considering the addition of several hundred million dollars a year to oil shipping costs that would be caused by this proposal, the Carter administration and the committee agreed on a modified version that would require 9.5 percent instead of 30 percent. The bill was approved by the committee but subsequently was defeated in the House.

This defeat occurred after the glare of publicity, generated by Common Cause and the media, revealed the alleged weaknesses of the legislation and the extensive use of political money by marine interests to support it. For example, from 1972 to 1977 Committee Chairman Murphy had received $43,650 in campaign contributions from maritime interests. Twenty-four of the 31 committee members voting for the bill had received a total of $82,263 during the 1976 congressional campaigns.

Moreover, had the bill made it to the Senate, it would have been reviewed by the Senate Commerce Committee, 12 of the 18 members of which had received a total of $129,059 from maritime unions in their most recent campaigns. During the 1976 campaigns, the maritime unions contributed almost one million dollars to various House and Senate candidates.[5] According to opponents of the legislation, only after public attention was drawn to this use of political money to influence policy was victory denied to the maritime interests.

Hospital Cost Containment. Although special-interest money failed to assure passage of the cargo preference bill, there are other occasions, reformers maintain, when the subtle direct influence of money has had an impact on the decision-making process. One of those occasions was the defeat of President Carter's Hospital Cost Containment Act of 1977. Strongly opposed to the bill, the American Medical Association led a well-financed attack on the efforts to control surging hospital costs. By 1977 AMPAC, the American Medical Association's political action arm, had become one of the largest group-contributors to congressional candidates. In 1974 and 1976, according to Common Cause, AMPAC led all political action committees with contributions of $1,460,000 and $1,790,000 respectively. Those figures, however, are disputed by AMPAC, which asserts that it has no branches or subsidiary groups and, accordingly, claims the designation by Common Cause of "American Medical Associations" is incorrect. According to AMPAC, some $969,405 was contributed by it to congressional candidates in 1974 and $1,076,421 in 1976.

Using Common Cause figures, but acknowledging that they may be wrong because they combine national and state association medical PACs during the 1976 election, such PACs if combined gave an average of $3,000 to each of 382 House candidates. In Senate campaigns, they jointly gave an average of $5,000 to each of 42 candidates. On February 28, 1978, the Health Subcommittee of the House Ways and Means Committee, 11 of the 13 members of which had received total contributions from such PACs of more than $63,132, voted down the bill. On July 18, the House Interstate and Foreign Commerce Committee voted 22 to 21 against the proposed health program. During the three and a half years prior to that vote, 19 members of this committee had received a total of $85,150 from those sources. Thus, according to Common Cause, legislation that advocates said would have saved American consumers $27 billion over the subsequent five years appeared to be killed by the actions of powerful medical interest groups.[6]

AMPAC officials are quick to point out that, during the period in question, its contributions also went to members of a variety of other congressional committees not immediately concerned with health care issues. In fact, according to AMPAC, the percentage of members of those other committees receiving contributions often was greater than the percentage of House Interstate and Foreign Commerce Committee members who did so. This diversified giving, the officials maintain, indicates that AMPAC did not seek a quid pro quo between contributions to representatives and subsequent action on health care legislation by those representatives. Of course all the representatives to whom AMPAC contributed would have had a vote on health care legislation if the bill had reached the floor of the House.

Not everyone, of course, accepts the assumption underlying the Common Cause charges; that is, that votes on key issues have been bought. Many elected officials resent the notion that their acceptance of a contribution indicates that they have been influenced by a particular interest group. Often, they rightfully maintain, they receive contributions because interest groups know where the elected officials stand on relevant issues and approve and support that stand.[7] Indeed, in most cases it is simplistic to think that a congressional vote can be bought for $500, $1,000 or even $5,000.

Nevertheless, whatever the precise figures or relationships in the hospital cost containment bill, the case raises the question whether some groups may achieve power to halt legislation even though they may not be able to get favorable legislation enacted.

REFORM PROPOSALS

The perceived special-interest influence on officeholders has been a major factor in the pressure to reform financing of congressional elections. Most of the proposed remedies call for some form of public funding, a concept that Congress has been reluctant to apply to its own elections.

Common Cause's reform proposals call for a mixed system of private and public financing. The basic goal is to increase the role of small individual contributors and limit the role of special-interest groups. To qualify for public funds, each House candidate would be required to raise a threshold amount of small private contributions from individuals, perhaps $10,000, to demonstrate viability as a candidate; candidates for the Senate would need to raise, say, $100,000. Having achieved this first step, a candidate's contributions from individuals up to perhaps $100 then would be matched with public funds from the voluntary tax checkoff. An overall spending limit would be imposed on those who accept public funds, and wealthy candidates would be limited in the amounts of their own money they could spend. Finally, the limit on group or PAC contributions would be reduced. Advocates claim this system would bring about more competition, lessening the financial advantage of incumbents and increasing the amount of money available to challengers.[8]

Public Financing

The most controversial reform proposal is public financing, which polls show the voters both approving and disapproving when it comes to congressional elections. Under some of the proposals, the money would go to political parties, rather than to candidates.

Conflicting Polls. A March 1979 poll by Civic Service Inc. of St. Louis showed voting age Americans strongly opposed to the use of public funds to finance campaigns for Congress.[9]

The pollsters asked 1,659 persons nationwide: "It has been proposed in Congress that the federal government provide public financing for congressional campaigns for the U.S. House of Representatives and Senate. Would you approve or disapprove of the proposal to use public funds, federal money, to pay the costs of congressional campaigns and how strongly do you feel?" Some 67 percent registered disapproval, compared with 22 percent who approved and 11 percent undecided. The results of the 1979 poll were consistent with two previous polls on the subject conducted by Civic Service for AMPAC (American Medical Political Action Committee).

The wording of the question that elicited the unfavorable response differed somewhat from that asked in a Gallup Poll on the same subject, and this may help account for the significantly different results of the two polls, both conducted at about the same time in March 1979.

The Gallup Poll indicated strong voter support for public funding of congressional campaigns.[10] In personal interviews, 1,512 adults were asked: "It has been suggested the federal government provide a fixed amount of money for the election campaigns of candidates for Congress and that all private contributions from other sources be prohibited. Do you think this is a good idea or a poor idea?" Some 57 percent answered that it was a good idea; 30 percent thought poorly of it and 13 percent had no opinion. These findings virtually duplicate the results of a 1977 Gallup Poll on the same matter.

To these conflicting results may be added the observation of Thomas F. McCoy in remarks prepared for presentation at a June 1979 Senate hearing (later cancelled) on public financing of Senate campaigns. "The only poll we have of any value on the subject of public financing of political campaigns," McCoy said, "is the checkoff on federal income tax returns." He noted that the highest percentage of taxpayers responding positively to the checkoff in any of the previous seven years was 29 percent. Further, preliminary information available from the Internal Revenue Service indicates that 25.4 percent responded positively on 1979 tax returns on 1978 income.

Public Funding and Political Parties. Some proponents of public financing maintain that the money should be channeled to congressional candidates through the political parties. Among supporters of that proposal is the Committee on Party Renewal, a voluntary association of political scientists and practitioners whose goal is to strengthen U.S. political parties.

There already has been some experience in funding nonfederal candidates through state or local party committees. That experience was summarized in Chapter 7. In House testimony, the chairmen of the Democratic and Republican parties in Iowa, where a public funding system has operated, endorsed the notion of strengthening the parties by permitting them some discretion in the distribution of public funds. And Morley Winograd, president of the Association of State Democratic Chairpersons, proposed on behalf of that group a system to return to the states the federal tax dollars checked off by state residents, with the taxpayer having the right to direct the money to the political party of his or her choice. The party then would distribute 75 percent to congressional candidates and retain 25 percent to finance its federal election activities, such as voter registration and voter turnout. This proposal, which would need to be meshed with presidential public funding, would permit parties to perform their crucial activity of contributing money to candidates' campaigns, or to undertake parallel campaigning on behalf of their candidates.

At present, portions of the Federal Election Campaign Act work to separate the candidate from the party. Limits on party activity for and contributions to candidates are imposed concurrently with limits on individual or interest-group activity and contributions. According to proponents of party renewal, the parties should be unrestricted in their ability to help candidates. The greater the dependence of the candidate upon the party, they maintain, the greater the leverage the party has in the potential to withhold funds, the greater the chance to achieve some policy coherence and discipline among candidates on the ticket, the greater the potential to mobilize party majorities for policy votes in Congress, and the more national unity and cooperation there should be on issues. This, they point out, holds true both for the majority party and the minority party. Strengthening the parties could lead to more sharply defined policy and issue differences between them, which some consider desirable in a two-party system.[11]

Supporters of public funding through the parties contend that it would serve three desirable ends: 1) Public funding would give candidates an alternative funding source, enabling them to refuse special-interest or PAC gifts at their discretion. 2) Presuming the parties would be allowed to retain a percentage of the public funds to finance their federal election activities such as voter registration and voter turnout, the new funding would enable them to strengthen both themselves and their relationships with their candidates. 3) Stronger political parties would have incentive to reform themselves, to be more issue-oriented than job-oriented, and to root out the corruption that has developed from time to time in the past.

In the current atmosphere, with the presidency changing and Congress asserting itself more aggressively, proponents of party renewal are persuaded that the parties could become new anchors of a political system in which they are dynamic and relevant instrumentalities responsive to the best combination of national interest and local concerns. If public funding through the parties helped to make the parties better able to exert some degree of control over candidates' campaigns, the result could be more policy coherence than now exists.

Floors Without Ceilings

Not all supporters of public funding think that it and expenditure limits are of necessity bound together, even though the Supreme Court's *Buckley* decision ruled out spending limits without public funding. A limited number of supporters advocate public funding floors rather than spending limit ceilings. This concept is favored by many of the mature democracies in Western Europe, where government subsidies are given to political parties with no limits on receiving and spending private contributions. The idea is that partial public funding, or a floor, gives candidates at least minimal access to the electorate and provides alternative funds so that candidates can reject private contributions with expressed or tacit obligations attached. At the same time, if this approach were used in the United States, the absence of spending limits would avoid the constitutional issues raised in the *Buckley* case. Some modifications, however, probably would be required to make this system workable in the United States, for in other countries subsidies are given to political parties, not candidates, and upon the basis of parliamentary strength, making for quite different systems.

Expenditure and Contribution Limits

One of the most significant problems with expenditure limitations is to find a ceiling that is equitable to incumbents and challengers alike. If the ceiling is too high, candidates try to spend up to the limit. If it is too low, the limit tends to hurt challengers who need to spend more money to get well enough known to compete against better known incumbents.

Contribution limits, according to critics, serve to exacerbate financial pressures instead of making candidates less dependent on large contributors. Such limits unfairly act as an indirect expenditure limit, critics maintain, since wealthy candidates can spend unlimited amounts on their own campaigns. Some reformers recommend increasing existing individual contribution limits to make election campaigns more competitive.[12]

The New Jersey Experience. The 1977 New Jersey gubernatorial general election campaign illustrated the problem of finding an equitable expenditure ceiling. Both major-party candidates in that campaign raised up to the maximum in private contributions and received matching public funds close to the limit. This gave an advantage to

Governor Brendan Byrne, who was better known across the state. But the expenditure limits additionally worked to the disadvantage of the governor's challenger, state Senator Ray Bateman, who late in the campaign wanted to change strategies and revise campaign themes because he was sinking in the polls. But Bateman was unable to take a new approach and still stay within the expenditure limit. Byrne won and spending limits in this case seemed to rigidify the system.

A majority of the New Jersey Election Law Enforcement Commission has since recommended dropping overall expenditure limits but retaining limitations on contributions and loans and candidates' use of personal funds, with a cap on public funds available to candidates.

San Diego and San Francisco. A 1976 study of the consequences of campaign finance reform in San Diego and San Francisco appears to lend support to some of the objections raised by critics of spending and contribution limits.[13] The mayoralty races there in 1975 were the first citywide contests since both cities adopted ordinances requiring full disclosure of campaign contributions and imposing limits on them. Neither ordinance made any provision for public funding of the elections.

The ordinances differed in several ways. The San Francisco ordinance established a ceiling on campaign expenditures — later invalidated by the *Buckley* decision. The San Diego ordinance allowed a maximum individual contribution of $250 to a candidate, while the San Francisco ordinance established a $500 maximum. Both ordinances limited mayoralty candidates to $2,500 gifts to their own campaigns.

The four political scientists who conducted the study found that total expenditures in San Diego's mayoralty race, in which there were no spending limits, fell by 16.5 percent when compared with the 1971 race. This they took as an indication that contribution limits do, in fact, serve as an indirect form of expenditure limit. They discovered that limits on contributions tended to increase the costs and difficulty of fund raising. Expenditures for fund-raising activities increased by 7.3 percent in San Diego and 11.5 percent in San Francisco between 1971 and 1975. The researchers reported that in San Francisco campaign staffs and managers expressed dissatisfaction with the spending limits. They also noted that many of the reforms in both ordinances increased bookkeeping costs and suggested that such costs might discourage the solicitation of very small contributions. The authors observed that the restrictions apparently increased the potential influence of organized groups because they increased candidates' need for inexpensive access to voters and contributors.

IMPACT OF EXISTING REFORMS

Some studies have found that federal election reform legislation currently in effect has had a significant impact on the competitive nature of the electoral process in congressional campaigns — but the impact has not always been what election reformers intended.

Incumbents vs. Challengers

Analyzing campaign spending data from the 1972 and 1974 congressional elections, Gary C. Jacobson has shown that campaign spending does not have the same consequences for incumbents and challengers alike. Jacobson's findings showed that spending by challengers has more impact on election outcomes than spending by incumbents. "In simple terms," claims Jacobson, "the more incumbents spend, the worse they do; the reason is that they raise and spend money in direct proportion to the magnitude of the electoral threat posed by the challenger, but this reactive spending fails to offset the progress made by the challenger that inspires it in the first place." [14]

To support his conclusions, Jacobson pointed out that 87 percent of the incumbents who lost in 1974 spent more in losing than they did in winning in 1972. For all incumbents who ran and were opposed in both elections, the mean expenditure was $61,799 in 1972 and $63,609 in 1974, an increase of 3 percent. For the 1974 losers, the mean expenditure was $69,218 in 1972 and $101,645 in 1974, a 47 percent increase.[15] When data from the 1976 election were included in another study, Jacobson continued to find that the amount spent by challengers had a stronger effect on election outcomes than that spent by incumbents.[16]

Simply being known and remembered by voters is a very important factor in electoral success. Jacobson contends that this suggests "an attractive theoretical explanation" for his findings. The average incumbent, provided with the resources of his office, already enjoys an advantage in voter recognition prior to the campaign. The dissemination of additional information about the incumbent during the campaign, therefore, may often be superfluous even though it helps reinforce voters' opinions. On the other hand, the challenger, not so well known to most voters, has everything to gain from an extensive and expensive effort to acquire voter awareness.

Translated into financial terms, this means that because senators and representatives are generally better known, they usually need less campaign money but are able to raise more. The challengers, while they may need more money, have difficulty in getting it. But when they do, either through providing it to their own campaigns out of their own wealth, or by attracting it, they become better known and are more likely to win. If the incumbent then raises money to meet the threat, spending money helps him or her less per dollar spent than additional dollars spent by the challenger. In summary, those votes that change as a result of campaign spending generally benefit challengers.

Jacobson concluded that any campaign finance policy, such as public subsidies, that would increase spending for both incumbent and challenger would work to the benefit of the latter, thus making elections more competitive. On the other hand, any policy that attempts to equalize the financial positions of candidates by limiting campaign contributions and spending would benefit incumbents, thus lessening electoral competition.[17]

PACs and Small Contributors

A comparison of fund raising in the 1972 and 1976 House campaigns by Roland D. McDevitt tends to add support to Jacobson's conclusions. The $1,000 limit on individual contributions has increased reliance on small contributions and has encouraged the proliferation of political action committees. These two groups, McDevitt discovered, tend to aid incumbents more than challengers: "Taken together in 1976, all PAC contributions and individual contributions of $100 or less constituted 69.1 percent of incumbents' receipts and 45.4 percent of challengers' receipts." [18] Thus challengers seem to need larger contributions if they are to compete effectively.

In a similar analysis of Senate campaigns, McDevitt also found an especially strong advantage for incumbents among small individual contributors. The growth trend in PAC contributions was not so great in the Senate campaigns, however, suggesting that PACs may prefer to support candidates having smaller constituencies where it costs less to elect. In the 1972 Senate races, PAC money totaled 12.8 percent of candidate receipts in the five largest states against 27.4 percent in the five smallest states. In 1976 the range was from 11.7 percent in the largest states to 24.2 percent in the smallest. That trend continued in 1978, even while the overall percentage of campaign income from PAC contributions increased, comprising for the general election about 13 percent of all receipts of Senate candidates and about 25 percent of receipts of House candidates.[19]

According to Federal Election Commission figures, one trend noted by McDevitt in the 1972 and 1976 congressional campaigns did continue in 1978 — PAC money continued to aid incumbents more than challengers.[20] Including primary and general elections, PACs contributed $19.9 million to 414 incumbents, $7.7 million to 986 challengers and $7.4 million to 521 candidates for open seats.

An analysis by W. P. Welch of contributions by 11 PACs to House candidates in 1974 and 1976 offers a useful clarification to the finding that PACs tend to favor incumbents more than challengers.[21] Welch determined that economic-interest groups contribute primarily to likely winners and that ideological groups tend to contribute mainly to candidates in close races.

In another study, reported while still in progress, Michael J. Malbin found evidence that "the larger corporations, like the umbrella labor organizations, are behaving as combined general interest/special interest groups." On the other hand, said Malbin, "the real 'special-interest' groups — the ones that give money to incumbents for the sake of narrow economic interests — are the single-product corporations, trade associations, and single industry labor unions."[22]

The Complexities of Compliance

In discussing the complexities of the Federal Election Campaign Act, the late Senator Lee Metcalf once wondered whether officeholders should not worry about serving time rather than constituents. His quip highlights the conflict between the goals proponents of election reform sought to achieve and the statutory and enforcement constraints that the implementation of the reforms has imposed on the democratic electoral process.

Though the election reforms of the 1970s have sought to involve more people in the electoral process, the new technologies and the professionalization of politics — brought on in part by the reform laws themselves — have often required candidates to substitute paid experts for free, usually unskilled, help. The requirements of compliance with the laws do not pose great difficulty for corporate and union PACs. Corporations and labor unions can use treasury money to cope with regulations and pass along the cost in higher prices or increased dues.

Candidates, parties and other political committees, however, are at a disadvantage. They cannot as readily pay salaries of individuals whose task is to ensure compliance nor can they pass along the costs of compliance. Money is always a scarce resource in politics. Whatever money they spend to comply with election regulations decreases their campaigning ability and increases financial pressures. When expenditure limits are in effect, it seems desirable to exempt compliance costs to free the maximum possible amount for direct campaigning.

The problems of compliance became so substantial and costly that changes in the laws were sought early in 1976. In one of the few bipartisan efforts during the campaign, Gerald Ford and Jimmy Carter sought and achieved a legislated exemption of compliance costs that was included in the 1976 Amendments. This provision enabled candidates who were close to the spending limits — Ford, Carter and Ronald Reagan — to isolate compliance costs retroactive to January 1, 1975, and to recalculate their other expenditures. It had no effect on candidates whose expenditures did not approach the limits.[23]

1980 AND BEYOND

Despite efforts to control political spending through the imposition of contribution limits, and of expenditure limits in campaigns in which candidates accept public funds, it appears that the cost of running for public office will remain high. Indeed, early in the 1979-80 election cycle, several trends emerged — some legislated, others not — that had a notable effect on campaign financing, particularly at the presidential level. In general, those trends indicated that for the foreseeable future political costs will continue to rise.

Early Starts

In August 1978 Representative Philip Crane of Illinois formally announced his candidacy for the 1980 Republican presidential nomination. By announcing so far in advance, Crane continued a trend started by George McGovern in 1971 and repeated by several Democratic candidates, including Jimmy Carter, in 1975. By June 1979 seven major contenders had announced their presidential candidacies and another, Senator Lowell Weicker of Connecticut, had announced and subsequently dropped out. The early formation of campaign committees indicated that the 1980 campaign would be the longest — and perhaps most costly — in recent memory.

Several contenders who did not formally declare their candidacies until 1979 — including President Carter, Senator Howard Baker of Tennessee, former California Governor Ronald Reagan and incumbent California Governor Jerry Brown — formed committees earlier to do the necessary organizational and fund-raising work.

In addition, Senator Edward Kennedy of Massachusetts took no steps to halt a draft-Kennedy movement that began in the early months of 1979. That movement, like the campaign committees of the announced and unannounced candidates, did raise and spend funds, thus contributing to the increase in political spending. Kennedy announced his candidacy in November 1979.

Long, Costly Campaigns

Several factors led to a lengthy and expensive 1980 prenomination campaign period. Like McGovern in 1971 and Carter in 1975, candidates who were not well-known nationally felt the need to establish name recognition among voters.

The campaign reform laws of the 1970s also contributed to a longer, costlier 1980 campaign. As in 1976, all federal candidates were bound by law limiting individual contributions to $1,000 and political action committee contributions to $5,000. Consequently they had to engage in often long and expensive drives to raise funds from a large number of smaller contributors. Presidential candidates who planned to accept matching funds for their prenomination campaigns were required to engage in fund raising broad-based enough to collect $5,000 in 20 or more states in individual contributions of $250 or less.

In 1980 candidates also had to contend with a larger number of primaries — 35 states plus the District of Columbia and Puerto Rico — compared with the 30 states that held primary elections in 1976. In addition, Democrats and Republicans in Florida and Republicans in Massachusetts held nonbinding presidential selection conventions. Finally, there was an unusual amount of maneuvering among candidates to gain potential election advantage. In California, for example, former Texas Governor John Connally, who announced early as a candidate for the Republican nomination, unsuccessfully sought to change California's winner-take-all primary rule. Connally backers lost the battle for proportional allocation of convention delegates, to overcome the apparent advantage of former Governor Ronald Reagan, an early favorite to win his state's primary. In Illinois and New York, Republican organizations sought to assure that delegates would appear on the primary ballots with no indication of presidential preference. That procedure would allow the state organizations to maintain greater control over the delegations and thus wield influence in favor of one candidate or a favorite son. Jockeying in these and other states required additional expenditures by candidates, announced and unannounced. For presidential candidates who planned to accept public funding, and thus subject themselves to expenditure limits, the cost of participating in additional primary elections, of influencing presidential selection conventions and of maneuvering for political advantage in individual states put further pressure on candidates' ability to stay within the spending ceilings. The increased financial pressure led early in the 1980 campaign to intensive fund-raising efforts. By the end of September 1979, the top 12 money-raisers among presidential candidates had collected $17.4 million, compared with $4.2 million through the corresponding period in 1975.[24] At least one candidate, John Connally, decided to do without federal matching funds so as to avoid the attached spending limits.[25] But on March 9, 1980, after a major setback in the South Carolina primary, Connally withdrew his candidacy.

Senate Campaigns

The early part of the 1979-80 election cycle also gave indications that the costs of Senate campaigns would continue to climb. The contest for the New York seat held by Republican Jacob Javits was expected to attract at least five candidates spending one million dollars each.[26] In addition, conservative ideological committees continued a trend that had been clearly discerned in the 1978 election, when they targeted large sums of money for media attacks on a number of liberal Democratic senators. The targeted senators in 1980 included South Dakota's George McGovern, Idaho's Frank Church, New Hampshire's John Durkin and Iowa's John Culver.[27] The planned spending increase by conservative groups and Republican committees could, of course, only lead to increased fund raising and spending by the officeholders whose seats were at stake. Long before the 1980 elections, then, it was clear that the ante had been raised — the costs of campaigning for many elective offices would be greater than ever.

Table 8-1 Federal Income Tax Checkoff

Tax Year	*Approximate Percentages of Taxpayers Using Checkoff*	*Approximate Amount*
1972[a]	7.0	$12,900,000
1973	13.6	17,300,000
1974	24.2	31,900,000
1975	25.8	33,700,000
Total available for 1976 presidential election (approx.)		95,800,00
Total funds certified to candidates		−72,000,000
Total remaining after 1976 election		$23,800,000
1976	27.0	36,600,000
1977	29.0	39,200,000
1978	25.8	35,600,000
Total		$135,200,000

[a] In its first year the tax checkoff form was separate from the 1040 form and was not readily available for many. In 1974 the tax checkoff form was included on the front page of the 1040 form. It also allowed taxpayers who had not checked off for 1972 to do so retroactively for that year. Only $4 million was checked off initially for 1972. Another $8.9 million was added retroactively, for a total of $12.9 million.

SOURCE: Testimony of Thomas E. Harris before the Committee on Rules and Administration, United States Senate. *Federal Election Reform Proposals of 1977,* Appendix B, p. 430. Figures for 1978 are from the Internal Revenue Service.

Income Tax Checkoff

The success of public financing of presidential campaigns depends in large part on taxpayers' continued willingness to contribute to the fund by using the income tax checkoff. Through the 1978 tax year, at least, they showed enough support for the system to assure adequate funds for the 1980 payout to eligible candidates and national nominating conventions.

The extent of support for the program is indicated in Table 8-1, which shows both the percentage of taxpayers using the checkoff and the amount checked off for each year since the program began in 1972. It was expected that approximately $135 million would be available for the 1980 payout. That figure includes an excess of about $23.8 million left from 1976 and held for the 1980 election.

Private Financing

Even with public financing in force for presidential elections and under consideration for congressional elections, a commitment to some forms of private financing seems likely to continue. Improved solicitation and collection systems are essential if tax or matching incentives are to work effectively. The political party, of course, is one possible "collection agency." The party can go beyond merely funding party committees to fund its candidates' campaigns as well. Other important collection systems include associational networks existing in membership groups. Labor unions, corporations, dairy cooperatives, trade associations and professional groups can solicit effectively because of two characteristics: 1) they include large groups of like-minded persons, and 2) they have ready-made channels for communicating with their members. Whether at meetings, through field men or even by mail, such groups possess internal and therefore inexpensive means of asking for political money.

Collection systems with bipartisan potential exist at places of employment. With safeguards (perhaps through the use of a neutral trusteeship program), even government employees could be asked on a nonpartisan basis to contribute. While such sources of funds may be controversial, their potential is immense if properly tapped.

Carleton Sterling has criticized the political reformer for seeking ". . . a direct dialogue between candidates and voters both free of outside influences."[28] Politics devoid of the influence of interest groups is not realistic. Politics probably cannot be sterilized and purified to the degree that would satisfy the most zealous reformers. Politics is about people and groups of people, their ideas, interests and aspirations. Since people seek political involvement partly through groups, a politics in which groups are shut out or seriously impaired is difficult to envision.

Government subsidies represent one alternative source of funds. But given the struggle to provide public funding at just the presidential level, private solicitation for campaigns at lower levels will be necessary in the indefinite future.

Participation as a Goal

Money is only one part of a complex political ecology in which voting is the single most important individual act. Persons who would replace private financing with total government funding might succeed unwittingly in changing fundamental balances in the political system. Critics who minimize individual efforts ignore history: A system of free elections cannot survive without voluntarism. In whatever form or quantity elections draw upon government assistance, freely contributed money and services will still be needed.

Success in attracting individuals to charitable giving has not been a matter of accident or a spontaneous result of general good will toward organizations with good causes. Rather, it reflects a serious effort to educate the public in its responsibilities and to organize collection systems. Political responsibilities must be similarly learned.

The value of contributing small sums for political activity is neither taught in schools nor widely understood as an act of good citizenship, although voting is both honored and respected, at least in principle. The challenge is to associate contributing with voting as an act of good citizenship, to upgrade and dignify political giving and to gain for the popular financing of politics the public approval accorded voting.

The major changes in our campaign finance laws in the 1970s have not always resulted in systematic or consistent reform. In part, this is because various aspects of the problem have been dealt with separately and at different times by the major actors in government — Congress, the president, the Federal Election Commission and the Supreme Court.

What the 1971 Federal Election Campaign Act, the 1974 Amendments and many state laws have lacked has been a philosophy about regulation that is both constitutional and pragmatically designed to keep the election process open and flexible rather than rigid, exclusionary and fragmented. It is not yet clear whether the 1976 Amendments, the 1979 Amendments or the revision of state laws following *Buckley v. Valeo* will lead to the openness and flexibility a democratic and pluralistic society require.

NOTES

1. Congressional Quarterly *Weekly Report.* December 4, 1976, pp. 3280-3286, and December 25, 1976, pp. 3367-3389. Author's compilation for 1978.
2. Testimony of Roy A. Schotland, *Hearings on Public Financing of Congressional Campaigns,* before the House Administration Committee, 95th Congress, 1st session, June 28, 1977, Table H-1, p. 4.
3. Lewis Perdue, "The Million-Dollar Advantage of Incumbency," *The Washington Monthly,* March 1977, p. 52.
4. Common Cause, *How Money Talks in Congress,* mimeograph, 1978, pp. 6-13.
5. Common Cause, *How Money Talks,* pp. 8-9.
6. Common Cause, *How Money Talks,* pp. 11-13.
7. Michael Malbin maintains that "on the whole, business and labor, like the ideological groups, give to people who share their broad views about public policy. . . . It is hard to justify the notion that campaign gifts, particularly ones from the more broadly based labor, corporate or ideological PACs, are a special-interest group downpayment for future special benefits." Michael J. Malbin, "Campaign Financing and the 'Special Interests,' " *The Public Interest,* 56 (Summer 1979), p. 27.
8. Common Cause, *How Money Talks,* pp. 24-25.
9. Civic Service Inc., "Attitudes Toward Campaign Financing," mimeograph, March 1979.
10. Reported in *Campaign Practices Reports,* newsletter, Plus Publications Inc., April 16, 1979, p. 5
11. Other proposals to strengthen the parties have been made by the Campaign Study Group of Harvard University's Institute of Politics. They include creating an additional tax credit for contributions to political parties and easing reporting requirements for state and local party committees that

contribute to federal candidates. See *Campaign Practices Reports,* July 10, 1979, p. 9.

12. The Campaign Study Group of Harvard's Institute of Politics is among the groups recommending increased individual contribution limits. See *Campaign Practices Reports,* July 10, 1979, p. 9. See also Herbert E. Alexander, "Public Financing of Congressional Campaigns," *Regulation,* January/February 1980, pp. 27-32.
13. Roger H. Davidson, Timothy A. Hodson, Roland D. McDevitt with Michael Semler, "An Investigation of the Consequences of Campaign Finance Reform," mimeograph, 1976, 136 pages.
14. Gary C. Jacobson, "The Effects of Campaign Spending in Congressional Elections," *American Political Science Review,* Vol. 72, No. 2 (June 1978), p. 469. See also Gary C. Jacobson, *Money In Congressional Elections* (New Haven and London: Yale University Press, 1980).
15. Jacobson, "Effects of Campaign Spending," p. 474.
16. Jacobson, "Public Funds for Congressional Campaigns: Who Would Benefit?" in *Political Finance,* Herbert E. Alexander, ed. (Beverly Hills: Sage Publications Inc., 1979), pp. 99-127.
17. Jacobson, "Effects of Campaign Spending," p. 479.
18. Roland D. McDevitt, "The Changing Dynamics of Fund Raising in House Campaigns," in *Political Finance,* p. 152.
19. Roland D. McDevitt, "The Changing Dynamics of Fund Raising in Senate Campaigns," unpublished paper.
20. Federal Election Commission news release, May 10, 1979.
21. W. P. Welch, "Patterns of Contributions: Economic Interest and Ideological Groups," in *Political Finance,* pp. 199-220.
22. Michael J. Malbin, "Neither a Mountain nor a Molehill," *Regulation,* May/June 1979, p. 43.
23. For a fuller discussion of compliance requirements and costs in the 1976 campaigns, see Herbert E. Alexander, *Financing the 1976 Election,* (Washington, D.C.: Congressional Quarterly Press, 1979), pp. 492-503.
24. Christopher Buchanan, "Presidential Campaign Finances," Congressional Quarterly *Weekly Report,* November 10, 1979, p. 2529.
25. Richard J. Cattani, "U.S. Candidates Amass Funds at Record Pace," *Christian Science Monitor,* September 5, 1979.
26. Cattani, "Candidates Amass Funds."
27. Cattani, "The 1980s Battle for Control of the Senate," *Christian Science Monitor,* August 6, 1979.
28. Carleton W. Sterling, "Control of Campaign Spending: The Reformer's Paradox," *American Bar Association Journal,* 59 (October 1973), p. 1153. ▮

Appendix

Federal Election Campaign Act of 1971*

The Federal Election Campaign Act of 1971 (FECA) was the first comprehensive revision of federal campaign legislation since the Corrupt Practices Act of 1925. The act established detailed spending limits and disclosure procedures. P.L. 92-225 contained the following major provisions:

General

- Repealed the Federal Corrupt Practices Act of 1925.
- Defined "election" to mean any general, special, primary or runoff election, nominating convention or caucus, delegate-selection primary, presidential preference primary or constitutional convention.
- Broadened the definitions of "contribution" and "expenditure" as they pertain to political campaigns, but exempted a loan of money by a national or state bank made in accordance with applicable banking laws.
- Prohibited promises of employment or other political rewards or benefits by any candidate in exchange for political support, and prohibited contracts between candidates and any federal department or agency.
- Provided that the terms "contribution" and "expenditure" did not include communications, nonpartisan registration and get-out-the-vote campaigns by a corporation aimed at its stockholders or by a labor organization aimed at its members.
- Provided that the terms "contribution" and "expenditure" did not include the establishment, administration and solicitation of voluntary contributions to a separate segregated fund to be utilized for political purposes by a corporation or labor organization.

Contribution Limits

- Placed a ceiling on contributions by any candidate or his immediate family to his own campaign of $50,000 for president or vice president, $35,000 for senator and $25,000 for representative.

Spending Limits

- Limited the total amount that could be spent by federal candidates for advertising time in communications media to 10 cents per eligible voter or $50,000, whichever was greater. The limitation would apply to all candidates for president and vice president, senator and representative, and would be determined annually for the geographical area of each election by the Bureau of the Census.

• Included in the term "communications media" radio and television broadcasting stations, newspapers, magazines, billboards and automatic telephone equipment. Of the total spending limit, up to 60 percent could be used for broadcast advertising time.

• Specified that candidates for presidential nomination, during the period prior to the nominating convention, could spend no more in primary or nonprimary states than the amount allowed under the 10-cent-per-voter communications spending limitation.

• Provided that broadcast and nonbroadcast spending limitations be increased in proportion to annual increases in the Consumer Price Index over the base year 1970.

Disclosure and Enforcement

• Required all political committees that anticipated receipts in excess of $1,000 during the calendar year to file a statement of organization with the appropriate federal supervisory officer, and to include such information as the names of all principal officers, the scope of the committee, the names of all candidates the committee supported and other information as required by law.

• Stipulated that the appropriate federal supervisory officer to oversee election campaign practices, reporting and disclosure was the Clerk of the House for House candidates, the Secretary of the Senate for Senate candidates and the Comptroller General for presidential candidates.

• Required each political committee to report any individual expenditure of more than $100 and any expenditures of more than $100 in the aggregate during the calendar year.

• Required disclosure of all contributions to any committee or candidate in excess of $100, including a detailed report with the name and address of the contributor and the date the contribution was made.

• Required the supervisory officers to prepare an annual report for each committee registered with the commission and make such reports available for sale to the public.

• Required candidates and committees to file reports of contributions and expenditures on the 10th day of March, June and September every year, on the 15th and fifth days preceding the date on which an election was held and on the 31st day of January. Any contribution of $5,000 or more was to be reported within 48 hours after its receipt.

• Required reporting of the names, addresses and occupations of any lender and endorser of any loan in excess of $100 as well as the date and amount of such loans.

• Required any person who made any contribution in excess of $100, other than through a political committee or candidate, to report such contribution to the commission.

• Prohibited any contribution to a candidate or committee by one person in the name of another person.

• Authorized the office of the Comptroller General to serve as a national clearinghouse for information on the administration of election practices.

• Required that copies of reports filed by a candidate with the appropriate supervisory officer also be filed with the secretary of state for the state in which the election was held.

Miscellaneous

• Prohibited radio and television stations from charging political candidates more than the lowest unit cost for the same advertising time available to commercial advertisers. Lowest unit rate charges would apply only during the 45 days preceding a primary election and the 60 days preceding a general election.

- Required nonbroadcast media to charge candidates no more than the comparable amounts charged to commercial advertisers for the same class and amount of advertising space. The requirement would apply only during the 45 days preceding the date of a primary election and 60 days before the date of a general election.
- Provided that amounts spent by an agent of a candidate on behalf of his candidacy would be charged against the overall expenditure allocation. Fees paid to the agent for services performed also would be charged against the overall limitation.
- Stipulated that no broadcast station could make any charge for political advertising time on a station unless written consent to contract for such time had been given by the candidate, and unless the candidate certified that such charge would not exceed the spending limit.

*Some provisions have been declared unconstitutional and some have been superseded by later amendments or repealed.

Revenue Act of 1971*

The Revenue Act of 1971, through tax incentives and a tax checkoff plan, provided the basis for public funding of presidential election campaigns. P.L. 92-178 contained the following major provisions:

Tax Incentives and Checkoff

• Allowed a tax credit of $12.50 ($25 for a married couple) or a deduction against income of $50 ($100 for a married couple) for political contributions to candidates for local, state or federal office. [NOTE: The Revenue Act of 1978, P.L. 96-600, raised the tax credit to $50 on a single tax return, $100 on a joint return. As in the 1971 Act, the credit equaled 50 percent of the contribution, up to those limits. The 1978 law eliminated the tax deduction for political contributions while increasing the tax credit.]

• Allowed taxpayers to contribute to a general fund for all eligible presidential and vice presidential candidates by authorizing $1 of their annual income tax payment to be placed in such a fund.

Presidential Election Campaign Fund

• Authorized to be distributed to the candidates of each major party (one which obtained 25 percent of votes cast in the previous presidential election) an amount equal to 15 cents multiplied by the number of U.S. residents age 18 or over.

• Established a formula for allocating public campaign funds to candidates of minor parties whose candidates received 5 percent or more but less than 25 percent of the previous presidential election vote.

• Authorized payments after the election to reimburse the campaign expenses of a new party whose candidate received enough votes to be eligible or to a minor party whose candidate increased its vote to the qualifying level.

• Prohibited major-party candidates who chose public financing of their campaign from accepting private campaign contributions unless their share of funds contributed through the income tax checkoff procedure fell short of the amounts to which they were entitled.

• Prohibited a major-party candidate who chose public financing and all campaign committees authorized by the candidate from spending more than the amount to which the candidate was entitled under the contributions formula.

• Provided that if the amounts in the fund were insufficient to make the payments to which each party was entitled, payments would be allocated according to the ratio of contributions in their accounts. No party would receive from the general fund more than the smallest amount needed by a major party to reach the maximum amount of contributions to which it was entitled.

• Provided that surpluses remaining in the fund after a campaign be returned to the Treasury after all parties had been paid the amounts to which they were entitled.

Enforcement

- Provided penalties of $5,000 or one year in prison, or both, for candidates or campaign committees that spent more on a campaign than the amounts they received from the campaign fund or who accepted private contributions when sufficient public funds were available.
- Provided penalties of $10,000 or five years in prison, or both, for candidates or campaign committees who used public campaign funds for unauthorized expenses, gave or accepted kickbacks or illegal payments involving public campaign funds, or who knowingly furnished false information to the Comptroller General.

*Some provisions have been declared unconstitutional and some have been superseded by later amendments or repealed.

Federal Election Campaign Act Amendments of 1974*

The 1974 Amendments set new contribution and spending limits, made provision for government funding of presidential prenomination campaigns and national nominating conventions, and created the bipartisan Federal Election Commission to administer election laws. P.L. 93-443 contained the following major provisions:

Federal Election Commission

- Created a six-member, full-time bipartisan Federal Election Commission to be responsible for administering election laws and the public financing program.
- Provided that the president, Speaker of the House and president pro tem of the Senate would appoint to the commission two members, each of different parties, all subject to confirmation by Congress. Commission members could not be officials or employees of any branch of government.
- Made the Secretary of the Senate and Clerk of the House ex officio, nonvoting members of the FEC; provided that their offices would serve as custodian of reports for House and Senate candidates.
- Provided that commissioners would serve six-year, staggered terms and established a rotating one-year chairmanship.

Contribution Limits

- $1,000 per individual for each primary, runoff or general election, and an aggregate contribution of $25,000 to all federal candidates annually.
- $5,000 per organization, political committee and national and state party organization for each election, but no aggregate limit on the amount organizations could contribute in a campaign nor on the amount organizations could contribute to party organizations supporting federal candidates.
- $50,000 for president or vice president, $35,000 for Senate and $25,000 for House races for candidates and their families to their own campaign.
- $1,000 for independent expenditures on behalf of a candidate.
- Barred cash contributions of over $100 and foreign contributions.

Spending Limits

- Presidential primaries — $10 million total per candidate for all primaries. In a state presidential primary, limited a candidate to spending no more than twice what a Senate candidate in that state would be allowed to spend.
- Presidential general election — $20 million per candidate.
- Presidential nominating conventions — $2 million each major political party, lesser amounts for minor parties.
- Senate primaries — $100,000 or eight cents per eligible voter, whichever was greater.

• Senate general elections — $150,000 or 12 cents per eligible voter, whichever was greater.

• House primaries — $70,000.

• House general elections — $70,000.

• National party spending — $10,000 per candidate in House general elections; $20,000 or two cents per eligible voter, whichever was greater, for each candidate in Senate general elections; and two cents per voter (approximately $2.9 million) in presidential general elections. The expenditure would be above the candidate's individual spending limit.

• Applied Senate spending limits to House candidates who represented a whole state.

• Repealed the media spending limitations in the Federal Election Campaign Act of 1971 (P.L. 92-225).

• Exempted expenditures of up to $500 for food and beverages, invitations, unreimbursed travel expenses by volunteers and spending on "slate cards" and sample ballots.

• Exempted fund-raising costs of up to 20 percent of the candidate spending limit. Thus the spending limit for House candidates would be effectively raised from $70,000 to $84,000 and for candidates in presidential primaries from $10 million to $12 million.

• Provided that spending limits be increased in proportion to annual increases in the Consumer Price Index.

Public Financing

• Presidential general elections — voluntary public financing. Major-party candidates automatically would qualify for full funding before the campaign. Minor-party and independent candidates would be eligible to receive a proportion of full funding based on past or current votes received. If a candidate opted for full public funding, no private contributions would be permitted.

• Presidential nominating conventions — optional public funding. Major parties automatically would qualify. Minor parties would be eligible for lesser amounts based on their proportion of votes received in a past election.

• Presidential primaries — matching public funds of up to $5 million per candidate after meeting fund-raising requirement of $100,000 raised in amounts of at least $5,000 in each of 20 states or more. Only the first $250 of individual private contributions would be matched. The matching funds were to be divided among the candidates as quickly as possible. In allocating the money, the order in which the candidates qualified would be taken into account. Only private gifts, raised after January 1, 1975, would qualify for matching for the 1976 election. No federal payments would be made before January 1976.

• Provided that all federal money for public funding of campaigns would come from the Presidential Election Campaign Fund. Money received from the federal income tax dollar checkoff automatically would be appropriated to the fund.

Disclosure and Enforcement

• Required each candidate to establish one central campaign committee through which all contributions and expenditures on behalf of a candidate must be reported. Required designation of specific bank depositories of campaign funds.

• Required full reports of contributions and expenditures to be filed with the Federal Election Commission 10 days before and 30 days after every election, and within 10 days of the close of each quarter unless the committee received or expended less than $1,000 in that quarter. A year-end report was due in nonelection years.

- Required that contributions of $1,000 or more received within the last 15 days before election be reported to the commission within 48 hours.
- Prohibited contributions in the name of another.
- Treated loans as contributions. Required a cosigner or guarantor for each $1,000 of outstanding obligation.
- Required any organization that spent any money or committed any act for the purpose of influencing any election (such as the publication of voting records) to file reports as a political committee.
- Required every person who spent or contributed more than $100, other than to or through a candidate or political committee, to report.
- Permitted government contractors, unions and corporations to maintain separate, segregated political funds.
- Provided that the commission would receive campaign reports, make rules and regulations (subject to review by Congress within 30 days), maintain a cumulative index of reports filed and not filed, make special and regular reports to Congress and the president, and serve as an election information clearinghouse.
- Gave the commission power to render advisory opinions, conduct audits and investigations, subpoena witnesses and information and go to court to seek civil injunctions.
- Provided that criminal cases would be referred by the commission to the Justice Department for prosecution.
- Increased existing fines to a maximum of $50,000.
- Provided that a candidate for federal office who failed to file reports could be prohibited from running again for the term of that office plus one year.

Miscellaneous

- Set January 1, 1975, as the effective date of the act (except for immediate preemption of state laws).
- Removed Hatch Act restrictions on voluntary activities by state and local employees in federal campaigns, if not otherwise prohibited by state law.
- Prohibited solicitation of funds by franked mail.
- Preempted state election laws for federal candidates.
- Permitted use of excess campaign funds to defray expenses of holding federal office or for other lawful purposes.

*Some provisions have been declared unconstitutional and some have been superseded by later amendments or repealed.

Federal Election Campaign Act Amendments of 1976*

The 1976 Amendments revised election laws following the Supreme Court decision in *Buckley v. Valeo.* The Amendments reopened the door to large contributions through "independent expenditures" and through corporate and union political action committees. P.L. 94-283 contained the following major provisions:

Federal Election Commission

- Reconstituted the Federal Election Commission as a six-member panel appointed by the president and confirmed by the Senate.
- Prohibited commission members from engaging in outside business activities; gave commissioners one year after joining the body to terminate outside business interests.
- Gave Congress the power to disapprove individual sections of any regulation proposed by the commission.

Contribution Limits

- Limited an individual to giving no more than $5,000 a year to a political action committee and $20,000 to the national committee of a political party (the 1974 law set a $1,000-per-election limit on individual contributions to a candidate and an aggregate contribution limit for individuals of $25,000 a year, both provisions remaining in effect).
- Limited a multicandidate committee to giving no more than $15,000 a year to the national committee of a political party (the 1974 law set only a limit of $5,000 per election per candidate, a provision remaining in effect).
- Limited the Democratic and Republican senatorial campaign committees to giving no more than $17,500 a year to a candidate (the 1974 law set a $5,000-per-election limit, a provision remaining in effect).
- Allowed campaign committees organized to back a single candidate to provide "occasional, isolated, and incidental support" to another candidate. (The 1974 law had limited such a committee to spending money only on behalf of the single candidate for which it was formed.)
- Restricted the proliferation of membership organization, corporate and union political action committees. All political action committees established by a company or an international union would be treated as a single committee for contribution purposes. The contributions of political action committees of a company or union would be limited to no more than $5,000 overall to the same candidate in any election.

Spending Limits

- Limited spending by presidential and vice presidential candidates to no more than $50,000 of their own, or their families', money on their campaigns, if they accepted public financing.

• Exempted from the law's spending limits payments by candidates or the national committees of political parties for legal and accounting services required to comply with the campaign law, but required that such payments be reported.

Public Financing

• Required presidential candidates who received federal matching subsidies and who withdrew from the prenomination election campaign to give back leftover federal matching funds.
• Cut off federal campaign subsidies to a presidential candidate who won less than 10 percent of the vote in two consecutive presidential primaries in which he ran.
• Established a procedure under which an individual who became ineligible for matching payments could have eligibility restored by a finding of the commission.

Disclosure and Enforcement

• Gave the commission exclusive authority to prosecute civil violations of the campaign finance law and shifted to the commission jurisdiction over violations formerly covered only in the criminal code, thus strengthening its power to enforce the law.
• Required an affirmative vote of four members for the commission to issue regulations and advisory opinions and initiate civil actions and investigations.
• Required labor unions, corporations and membership organizations to report expenditures of over $2,000 per election for communications to their stockholders or members advocating the election or defeat of a clearly identified candidate. The costs of communications to members or stockholders on issues would not have to be reported.
• Required that candidates and political committees keep records of contributions of $50 or more. (The 1974 law had required records of contributions of $10 or more.)
• Permitted candidates and political committees to waive the requirement for filing quarterly campaign finance reports in a nonelection year if less than a total of $5,000 was raised or spent in that quarter. Annual reports would still have to be filed. (The exemption limit was $1,000 under the 1974 law.)
• Required political committees and individuals making an independent political expenditure of more than $100 that advocated the defeat or election of a candidate to file a report with the election commission. Required the committee and individual to state, under penalty of perjury, that the expenditure was not made in collusion with a candidate.
• Required that independent expenditures of $1,000 or more made within 15 days of an election be reported within 24 hours.
• Limited the commission to issuing advisory opinions only for specific fact situations. Advisory opinions could not be used to spell out commission policy. Advisory opinions were not to be considered as precedents unless an activity was "indistinguishable in all its material aspects" from an activity already covered by an advisory opinion.
• Permitted the commission to initiate investigations only after it received a properly verified complaint or had reason to believe, based on information it obtained in the normal course of its duties, that a violation had occurred or was about to occur. The commission was barred from relying on anonymous complaints to institute investigations.
• Required the commission to rely initially on conciliation to deal with alleged campaign law violations before going to court. The commission was allowed to

refer alleged criminal violations to the Department of Justice for action. The attorney general was required to report back to the commission within 60 days an action taken on the apparent violation and subsequently every 30 days until the matter was disposed of.

• Provided for a one-year jail sentence and a fine of up to $25,000 or three times the amount of the contribution or expenditure involved in the violation, whichever was greater, if an individual was convicted of knowingly committing a campaign law violation that involved more than $1,000.

• Provided for civil penalties of fines of $5,000 or an amount equal to the contribution or expenditure involved in the violation, whichever was greater. For violations knowingly committed, the fine would be $10,000 or an amount equal to twice the amount involved in the violation, whichever was greater. The fines could be imposed by the courts or by the commission in conciliation agreements. (The 1974 law included penalties for civil violations of a $1,000 fine and/or a one-year prison sentence.)

Miscellaneous

• Restricted the fund-raising ability of corporate political action committees. Company committees could seek contributions only from stockholders and executive and administrative personnel and their families. Restricted union political action committees to soliciting contributions only from union members and their families. However, twice a year the law permitted union and corporate political action committees to seek campaign contributions only by mail from all employees not initially included in the restriction. Contributions would have to remain anonymous and would be received by an independent third party that would keep records but pass the money to the committees.

• Permitted trade association political action committees to solicit contributions from member companies' stockholders, executive and administrative personnel and their families.

• Permitted union political action committees to use the same method to solicit campaign contributions that the political action committee of the company uses. The union committee would have to reimburse the company at cost for the expenses the company incurred for the political fund raising.

*Some provisions have been declared unconstitutional and some have been superseded by later amendments or repealed.

Federal Election Campaign Act Amendments of 1979

The 1979 Amendments were enacted to lighten the burden the law imposed on candidates and political committees by reducing paperwork, among other changes. P.L. 96-187 contained the following major provisions:

Disclosure

- Required a federal candidate to file campaign finance reports if he or she received or expended more than $5,000. Previously any candidate, regardless of the amount raised or spent, had to file.
- Allowed local political party organizations to avoid filing reports with the FEC if expenditures for certain voluntary activities (get-out-the-vote and voter registration drives for presidential tickets and purchase of buttons, bumper stickers and other materials) were less than $5,000 a year. If other types of expenditures were more than $1,000 a year, then such a group would be required to file. Previously local political party organizations were required to file when any class of expenditure exceeded $1,000 a year.
- Permitted an individual to spend up to $1,000 in behalf of a candidate or $2,000 in behalf of a political party in voluntary expenses for providing his home, food or personal travel without it being counted as a reportable contribution.
- Eliminated the requirement that a political committee have a chairman, but continued the requirement that each have a treasurer.
- Allowed 10 days, instead of the previous five, for a person who received a contribution of more than $50 on behalf of a candidate's campaign committee to forward it to the committee's treasurer.
- Required a committee's treasurer to preserve records for three years. Previously, the FEC established the period of time that committee treasurers were required to keep records.
- Required a candidate's campaign committee to have the candidate's name in the title of the committee. Also, the title of a political action committee was required to include the name of the organization with which it was affiliated.
- Reduced to six from 11 the categories of information required on registration statements of political committees. One of the categories eliminated was one requiring political action committees to name the candidates supported. That requirement meant that PACs were forced frequently to file lists of candidates to whom they contributed when that information already was given in their contribution reports.
- Reduced to nine from 24 the maximum number of reports that a candidate would be required to file during a two-year election cycle. Those nine reports would be a preprimary, a pregeneral, a postgeneral, four quarterly reports during an election year and two semiannual reports during the nonelection year. The preelection reports would be due 12 days before the election; the postgeneral report would be due 30 days after the election; the quarterly reports would be due 15 days after the end of each quarter and the semiannual reports would be due July 31 and January 31.

• Required presidential campaign committees to file monthly reports, as well as pre- and postgeneral reports, during an election year if they had contributions or expenditures in excess of $100,000. All other presidential campaign committees would be required to file quarterly reports, as well as pre- and postgeneral reports, during an election year. During a nonelection year presidential campaign committees could choose whether to file monthly or quarterly reports.

• Required political committees other than those affiliated with a candidate to file either monthly reports in all years or nine reports during a two-year election cycle.

• Provided that the FEC be notified within 48 hours of contributions of $1,000 or more that were made between 20 days and 48 hours before an election. Previously the period had been between 15 days and 48 hours before an election.

• Required the names of contributors to be reported if they gave $200 or more instead of $100 or more.

• Required expenses to be itemized if they were $200 or more instead of $100 or more.

• Increased the threshold for reporting independent expenditures to $250 from $100.

Federal Election Commission

• Established a "best effort" standard for the FEC to determine compliance by candidates' committees with the law. This was intended to ease the burden on committees, particularly in the area of meeting the requirement of filing the occupations of contributors.

• Allowed any person who had an inquiry about a specific campaign transaction — not just federal officeholders, candidates, political committees and the national party committees — to request advisory opinions from the FEC.

• Required the FEC to respond to advisory opinion requests within 60 days instead of within a "reasonable time." If such a request were made within the 60-day period before an election, the FEC would be required to issue an opinion within 20 days.

• Provided that within five days of receiving a complaint that the election campaign law had been violated the FEC must notify any person alleged to have committed a violation. The accused has 15 days in which to respond to the complaint.

• Required a vote of four of the six members of the FEC to make the determination it had "reason to believe" a violation of the law had occurred. An investigation then would be required, and the accused had to be notified.

• Provided that four votes of the FEC were necessary to determine "probable cause" that a violation had occurred. The commission then would be required to attempt to correct the violation by informal methods and to enter into a conciliation agreement within 90 days. Commission action required the vote of four FEC members.

• Narrowed the scope of the FEC's national clearinghouse function from all elections to federal elections.

• Eliminated random audits of committees by the FEC and required a vote of four FEC members to conduct an audit after it had determined that a committee had not substantially complied with the election campaign law.

• Required secretaries of state in each state to keep copies of FEC reports on file for only two years compared with the previous requirement that all House candidate reports be retained for five years and all other reports for 10 years.

• Provided an expedited procedure for the Senate, as well as for the House, to disapprove a regulation proposed by the FEC.

Enforcement

- Retained the substance of the existing law providing for civil and criminal relief of election campaign law violations.
- Continued the prohibition on the use of the contents of reports filed with the FEC for the purpose of soliciting contributions or for commercial purposes, but added the exception that the names of PACs registered with the FEC may be used for solicitation of contributions.
- Permitted political committees to include 10 pseudonyms on each report to protect against illegal use of the names of contributors. A list of those names would be provided to the FEC and would not be made public.

Political Parties

- Allowed state and local party groups to buy, without limit, buttons, bumper stickers, handbills, brochures, posters and yard signs for voluntary activities.
- Authorized state and local party groups to conduct voter registration and get-out-the-vote drives on behalf of presidential tickets without financial limit.

Public Financing

- Increased the allotment of federal funds for the Democrats and Republicans to finance their nominating conventions to $3 million from $2 million.

Miscellaneous

- Permitted buttons and similar materials, but not commercial advertisements, that promoted one candidate to make a passing reference to another federal candidate without its being treated as a contribution to the second candidate.
- Permitted leftover campaign funds to be given to other political committees, as well as charities.
- Prohibited anyone, with the exception of members of Congress at the time of P.L. 96-187's enactment, to convert leftover campaign funds to personal use.
- Continued the ban on solicitation by candidates for Congress or members of Congress and by federal employees of other federal workers for campaign contributions, but dropped the prohibition on the receipt of such contributions by federal employees. An inadvertent solicitation of a federal employee would not be a violation.
- Permitted congressional employees to make voluntary contributions to members of Congress other than their immediate employers.
- Continued the ban on solicitation and receipt of contributions in a federal building. But it would not be a violation if contributions received at a federal building were forwarded within seven days to the appropriate political committee and if the contribution had not been directed initially to the federal building. ∎

Selected Bibliography

Books

Adamany, David. *Campaign Finance in America.* North Scituate, Mass.: Duxbury Press, 1972.

———, and Agree, George E. *Political Money: A Strategy For Campaign Financing In America.* Baltimore: The Johns Hopkins University Press, 1975.

Agranoff, Robert. *The Management of Election Campaigns.* Boston: Holbrook Press Inc., 1976.

———. *The New Style in Election Campaigns.* Boston: Holbrook Press Inc., 1976.

Alexander, Herbert E. *Financing the 1960 Election.* Princeton, N.J.: Citizens' Research Foundation, 1962.

———. *Financing the 1964 Election.* Princeton, N.J.: Citizens' Research Foundation, 1966.

———. *Financing the 1968 Election.* Lexington, Mass.: Lexington Books, D. C. Heath and Co., 1971.

———. *Financing the 1972 Election.* Lexington, Mass.: Lexington Books, D. C. Heath and Co., 1976.

———. *Financing the 1976 Election.* Washington, D.C.: Congressional Quarterly Press, 1979.

———. *Money in Politics.* Washington, D.C.: Public Affairs Press, 1972.

———, ed. *Campaign Money: Reform and Reality in the States.* New York: The Free Press, 1976.

———, ed. *Political Finance.* Beverly Hills: Sage Publications, 1979.

Barber, James David, ed. *Choosing the President.* Englewood Cliffs, N.J.: Prentice-Hall Inc., 1974.

Berg, Larry L., Hahn, Harlan, and Schmidhauser, John R. *Corruption in the American Political System.* Morristown, N.J.: General Learning Press, 1976.

Bernstein, Carl and Woodward, Bob. *All the President's Men.* New York: Simon and Schuster, 1974.

Bickel, Alexander M. *Reform and Continuity: The Electoral College, the Convention, and the Party System.* New York: Harper & Row, Publishers, 1971.

Bishop, George F., Meadow, Robert G., Jackson-Beeck, Marilyn, eds. *The Presidential Debates: Media, Electoral, and Policy Perspectives.* New York: Praeger Publishers, 1979.

Broder, David S. *The Party's Over: The Failure of Politics in America.* New York: Harper & Row, Publishers, 1972.

Caddy, Douglas. *The Hundred Million Dollar Payoff.* New Rochelle, N.Y.: Arlington House, Publishers, 1974.

Chester, Edward W. *Radio, Television and American Politics.* New York: Sheed and Ward, 1969.

Claude, Richard O. *The Supreme Court and the Electoral Process.* Baltimore: The Johns Hopkins Press, 1970.

Crotty, William J. *Decision for the Democrats: Reforming Party Structure.* Baltimore: The Johns Hopkins University Press, 1978.

______. *Political Reform and the American Experiment.* New York: Thomas Y. Crowell Co., 1977.

Demaris, Ovid. *Dirty Business: The Corporate-Political Money-Power Game.* New York: Harper's Magazine Press, 1974.

DeVries, Walter and Tarrance, Lance, Jr. *The Ticket-Splitter: A New Force in American Politics.* Grand Rapids, Mich.: William B. Eardmans Publishing Co., 1972.

Domhoff, G. William. *Fat Cats and Democrats: The Role of the Big Rich in the Party of the Common Man.* Englewood Cliffs, N.J.: Prentice-Hall, 1972.

Dunn, Delmer. *Financing Presidential Campaigns.* Washington, D.C.: The Brookings Institution, 1972.

Epstein, Edwin M. *The Corporation in American Politics.* Englewood Cliffs, N.J.: Prentice-Hall Inc., 1969.

Gilson, Lawrence. *Money and Secrecy: A Citizen's Guide to Reforming State and Federal Practices.* New York: Praeger Publishers, 1972.

Greenwald, Carol. *Group Power: Lobbying and Public Policy.* New York: Praeger Publishers, 1977.

Heard, Alexander. *The Costs of Democracy.* Chapel Hill, N.C.: University of North Carolina Press, 1960.

Heidenheimer, Arnold J., ed. *Comparative Political Finance: The Financing of Party Organizations and Election Campaigns.* Lexington, Mass.: Lexington Books, D. C. Heath and Co., 1970.

Hess, Stephen. *The Presidential Campaign: The Leadership Selection Process After Watergate.* Washington, D.C.: The Brookings Institution, 1974.

Hiebert, Ray, Jones, Robert, Lotito, Ernest and Lorenz, John, eds. *The Political Image Merchants: Strategies in the New Politics.* Washington, D.C.: Acropolis Books Ltd., 1971.

Kelley, Stanley, Jr. *Political Campaigning: Problems in Creating an Informed Electorate.* Washington, D.C.: The Brookings Institution, 1960.

______. *Professional Public Relations and Political Power.* Baltimore: The Johns Hopkins Press, 1956.

Kraus, Sidney. *The Great Debates: Background — Perspective — Effects.* Bloomington, Ind.: Indiana University Press, 1962.

Ladd, Everett Carll, Jr. *Where Have All the Voters Gone? The Fracturing of America's Political Parties.* New York: W. W. Norton & Co. Inc., 1978.

Leonard, Dick. *Paying for Party Politics: The Case For Public Subsidies.* London: PEP, 1975.

Leuthold, David A. *Electioneering in a Democracy: Campaigns for Congress.* New York: John Wiley and Sons, 1968.

Lipset, Seymour Martin, ed. *Emerging Coalitions in American Politics.* San Francisco: Institute for Contemporary Studies, 1978.

McCarthy, Max. *Elections for Sale.* Boston: Houghton-Mifflin Co., 1972.

McGinniss, Joe. *The Selling of the President, 1968.* New York: Trident Press, 1969.

MacNeil, Robert. *The People Machine: The Influence of Television on American Politics.* New York: Harper & Row, Publishers, 1968.

Malbin, Michael J., ed. *Parties, Interest Groups, and Campaign Finance Laws.* Washington, D.C.: American Enterprise Institute for Public Policy Research, 1980.

May, Ernest R. and Fraser, Janet, eds. *Campaign '72: The Managers Speak.* Cambridge: Harvard University Press, 1973.

Mazmanian, Daniel A. *Third Parties in Presidential Elections.* (Studies in Presidential Selection.) Washington, D.C.: The Brookings Institution, 1974.

Mickelson, Sig. *The Electric Mirror: Politics in an Age of Television.* New York: Dodd, Mead & Co., 1972.

Minow, Newton N., Martin, John Bartlow and Mitchell, Lee M. *Presidential Television.* New York: Basic Books, 1973.

Napolitan, Joseph. *The Election Game and How to Win It.* Garden City, New York: Doubleday & Co. Inc., 1972.

Nichols, David. *Financing Elections: The Politics of an American Ruling Class.* New York: New Viewpoints, A Division of Franklin Watts Inc., 1974.

Nie, Norman H., Verba, Sidney and Petrocik, John R. *The Changing American Voter.* Cambridge: Harvard University Press, 1976.

Nimmo, Dan. *The Political Persuaders.* Englewood Cliffs, N.J.: Prentice Hall, 1970.

Ornstein, Norman J. and Elder, Shirley. *Interest Groups, Lobbying, and Policymaking.* Washington, D.C.: Congressional Quarterly Press, 1978.

Overacker, Louise. *Money in Elections.* New York: The Macmillan Co., 1932.

Patterson, Thomas E. and McClure, Robert D. *The Unseeing Eye: The Myth of Television Power in National Politics.* New York: G. P. Putnam's Sons, 1976.

Peabody, Robert L., Berry, Jeffrey M., Frasure, William G. and Goldman, Jerry. *To Enact A Law: Congress and Campaign Financing.* New York: Praeger Publishers, 1972.

Pollock, James K., Jr. *Party Campaign Funds.* New York: Knopf, 1926.

———. *Money and Politics Abroad.* New York: Alfred A. Knopf, 1932.

Pomper, Gerald, Baker, Ross K., Jacob, Charles E., McWilliams, Wilson Carey, Plotkin, Henry A., Pomper, Marlene M., eds. *The Election of 1976: Reports and Interpretations.* New York: David McKay Co. Inc., 1977.

Rae, Douglas W. *The Political Consequences of Electoral Laws.* New Haven: Yale University Press, 1967.

Ranney, Austin. *Curing the Mischiefs of Faction: Party Reform in America.* Berkeley: University of California Press, 1975.

Rosenbloom, David Lee. *The Election Men: Professional Campaign Managers and American Democracy.* New York: Quadrangle Books, 1973.

Schwarz, Thomas J. *Public Financing of Elections: A Constitutional Division of the Wealth.* Chicago: The American Bar Association, Special Committee on Election Reform, 1975.

Shannon, Jasper B. *Money and Politics.* New York: Random House, 1959.

Steinberg, Arnold. *Political Campaign Management: A Systems Approach.* Lexington, Mass.: Lexington Books, D. C. Heath and Co., 1976.

———. *The Political Campaign Handbook: Media, Scheduling, and Advance.* Lexington, Mass.: Lexington Books, D. C. Heath and Co., 1976.

Stewart, John G. *One Last Chance: The Democratic Party, 1974-76.* New York: Praeger Publishers, 1974.

Sundquist, James L. *Dynamics of the Party System: Alignment and Realignment of Political Parties in the United States.* Washington, D.C.: The Brookings Institution, 1973.

Thayer, George. *Who Shakes the Money Tree? American Campaign Financing Practices from 1789 to the Present.* New York: Simon and Schuster, 1973.

Van Doren, John. *Big Money in Little Sums.* Chapel Hill: Institute for Research in Social Science, University of North Carolina, 1956.

White, George H. *A Study of Access to Television for Political Candidates.* Cambridge: John F. Kennedy Institute of Politics, May 1978.

White, Theodore H. *The Making of the President, 1960.* New York: Atheneum Publishers, 1961.

______. *The Making of the President, 1964*. New York: Atheneum Publishers, 1965.
______. *The Making of the President, 1968*. New York: Atheneum Publishers, 1969.
______. *The Making of the President, 1972*. New York: Atheneum Publishers, 1973.
Woodward, Bob and Bernstein, Carl. *The Final Days*. New York: Simon and Schuster, 1976.

Reports and Articles

Agree, George E. "Public Financing After the Supreme Court Decision," in "Political Finance: Reform and Reality," *The Annals,* vol. 425, Philadelphia: The American Academy of Political and Social Science, May 1976.
Alexander, Herbert E., ed. "Political Finance: Reform and Reality," *The Annals,* vol. 425. Philadelphia: The American Academy of Political and Social Science, May 1976.
Alexander, Herbert E. and Molloy, J. Paul. *Model State Statute: Politics, Elections and Public Office.* Princeton, N.J.: Citizens' Research Foundation, August 1974.
American Bar Association, Special Committee on Election Reform. *Symposium on Campaign Financing Regulation.* Tiburon, Calif., April 25-27, 1975.
An Analysis of the Impact of the Federal Election Campaign Act, 1972-1978. Report by the Campaign Finance Study Group to the Committee on House Administration of the U.S. House of Representatives, Institute of Politics, John Fitzgerald Kennedy School of Government, Harvard University, May 1979.
Anonymous. "Developments in the Law — Elections," *Harvard Law Review,* Vol. 88, No. 6, Cambridge, Mass.: Gannett House, April 1975.
Cohen, Richard E. "Public Financing for House Races — Will It Make a Difference?", *National Journal,* May 12, 1979.
Electing Congress: The Financial Dilemma. Report of the Twentieth Century Fund Task Force on Financing Congressional Campaigns. (Background Paper by David Lee Rosenbloom) New York, 1970.
Epstein, Edwin M. "An Irony of Electoral Reform," *Regulation,* May/June 1979.
Federal Election Commission, Review of the Political Campaign Auditing Process. Report by Arthur Andersen & Co. to the Federal Election Commission, Washington, D.C., September 1979.
Financing a Better Election System. A Statement on National Policy by the Research and Policy Committee of the Committee for Economic Development. New York: Committee for Economic Development, December 1968.
Financing Presidential Campaigns. Report of the President's Commission on Campaign Costs. Washington, D.C., April 1962.
Fling, Karen, ed. "A Summary of Campaign Practices Laws of the 50 States," Report 4, *Campaign Practices Reports,* Washington, D.C., October 1978.
How Money Talks in Congress, a Common Cause Study of the Impact of Money on Congressional Decision-Making. Common Cause, Washington, D.C., 1979.
Jacobson, Gary C. "The Effects of Campaign Spending in Congressional Elections," *American Political Science Review,* Vol. 72, No. 2, June 1978.
Jones, Ruth S. "State Public Financing and the State Parties," in Michael J. Malbin, ed. *Parties, Interest Groups, and Campaign Finance Laws,* Washington, D.C.: American Enterprise Institute for Public Policy Research, 1980.

Kirby, James C., Jr. *Congress and the Public Trust.* Report of the Association of the Bar of the City of New York Special Committee on Congressional Ethics. New York: Atheneum, 1970.

Lydenberg, Steven D. *Bankrolling Ballots: The Role of Business in Financing State Ballot Question Campaigns.* New York: Council on Economic Priorities, 1979.

Malbin, Michael J. "Campaign Financing and the Special Interests," *The Public Interest,* No. 56, Summer 1979.

———. "Labor, Business, and Money — A Post-Election Analysis," *National Journal,* March 19, 1977.

———. "Neither a Mountain nor a Molehill," *Regulation,* May/June, 1979.

Moore, Jonathan and Albert C. Pierce, eds. *Voters, Primaries and Parties.* Selections from a Conference on American Politics. Institute of Politics, John Fitzgerald Kennedy School of Government, Harvard University, 1976.

1972 Congressional Campaign Finances. Prepared by the Campaign Finance Monitoring Project, 3 vols., Washington, D.C.: Common Cause, 1974.

1972 Federal Campaign Finances: Interest Groups and Political Parties. Prepared by the Campaign Finance Monitoring Project, 10 vols., Washington, D.C.: Common Cause, 1974.

1974 Congressional Campaign Finances. Prepared by the Campaign Finance Monitoring Project, 5 vols., Washington, D.C.: Common Cause, 1976.

1976 Federal Campaign Finances. Prepared by the Campaign Finance Monitoring Project, 3 vols., Washington, D.C.: Common Cause, 1977.

Nomination and Election of the President and Vice President of the United States. Compiled by Thomas M. Durbin, Rita Ann Reimer and Thomas B. Riby, Congressional Research Service, Library of Congress for the United States Senate Library, under the direction of Francis R. Valeo, Secretary of the Senate, Washington, D.C.: U.S. Government Printing Office, 1976.

Rosenthal, Albert J. *Federal Regulation of Campaign Finance: Some Constitutional Questions.* Milton Katz, ed. Princeton, N.J.: Citizens' Research Foundation, 1972.

Schwarz, Thomas J. *Public Financing of Elections: A Constitutional Division of the Wealth.* Chicago: American Bar Association, Special Committee on Election Reform, 1975.

Senate Campaign Information, A Compilation of Federal Laws and Regulations Governing United States Senate Elections in 1978. Compiled by the Senate Library under the direction of J. S. Kimmitt, Secretary of Senate, Roger K. Haley, Librarian. Washington: Government Printing Office, 1978.

Study of the Federal Election Commission's Audit Process. Report by Accountants for the Public Interest to the Federal Election Commission. New York, September 10, 1979.

U.S. Congress, House of Representatives. Committee on House Administration. *Public Financing of Congressional Elections.* Hearings on a Bill to Amend the Federal Election Campaign Act of 1971 to Provide for the Public Financing of General Election Campaigns for the House of Representatives and for Other Purposes, 95th Cong., 1st Sess. Washington, D.C.: U.S. Government Printing Office, 1977.

U.S. Congress, Senate. Select Committee on Presidential Campaign Activities. *Final Report.* Pursuant to S. Res. 60, February 7, 1973. Senate Report No. 93-981. 93rd Cong., 2d sess. Washington, D.C.: U.S. Government Printing Office, 1974.

U.S. Congress, Senate. Select Committee on Presidential Campaign Activities. *Election Reform: Basic References.* Pursuant to S. Res. 60. Committee Print, 93rd Cong., 1st sess. Washington, D.C.: U.S. Government Printing Office, 1973.

Voters' Time. Report of the Twentieth Century Fund Commission on Campaign Costs in the Electronic Era. New York, 1969.

Winter, Ralph K., Jr. *Watergate and the Law: Political Campaigns and Presidential Power.* (Domestic Affairs Study No. 22.) Washington, D.C.: American Enterprise Institute for Public Policy Research, 1974.

———, in association with John R. Bolton. *Campaign Financing and Political Freedom.* (Domestic Affairs Study No. 19.) Washington, D.C.: American Enterprise Institute for Public Policy Research, 1973.

Index